Cover: Jacques Louis David, **The Death of Socrates** *[1787]*
(The Metropolitan Museum of Art, New York)

Though Socrates' trial and execution include none of the brutalities to which the twentieth century—on which this book will focus—will accustom us, the drama here depicted of a Socrates condemned to death, a Socrates whose one hand can be seen as raised in protestation, and could possibly materialize the witness oath in a gesture of an ultimate appeal (to Justice, to the law, to the Jurors, to his students, to posterity, to memory, to Truth), while his other hand, in an opposed gesture of a philosophical and acquiescent reconciliation, is reaching toward the poison cup, the drama of this trial, of the division and yet the integrity of the Socratic testimony in the face of death, here stands at once for the political and ethical dimensions of the archetypal testimonial crisis of an accused in the face of overpowering, oppressive violence, for the crisis of witnessing of the bystanders (whether in the role of judges or of students), and for the quintessential claim of testimony to originate in, and yet to fundamentally transcend, the witness.

"From me you will hear the whole truth, though not, by Zeus, gentlemen, expressed in embroidered and stylized phrases . . . but things spoken at random and expressed in the first words that come to mind, for I put my trust in the justice of what I say". (Socrates, *Apology*)

TESTIMONY

Published in 1992 by

Routledge
An imprint of Routledge, Chapman and Hall, Inc.
29 West 35 Street
New York, NY 10001

Published in Great Britain by

Routledge
11 New Fetter Lane
London EC4P 4EE

Library of Congress Cataloging in Publication Data

Felman, Shoshana.
    Testimony : crises of witnessing in literature, psychoanalysis,
and history / Shoshana Felman and Dori Laub, M.D.
    p. cm.
    Includes index.
    ISBN 0-415-90391-2 (cloth)   ISBN 0-415-90392-0 (paper)
    1. Psychoanalysis and literature.   2. Authors—Psychology.
3. Psychic trauma.   I. Laub, Dori.   II. Title.
PN56.P92F45   1991
801'.92—dc20   91-32891

British Library cataloguing in publication data also available

6-25-93

TESTIMONY

CRISES OF WITNESSING IN
LITERATURE, PSYCHOANALYSIS, AND HISTORY

SHOSHANA FELMAN AND DORI LAUB, M.D.

PN
56
.P92
F45
1992

KbS

ROUTLEDGE NEW YORK AND LONDON

Contents

Photo Credits

Stéphane Mallarmé, by Edouard Manet (page 22) courtesy of Giraudon/Art Resource, N.Y.; Mallarmé's handwriting and signature (page 24) courtesy of the Beinecke Rare Book and Manuscript Library, Yale University; Camus by Cartier-Bresson (page 113) courtesy of Magnum Photos, Inc.; Paul de Man in Galerie des Traitres (page 134) courtesy of the personal archives of Myriam Abramowicz; Paul de Man at Bard College (page 138) courtesy of Patricia de Man, photograph by David Brochs; Camus by Cartier-Bresson (page 166) courtesy of Magnum Photos, Inc.; Camus by Izis (page 200) courtesy of Photo *Izis*; All photos from the film *Shoah* (chapter 7) courtesy of Claude Lanzmann; Menachem S. (pages 45, 77, 87, 89, 90) courtesy of Menachem S.; Helen K. (page 43) courtesy of Helen K.

Acknowledgments

Portions of this book have previously appeared in the following publications: Chapter 1 (in a modified, earlier version) and Chapter 3, in *American Imago,* vol. 48, no. 1, Spring 1991 ("Psychoanalysis, Culture and Trauma", Cathy Caruth, ed.); Chapter 4 (abridged), in *Reading Narrative: Form, Ethics, Ideology,* James Phelan, ed., Columbus, Ohio University Press: 1989; chapter 5 in *Critical Inquiry,* Summer 1989; An excerpt of Chapter 7 in *Yale French Studies* no. 79, winter 1991 ("Literature and the Ethical Question", Claire Nouvet, ed.).

Both authors wish to thank Cathy Caruth for her patient reading of portions of the manuscript, her insightful feedback on both the clinical and the literary chapters, and her enriching comments and suggestions; Michal Shaked for the sharpness of the legal and critical perspective she afforded, in particular on Chapters 1 and 3; and Claude Lanzmann for his ongoing dialogue with both of us and for his inspiring presence.

We are grateful as well to Katherine Profeta, who assisted us through the actual process of production of the book, and whose intelligence, discrimination and resourceful dedication to details enabled us to bring the work to completion.

Shoshana Felman and *Dori Laub, M.D.*

Deeds which populate the dimensions of space and which reach their end when someone dies may cause us wonderment, but one thing, or an infinite number of things, dies in every final agony, unless there is a universal memory. . . . What will die with me when I die . . . ?

(Jorge Luis Borges, *The Witness*)

Where men and women are forced to endure terrible things at the hand of others—whenever, that is, extremity involves moral issues—the need to remember becomes a general response. Spontaneously, they make it their business to record the evil forced upon them. . . . Here—and in similar situations—survival and bearing witness become reciprocal acts.

(Terrence Des Pres, *The Survivor*)

The writer's function is not without its arduous duties. By definition, he cannot serve today those who make history; he must serve those who are subject to it.

(Albert Camus, *1957 Nobel Prize Address*)

Foreword

SHOSHANA FELMAN AND DORI LAUB, M.D.

"We have all the answers," Dostoevsky said: "It is the questions we do not know." This is a book on memory and on questions. On questions that we do not know, that we do not as yet possess as questions, but which nonetheless compellingly address us from within contemporary art and from within contemporary history. As readers, we are witnesses precisely to these questions we do not own and do not yet understand, but which summon and beseech us from within the literary texts. What is the relation between literature and testimony, between the writer and the witness? What is the relation between the act of witnessing and testifying, and the acts of writing and of reading, particularly in our era?

What is, furthermore, this book will ask, the relation between narrative and history, between art and memory, between speech and survival? Through an alternation of a literary and a clinical perspective, the present study strives to grasp and to articulate the obscure relation between witnessing, events and evidence, as what defines at once the common ground between literature and ethics, and the meeting point between violence and culture, the very moment when, precisely, the phenomenon of violence and the phenomenon of culture come to clash—and yet to mingle—in contemporary history.

It is no coincidence if this book proceeds from the collaboration of two authors, engaged in separate, yet complementary, fields of endeavor: one of us is a professional interpreter of texts, the other—a professional interpreter of people; one of us is a literary critic and a literary educator at Yale University, training graduate and undergraduate students in the complex relationship between language and life and in the methods and techniques of reading, and of listening to, truths that are unspoken—or unspeakable—and that are yet inscribed

xiii

in texts; the other is a psychiatric educator trained to decipher traces of trauma in human narrative, a psychoanalyst pragmatically engaged in the treatment of trauma survivors, and the cofounder of a testimonial enterprise: the Video Archive for Holocaust Testimonies at Yale. This book has grown out of the mutual interest we each had in the other's work, and has gradually evolved—over a period of six years—out of the encounter and the dialogue between these two professional perspectives, and between the mutually enhancing lessons of these different practices.

The chapters that will follow, while primarily conceived and written (as their signature will indicate) by one of us or by the other, are in fact the product of this intellectual and conceptual interaction and of this continuous dialogue of insights, that has served both as the motivating and as the enabling force in the process of the writing.

*

With the exception of the nineteenth-century and early twentieth-century writers and theorists discussed in Chapter 1 (among them Freud, Dostoevsky, Mallarmé), the major texts, films and documents submitted to the scrutiny of this book (Camus' novels, de Man's essays, the poetic project of Celan, videotaped Holocaust testimonies, and the film *Shoah* by Claude Lanzmann) were all written and produced consequent to the historic trauma of the Second World War, a trauma we consider as the watershed of our times and which the book will come to view not as an event encapsulated in the past, but as a history which is essentially *not over,* a history whose repercussions are not simply omnipresent (whether consciously or not) in all our cultural activities, but whose traumatic consequences are still actively *evolving* (Eastern Europe and the Gulf War are two obvious examples) in today's political, historical, cultural and artistic scene, the scene in which we read and psychoanalyze, and from within whose tumult and whose fluctuations we strive both to educate and write.

If our readings, in the studies that will follow, thus extend, indeed, not merely to the texts themselves but to the intellectual, political, historical and biographical context of their actual production, it is not, however, so as to return, once again, to the purely academic "mirror-games" between "novel" and "life" and to the traditional, all-too-familiar critical accounts of the mutual "reflection" (or "representation") between "history" and "text." It is rather, and more challengingly, so as to attempt to see—in an altogether different and exploratory light—how issues of biography and history are neither simply represented nor simply reflected, but are reinscribed, translated, radically rethought and fundamentally worked over by the text. In order to gain insight into the significance and impact of the context on the text, the empirical context needs not just to be *known,* but to be *read;* to be read in conjunction with, and as part of, the reading of the text. We thus propose to show how the basic and legitimate critical demand for *contextualization of the text* itself needs to be complemented, simultaneously, by the less familiar and yet necessary work of *texualization of the context;* and how this shuttle movement or this shuttle reading in the critic's work—the very *tension between textualization and contextualization*—might yield new avenues of insight, both into the texts at stake and into their context—the political, historical, and biographical realities with which the texts are dynamically involved and within which their particular creative possibilities are themselves inscribed.

In moving in between the questions of the text and the questions of the context, the overriding effort of the chapters that will follow is to offer new articulations of *perspective:* we underscore the question of the witness, and of witnessing, as nonhabitual, estranged *conceptual prisms* through which we attempt to apprehend—and to make tangible to the imagination—the ways in which our cultural frames of reference and our preexisting categories which delimit and determine our perception of reality have failed, essentially, both to contain, and to account for, the scale of what has happened in contemporary history.

The various chapters cover a whole spectrum of concerns, issues, works and media of transmission, moving from the literary to the visual, from the artistic to the autobiographical, and from the psychoanalytical to the historical. In the end, what is maintained is the multilayered vision offered by all these perspectives held together, and by the mutual light the various media shed on one another. The outline of the book revolves around a *movement,* a dynamic, a development based in the increasingly articulate pursuit, and in the increasingly complex progression, of some organizing questions. The exploratory structure and process of unfolding put in motion by the book is underscored at once by the concrete transitions from one chapter to another, by the momentum marking the progression of the table of contents as a whole, and by the shifting global vision offered by the volume, as it moves from concrete questions of practice into vaster questions of the mutual interaction between theory and history. "We have all the answers: it is the questions we do not know." This book indeed is looking not so much for answers as for new *enabling questions,* questions that would open new directions for research and new conceptual spaces for the yet unborn answers.

In the space engendered by—and in between—the disciplines we work in, the process of the questioning starts here *in medias res,* in the midst of the fulfillment of our daily tasks. The opening chapters thus proceed from a description of the differing nature of our practices—the practice of *reading* and the practice of *listening*—insofar as those two practical approaches bring into focus the different emphases, the different kinds of pragmatic situations and the different kinds of difficulties inherent to the exercises of the disciplines in which we work and by which our insights and our methods are informed: literature on the one hand, psychoanalysis on the other.

But into those two practices, we propose to introduce the dimension of the real—the events and implications of contemporary history. Both practices will thereby here confront at once their limits and their critical dimensions. As our ventures will bear witness to and as the concrete examples we narrate will show, the encounter with the real leads to the experience of an existential crisis in all those involved: students as well as teachers, narrators as well as listeners, testifiers as well as interviewers.

*

Chapter 1 narrates, indeed, the story of a class in which the reading of a chain of testimonial literary texts in conjunction with the viewing of videotaped autobiographical accounts of Holocaust survivors, brings about such an encounter with the real that the class, all of a sudden, finds itself entirely at a loss, uprooted and disoriented, and profoundly shaken in its anchoring world views and in its commonly held life-perspectives.

The book thus moves from the description of the unexpected educational experience of this crisis—and from the *pedagogical* lesson learnt in its wake—to a more directly focused *clinical* analysis, in Chapter 2, of the risks and the vicissitudes of listening: of listening to human suffering and to traumatic narratives. Even when the listener—in his capacity as psychoanalyst—is trained by discipline and by profession to treat trauma and to be its witness, the experience of the witnessing—of the listening to extreme limit-experiences—entails its hazards and might equally, like reading and like viewing in the story of the previous chapter, suddenly—without a warning—shake up one's whole grip on one's experience and one's life. The professionally trained receivers of the testimonies which bear witness to the war atrocities—the listeners and interviewers whose own listening in fact *enables* the unfolding of the testimonial life accounts of Holocaust survivors—cannot fulfill their task without, in turn, passing through the crisis of experiencing their boundaries, their separateness, their functionality, and indeed their sanity, at risk. They have to learn how to recognize these hazards, how to integrate these pitfalls of the witnessing into the fulfillment of their professional and human task, and how to bond with the narrator in a common struggle to release the testimony which, in spite of inhibitions on both sides, will allow the telling of the trauma to proceed and to reach its testimonial resolution.

The practical hazards of listening—of coming to know—lead to a rethinking of the crucial role the (always threatened) preservation of the truth, of knowledge and reality, plays in the enablement of psychological survival—in the very ability to sustain and to continue life after catastrophes. Chapter 3, in this way, moves from a description of the *practice of the testimonial* to a first attempt at working out a *theory of testimony*—at theorizing, that is, both the historical and philosophical lessons, and the psychoanalytic implications, of this practice. On the basis of a close analysis of concrete examples of historical and autobiographical accounts, the process of the testimony indeed sheds new light, both on the psychoanalytical relation between speech and survival, and on the historical processes of the Holocaust itself, whose uniquely devastating aspect is here interpreted for the first time as a radical historical *crisis of witnessing,* and as the unprecedented, inconceivable, historical occurrence of "an event without a witness"—an event eliminating its own witness.

Chapter 4 (on Camus' *The Plague*), Chapter 5 (on de Man's mature work in its historical and philosophical relation to his early writings) and Chapter 6 (on Camus' *The Fall*) test, attest and amplify this theory through the close analysis of postwar critical and literary texts which, indirectly or directly, testify precisely to this cataclysmic trauma. From Camus' *The Plague,* a wartime piece of writing and an immediate postwar publication, to Camus' *The Fall,* written a decade after the war but here interpreted as a crucial transformation and revision of *The Plague,* as a delayed effect and a belated thinking—and rethinking—of the trauma, literature—of which Camus becomes in our analysis a profound emblem—undergoes at once a stylistic and a philosophical transvaluation. We read both this stylistic transformation and this philosophical transvaluation taking place in Camus' writing as the indirect expressions of—or the belated testimonies to—the radical crisis of witnessing the Holocaust has been, and to the consequent, ongoing, as yet unresolved *crisis of history,* a crisis which in turn is translated into a *crisis of literature* insofar as literature becomes a witness, and perhaps the only witness, to the crisis within history which precisely cannot be articulated, witnessed in the given categories of history itself.

Surprisingly, but with an eloquence whose objective and coincidental nature is almost uncanny, it is a similar kind of philosophical and ethical transvaluation that we find in Paul de Man's critical writings (to which we turn in Chapter 5). Like Camus' *The Fall,* we read de Man's work—both his philosophical and existential dealings with literary theory and his practical engagement with specific texts (Rousseau, Shelley or Benjamin)—as a testimony, similarly, to a radical crisis of the literary text which is itself a witness to the crisis—and to the critical dimensions—of a history that nonetheless remains, as such, at once unspeakable and inarticulatable—a history that can no longer be accounted for, and formulated, in its own terms.

Although de Man's political position, at its starting point, is very different from Camus'; although Camus' war pieces are written by a member of the French Resistance, whereas de Man, at the beginning of the war, writes as a collaborating journalist, the *transformation* they both undergo *from their early to their later writings* bears striking underlying similarities. Paul de Man's personal and literary journey from his youthfully, simplistically embraced position as the journalistic chronicler and as the would-be historian of World War II, to his withdrawal into silence, and to his consequent retreat into a prose profoundly questioning the very possibility of representation, and into the ascetic, self-denying and uncompromising rigor of the author of the later writings, seems to follow the same cognitive itinerary as the one which leads Camus from the naïve, idealistic faith in witnessing embodied by *The Plague* to the sobering discovery, narrated by *The Fall,* of the failure and of the betrayal of the witness, as well as of the radical collapse inherent to the historical experience of witnessing as such.

The failed confession of *The Fall* could thus stand in the place of de Man's missing confession: insofar as it belatedly accounts for the aftermath of the trauma—and for the belated transformation—occasioned by the war, *The Fall* indeed can be read as de Man's unspoken autobiographical story.

And yet, in its deliberate conception and design, *The Fall* in fact enacts the story of Camus and Sartre—the story of the rupture of their friendship and of the disruption of their intellectual alliance, through the polemics of their views on history and the explosive political and philosophical debate that marks the parting of their ways. Encompassing uncannily the story of de Man as well as that which separates Camus from Sartre, *The Fall* turns out to be—beyond the personal and beyond any reductive psychological trivialization—the fated and ill-understood story of the baffling fall of an entire generation, a story (and a history) from whose bewildering complexity and from whose chaotic implications we have not as yet emerged.

In the final chapter of the book, however, Claude Lanzmann's *Shoah*—the ground breaking film which we here consider as the work of art of our times—takes us one step further. From the impossible confession of the Holocaust, pronounced as such and testified to philosophically and literarily both by Camus' *The Fall* and by the later writings of de Man, both by the ex-Belgian and former collaborator who has radically broken his ties with his country and his past, and by the French Resistant and the former wartime spokesman for Free France, *Shoah* leads us, through an exploration of the depths of history defined precisely as historical unspeakability, to a retrieval of the possibility of speaking and to a recovery and a return of the voice.

The impossible, unspeakable confession reverberates as well, throughout the film, in the bewildered muteness of the survivors of the holocaust themselves, who have continued, willingly or not, to be "the bearers of the silence," the very bearers, that is, of the secrecy and the secret of contemporary history. In its interviews with the survivors, the ex-Nazis, the bystanders, *Shoah* acutely shows how the Holocaust still functions as a cultural secret, a secret which, essentially, we are still keeping from ourselves, through various forms of communal or of personal denial, of cultural reticence or of cultural canonization. The film bursts this secret open. Its whole effort is, precisely, to decanonize the silence, to desacralize the witness and, in so doing, to enact the *liberation of the testimony* from the bondage of the secret. The film thus accomplishes at once a journey into history as fall to silence and a triumph, a return and a repossession of the living voice, for which art has now recovered the historically lost power to transmit and to convey.

*

It is this power which has summoned our act of listening in this book, and to whose call and whose imperative we have tried, in the essays here presented, to respond.

The present volume will endeavor to suggest, therefore, the first stage of a theory of a yet uncharted, nonrepresentational but performative, relationship between art and culture, on the one hand, and the conscious or unconscious witnessing of historical events, on the other. This is then a book about how art inscribes (artistically bears witness to) *what we do not yet know of our lived historical relation to events of our times.*

In considering, in this way, literature and art as a precocious mode of witnessing—of accessing reality—when all other modes of knowledge are precluded, our ultimate concern has been with the preservation, in this book, both of the uniqueness of experience in the face of its theorization, and of the shock of the unintelligible in the face of the attempt at its interpretation; with the preservation, that is, of reality itself in the midst of our own efforts at interpreting it and through the necessary process of its textualization.

O N E

Education and Crisis, Or the Vicissitudes of Teaching

SHOSHANA FELMAN

I

Trauma and Pedagogy

Is there a relation between crisis and the very enterprise of education? To put the question even more audaciously and sharply: Is there a relation between trauma and pedagogy? In a post-traumatic century, a century that has survived unthinkable historical catastrophes, is there anything that we have learned or that we should learn about education, that we did not know before? Can trauma *instruct* pedagogy, and can pedagogy shed light on the mystery of trauma? Can the task of teaching be instructed by the clinical experience, and can the clinical experience be instructed, on the other hand, by the task of teaching?

Psychoanalysis, as well as other disciplines of human mental welfare, proceed by taking testimonies from their patients. Can educators be in turn edified by the practice of the testimony, while attempting to enrich it and rethink it through some striking literary lessons? What does literature tell us about testimony? What does psychoanalysis tell us about testimony? Can the implications of the psychoanalytic lesson and the literary lesson about testimony *interact* in the pedagogical experience? Can the process of the testimony—that of bearing witness to a crisis or a trauma—be made use of in the classroom situation? What, indeed, does testimony mean in general, and what in general does it attempt to do? In a post-traumatic century, what and how can testimony teach us, not merely in the areas of law, of medicine, of history, which routinely use it in their daily practice, but in the larger areas of the *interactions between the clinical and the historical, between the literary and the pedagogical?*

1

The Alignment between Witnesses

In his book entitled *Kafka's Other Trial*, writer, critic and Nobel prize laureate for literature Elias Canetti narrates the effect that Kafka's correspondence has had on him:

> I found those letters more gripping and absorbing than any literary work I have read for years past. They belong among those singular memoirs, autobiographies, collection of letters from which Kafka himself drew sustenance. He himself . . . [read] over and over again, the letters of Kleist, of Flaubert, and of Hebbel . . .
>
> To call these letters documents would be saying too little, unless one were to apply the same title to the *life-testimonies* of Pascal, Kierkegaard, and Dostoevsky. For my part, I can only say that these letters have *penetrated me like an actual life.*[1]

A "life-testimony" is not simply a testimony to a private life, but a point of conflation between text and life, a textual testimony which can *penetrate us like an actual life*. As such, Kafka's correspondence is testimony not merely to the life of Kafka, but to something larger than the life of Kafka, and which Canetti's title designates, suggestively and enigmatically, as *Kafka's Other Trial*. Both through Kafka's life and through his work, something crucial takes place which is of the order of a *trial*. Canetti's very reading of Kafka's correspondence, in line with Kafka's reading of the letters of Kleist, Hebbel and Flaubert, thus adds its testimony—adds as yet another witness–to Kafka's *Trial*. Canetti writes:

> In the face of life's horror—luckily most people notice it only on occasion, but a few whom inner forces *appoint* to *bear witness* are always conscious of it—there is only one comfort: *its alignment with the horror experienced by previous witnesses.*[2]

How is the act of *writing* tied up with the act of *bearing witness*— and with the experience of the trial? Is the act of *reading* literary texts itself inherently related to the act of *facing horror*? If literature is the *alignment between witnesses*, what would this alignment mean? And by virtue of what sort of agency is one *appointed* to bear witness?

[1]Elias Canetti, *Kafka's Other Trial*, New York-Schocken Books, 1974, p. 4. Emphasis mine.

[2]Ibid. emphasis mine.

The Appointment

It is a strange appointment, from which the witness-appointee cannot relieve himself by any delegation, substitution or representation. "If someone else could have written my stories," says Elie Wiesel, "I would not have written them. I have written them in order to testify. And this is the origin of the loneliness that can be glimpsed in each of my sentences, in each of my silences."[3] Since the testimony cannot be simply relayed, repeated or reported by another without thereby losing its function as a testimony, the burden of the witness—in spite of his or her alignment with other witnesses—is a radically unique, noninterchangeable and solitary burden. "No one bears witness for the witness," writes the poet Paul Celan.[4] To bear witness is to *bear the solitude* of a responsibility, and to *bear the responsibility*, precisely, of that solitude.[4 - bis]

And yet, the *appointment* to bear witness is, paradoxically enough, an appointment to transgress the confines of that isolated stance, to speak *for* other and *to* others. The French philosopher Emmanuel Levinas can thus suggest that the witness's speech is one which, by its very definition, transcends the witness who is but its medium, the medium of realization of the testimony. "The witness," writes Levinas, "testifies to what has been said *through* him. Because the witness has said 'here I am' before the other."[5] By virtue of the fact that the testimony is *addressed* to others, the witness, from within the solitude of his own stance, is the vehicle of an occurrence, a reality, a stance or a dimension *beyond himself.*

---

[3]"The Loneliness of God," published in *Dvar Hashavu'a* (magazine of the newspaper *Davar*), Tel-Aviv, 1984. My translation from the Hebrew. For a further elaboration of the significance of Wiesel's statement, see chapter 7, I.

[4]In "Aschenglorie" ("Ashes-Glory"): "Niemand / zeugt für den / Zeugen."

[4 - bis]Celan's verse, "No one bears witness for the witness," is in effect so charged with absolute responsibility and utter solitude, so burdened with the uniqueness of the witnessing, that it becomes itself not a simple statement but a speech act which repeats, performs its own meaning in resisting our grasp, in resisting our replicating or recuperative witnessing. It thus performs its own solitude: it puts into effect what cannot be understood, transmitted, in the mission of transmission of the witness. It is the resonances of this *bearing*, of this burden of the performance of the witness, that will become, in all the senses of the word, the *burden* of this book—its leitmotif. In different forms and in a diversity of contexts, Celan's verse will indeed itself return through the various chapters of the present volume, like a compelling, haunting melody, like a directed beacon, an insistent driving force in the quest toward something which is not entirely within reach.

[5]Emmanuel Levinas, *Ethique et infini: Dialogues avec Philippe Nemo,* Paris: Fayard, 1982, p. 115. My translation from the French; emphasis mine.

Is the appointment to the testimony voluntary or involuntary, given *to* or *against* the witness's will? The contemporary writer often dramatizes the predicament (whether chosen or imposed, whether conscious or unconscious) of a voluntary or of an unwitting, inadvertent, and sometimes *involuntary witness*: witness to a trauma, to a crime or to an outrage; witness to a horror or an illness whose effects explode any capacity for explanation or rationalization.

The Scandal of an Illness

In Albert Camus' *The Plague*, for instance, the narrator, a physician by profession, feels historically appointed—by the magnitude of the catastrophe he has survived and by the very nature of his vocation as a healer—to narrate the story and bear witness to the history of the deadly epidemic which has struck his town:

> This chronicle is drawing to an end, and this seems to be the moment for Dr. Bernard Rieux to confess that he is the narrator . . . His profession put him in touch with a great many of our townspeople while plague was raging, and he had opportunities of hearing their various opinions. Thus he was well placed for giving a true account of all he saw and heard . . .
>
> Summoned to give evidence [appelé á tèmoigner] regarding what was a sort of crime, he has exercised the restraint that behooves a conscientious witness. All the same, following the dictates of his heart, he had deliberately taken the victims' side and tried to share with his fellow citizens the only certitudes they had in common—love, exile and suffering . . . Thus, decidedly, it was up to him to speak for all . . . Dr. Rieux resolved to compile this chronicle, so that he should not be one of those who hold their peace but should bear witness in favor of those plague-stricken people; so that some memorial of the injustice done them might endure.[6]

Camus' choice of the physician as the privileged narrator and the designated witness might suggest that the capacity to witness and the act of bearing witness in themselves embody some remedial quality and belong already, in obscure ways, to the healing process. But the presence of the doctor as key-witness also tells us, on the other hand, that what there is to witness urgently in the human world, what alerts and mobilizes the attention of the witness and what necessitates the testimony is always fundamentally, in one way or another, the scandal

[6]The Plague, trans. Stuart Gilbert, New York: Random House, 1972, pp. 270–287.

4

of an illness, of a metaphorical or literal disease; and that the imperative of bearing witness, which here proceeds from the contagion of
the plague—from the eruption of an evil that is radically incurable—
is itself somehow a philosophical and ethical correlative of a situation
with no cure, and of a radical human condition of exposure and
vulnerability.

In an Era of Testimony

Oftentimes, contemporary works of art use testimony both as the
subject of their drama and as the medium of their literal transmission.
Films like *Shoah* by Claude Lanzmann, *The Sorrow and the Pity* by
Marcel Ophuls, or *Hiroshima mon amour* by Marguerite Duras and
Alain Resnais, instruct us in the ways in which testimony has become
a crucial mode of our relation to events of our times—our relation to
the traumas of contemporary history: the Second World War, the
Holocaust, the nuclear bomb, and other war atrocities. As a relation
to events, testimony seems to be composed of bits and pieces of a
memory that has been overwhelmed by occurrences that have not
settled into understanding or remembrance, acts that cannot be con-
structed as knowledge nor assimilated into full cognition, events in
excess of our frames of reference.

What the testimony does not offer is, however, a completed statement, a totalizable account of those events. In the testimony, language
is in process and in trial, it does not possess itself as a conclusion, as
the constatation of a verdict or the self-transparency of knowledge.
Testimony is, in other words, a discursive *practice,* as opposed to a
pure *theory.* To testify—to *vow to tell,* to *promise* and *produce* one's
own speech as material evidence for truth—is to accomplish a *speech
act,* rather than to simply formulate a statement. As a performative
speech act, testimony in effect addresses what in history is *action* that
exceeds any substantialized significance, and what in happenings is
impact that dynamically explodes any conceptual reifications and any
constative delimitations.

Crisis of Truth

It has been suggested that testimony is the literary—or discursive—mode par excellence of our times, and that our era can precisely
be defined as the age of testimony. "If the Greeks invented tragedy,

the Romans the epistle and the Renaissance the sonnet," writes Elie Wiesel, "our generation invented a new literature, that of testimony."[7] What is the significance of this growing predominance of testimony as a privileged contemporary mode of transmission and communication? *Why has testimony in effect become at once so central and so omnipresent in our recent cultural accounts of ourselves?*

In its most traditional, routine use in the legal context—in the courtroom situation—testimony is provided, and is called for, when the facts upon which justice must pronounce its verdict are not clear, when historical accuracy is in doubt and when both the truth and its supporting elements of evidence are called into question. The legal model of the trial dramatizes, in this way, a contained, and culturally channeled, institutionalized, *crisis of truth.* The trial both derives from and proceeds by, a crisis of evidence, which the verdict must resolve.

What, however, are the stakes of the larger, more profound, less definable crisis of truth which, in proceeding from contemporary trauma, has brought the discourse of the testimony to the fore of the contemporary cultural narrative, way beyond the implications of its limited, restricted usage in the legal context?

II

The Story of a Class

As a way of investigating the significance of such a question, as well as of the questions raised in the beginning of this essay concerning the interaction between the clinical and the historical and the instructional relation between trauma, testimony and the enterprise of education, I devised some years ago a course entitled "Literature and Testimony." I subtitled it: "(Literature, Psychoanalysis, and History)". I announced it as a graduate seminar at Yale. The title drew some thirty graduate students, mainly from the literary disciplines, but also from psychology, philosophy, sociology, history, medicine and law.

I did not know then that I would myself, one day, have to articulate my testimony to that class, whose lesson—and whose unforeseeable eventness—turned out to be quite unforgettable, but not in ways that anyone could have predicted. I had never given—and have never given since—any other class like it, and have never been as stupefied

---

[7]"The Holocaust as a Literary Inspiration," in *Dimensions of the Holocaust,* Evanston: Northwestern University Press, 1977, p. 9.

by the inadvertent lessons and the unforeseeable effects of teaching as I was by the experience of this course. I would like to recount that uncanny pedagogical experience as my own "life-testimony," to share now the peculiar story of that real class whose narrative, in spite of its unique particularity, I will propose as a generic (testimonial) story (in a sense to which I will return, and from which I will later draw the implications): the story of how I became, in fact, myself a witness to the shock communicated by the subject-matter; the narrative of how the subject-matter was unwittingly *enacted*, set in motion in the class, and how testimony turned out to be at once more critically surprising and more critically important than anyone could have foreseen.

I have now repeated this course several times, but never with the same series of texts, never again in the say way and with the same framework of evidence. It was in the fall of 1984.

I organized my choice of texts around literary, psychoanalytic and historical accounts, which dramatize in different ways, through different genres and around different topics, the accounts of—or testimonies to—a crisis. The textual framework of the course included texts (or testimonies) by Camus, Dostoevsky, Freud, Mallarmé, Paul Celan, as well as autobiographical/historical life accounts borrowed from the Video Archive for Holocaust Testimonies at Yale. By thus conceiving of the course at once as a focused avenue of inquiry and as a varied constellation of texts, a diversity of works and genres in which testimony was inscribed in many ways and with a whole variety of implications, I had two tentative pedagogical objectives in mind: 1) to make the class feel, and progressively discover, how testimony is indeed *pervasive*, how it is implicated—sometimes unexpectedly— in almost every kind of writing; 2) to make the class feel, on the other hand, and—there again—progressively discover, how the testimony cannot be subsumed by its familiar notion, how the texts that testify do not simply *report facts* but, in different ways, encounter—and make us encounter—*strangeness*; how the concept of the testimony, speaking from a stance of superimposition of literature, psychoanalysis and history, is in fact quite unfamiliar and *estranging*, and how, the more we look closely at texts, the more they show us that, unwittingly, we do not even know what testimony is and that, in any case, it is not simply what we thought we knew it was.

How, indeed, has the significance of testimony itself been set in motion by the course, and how has it emerged, each time, at once in a new light and yet always still estranged, still a challenge for the task of understanding?

7

III

Narrative and Testimony: Albert Camus

It is the most familiar notion of the testimony, the one which we encounter daily through its usage by the media and are thus the most prepared for, because most acquainted with, with which we began the process of the exploration of the class. Taking as a starting point Camus' *The Plague*, we came first to believe—through the novel's underscored and most explicit indications—that the essence of the testimony is historical, and that its function is to record events and to report the facts of a historical occurrence. "To some," says the narrator of the novel, "these events [the outbreak of the plague] will seem quite unnatural; to others, all but incredible":

> But, obviously, a narrator cannot take account of these differences of outlook. His business is only to say: "This is what happened," when he knows that it actually did happen, that it closely affected the life of a whole populace, and that there are thousands of eyewitnesses who can appraise in their hearts the truth of what he writes.[6]

Thus, the narrator-doctor-witness feels both obligated and compelled to "chronicle" the "grave events" of the catastrophe he has survived and to "play the part of a historian" (6), to "bear witness," as he puts it, "in favor of those plague-stricken people, so that some memorial of the injustice done them might endure" (287). Since *The Plague* is a transparent allegory for the massive death inflicted by the Second World War and for the trauma of a Europe "quarantined" by German occupation and desperately struggling against the overwhelming deadliness of Nazism; since, indeed, a fragment of the novel was published literally as an *underground testimony*, as a French Resistance publication in Occupied France (in 1942), the witness borne by the doctor underscores, and at the same time tries to grasp and comprehend, the historical dimension of the testimony.

So did we, in class, focus, at the start, on this historical dimension. Surprisingly, however, the historical event *fails* to exhaustively account for the nature of the testimony, since the bearer of the testimony is not simply a "historian" but, primarily, a *doctor*, and since history appears, and is recorded, in the striking metaphor of a disease, a plague. Since the testimony dwells on historicity as a relationship to death, and since the act of writing—the act of making the artistic statement of the novel—is itself presented as an act of bearing witness to the trauma of survival, the *event* to which the testimony points and

8

Albert Camus as editor of "Combat," World War II

which it attempts to comprehend and grasp is enigmatically, at once historical and clinical. Is the testimony, therefore, a simple medium of historical transmission, or is it, in obscure ways, the unsuspected medium of a healing? If history has clinical dimensions, how can testimony *intervene*, pragmatically and efficaciously, at once historically (politically) *and* clinically?

Confession and Testimony: Fyodor Dostoevsky

If the testimony is, however, always an agent in a process that, in some ways, bears upon the clinical, how should we understand this clinical dimension when the testimony, in the course of its own utterance, quite explicitly rejects the very goal of healing and precludes any therapeutic project? This, as the class was to discover, is the case of Dostoevsky's hero or narrator, writing his *Notes from Underground*:

> I'm a sick man . . . a mean man. I think there's something wrong with my liver . . . But, actually, I don't understand a damn thing about my sickness; I'm not even too sure what it is that's ailing me. I'm not

Fyodor Dostoevsky, 1880

under treatment and never have been, although I have great respect for medicine and doctors. Moreover, I'm morbidly superstitious, enough, at least, to respect medicine. With my education, I shouldn't be superstitious, but I am just the same. No, I'd say I refuse medical help just out of contrariness. I don't expect *you* to understand that, but it's so. Of course, I can't explain who I am trying to fool this way. I'm fully aware that I can't spite the doctors by refusing their help. I know very well that I'm harming myself and no one else. But still, it's out of spite that I refuse to ask for the doctors' help. So my liver hurts? Good, let it hurt even more.[8]

[8]Dostoevsky, *Notes from Underground*, trans. Andrew MacAndrew, New York: Signet, 1961, pp. 90–91.

In thus presenting us with the "confession" of an illness that spites healing and does not seek cure, Dostoevsky's testimony, unlike Camus', seems to find its predilection in the clinical in a manner which subverts its very raison d'être and with such an exclusivity as to entirely preclude any larger perspective, any political or historical preoccupation. And yet, the clinical description, although crucial, is also crucially deceptive, and does not truly exhaust the testimonial stakes of Dostoevsky's text, whose complexity encompasses unwittingly a latent historical dimension: even through its very title, *Notes from the Underground* (1864) is written as a latent echo to a work Dostoevsky published two years earlier, *Notes from the House of the Dead*, in which the writer testifies to his historical and autobiographical experience as a political prisoner in a penitentiary in Siberia. Dostoevsky's early writings had placed him politically as a Russian liberal. Having joined a liberal circle of enthusiastic young men who met to discuss socialism, Dostoevsky was arrested, accused of complicity in a conspiracy (to set up a printing press), and condemned to death. The sentence was commuted to imprisonment, but, in a calculatedly cold-blooded farce devised by the tsarist authorities for

Before the execution.

11

the edification of subversives, the announcement of the pardon was made only in the middle of the ceremony of the execution, in the very face of the firing-squad. Some prisoners fainted. Two went permanently insane. Dostoevsky's epileptic fits, to which he had been subject since his childhood, were immeasurably aggravated.

In the guise of a confession that seeks above all to demystify and deconstruct itself, *Notes from Underground* can indeed be read as a belated *testimony to a trauma*, a trauma which endows Dostoevsky with the sickness of the one who "knows"—with the underground vision of the one who has been made into a *witness* of his own firing-squad. The testimony to the sickness encompasses, in fact, at once the history that lurks behind the clinical manifestations and the political oppression that signals mutely from behind the clinical "confession."

Unpredictably, the notion of the testimony thus turns out to be tied up, precisely, with the notion of the underground. In much the same way as Camus published *The Plague* as a literal member of the so-called "underground"—of the French Resistance during Nazi occupation—Dostoevsky's testimony from the underground equally, though unpredictably, encompasses not just the subterranean drift of the apparent clinical event, but the political dimension of oppression and the ethical dimension of resistance which proceed from, and inscribe within the testimony, the historical occurrence.

IV

Psychoanalysis and Testimony: Sigmund Freud

It was at this point that psychoanalysis was introduced into the course, and that the import of its lesson brought about a turning point in the insight of the class. We studied in particular Chapter 2 of *The Interpretation of Dreams*, with Freud's detailed account and interpretation of his "Irma dream." In our tentative awakening into the latent *clinical* dimension of the literary testimonies we had been examining, it was significant to note that Freud's narrated dream at once derives from (in reality), and enacts (in phantasy), the problematization of a setting that, this time explicitly, is clinical: the dream is triggered by the doctor's concern with his only partially successful treatment of his patient Irma: "the patient was relieved of her hysterical anxiety

12

Sigmund Freud in 1891, age thirty-five.

but did not lose all her somatic symptoms."[9] In the dream, the patient Irma is in fact complaining to the doctor, Freud, about her suffering and her continued pain. When Freud, while thinking of his dream, resorts to writing down for the first time ever all his free associations, he unexpectedly discovers, all at once, the dream's specific latent *meaning*, an unprecedented *method* of dream interpretation and a *theory* of dreams as psychical fulfillments of unconscious wishes:

> The dream acquitted me of the responsibility for Irma's condition by showing that it was due to other factors—it produced a whole series of reasons. The dream represented a particular state of affairs as I should have wished it to be. *Thus its content was the fulfillment of a wish and its motive was a wish.* [118–119]

[9]Freud, *The Interpretation of Dreams*, Chapter 2, "Analysis of a Specimen Dream," in *The Standard Edition of the Complete Psychological Works of Sigmund Freud*, translated from the German under the general editorship of James Strachey, Vol. IV, p. 106. Subsequent quotations from Freud's chapter, designating (in the body of the text) only page numbers in parenthesis, will refer to this edition.

13

Like Dostoevsky's *Notes* (although with an intention altogether different), Freud's *Dreams* in turn offer us, surprisingly enough, at once an autobiographical and a clinical *confession.* "I have other difficulties to overcome, which lie within myself," writes Freud. "There is some natural hesitation about revealing so many intimate facts about one's own mental life; nor can there be any guarantee against misinterpretation by strangers":

> [But] it is safe to assume that my readers . . . will very soon find their
> initial interest in the indiscretions which I am bound to make replaced
> by an absorbing immersion in the psychological problems upon which
> they throw light. [105]

Once again, then, in Freud's writing of his dreams, as in Dostoevsky's writing of his notes, the *testimony* differentiates itself from the content of the *manifest confession* which it uses as its vehicle, the confession is *displaced*, precisely, at the very moment that we think we grasp it, and it is in this surprise, in this displacement, that our sense of testimony will be shifted once again.

Considered as a testimony, Freud's discourse as a whole has an unprecedented status in the history of culture, in three respects: 1) the radical displacement that it operates in our understanding of the clinical dimension; 2) the validity and scientific recognition that it for the first time gives to unconscious testimony; 3) its unprecedented status as both a narrative and a theoretical event, as a narrative, in fact, of the advent of theory.

Freud's innovations as clinician stem, indeed, from his concern with how not to dismiss the patient's testimony—as medical doctors were accustomed to do in hysterics' cases—even when the physician does not understand this testimony. "So far," says Freud in the first of his *Five Lectures on Psychoanalysis*, "it has been an advantage to us to accompany the doctors; but the moment of parting is at hand. For you must not suppose that a patient's prospects of medical assistance are improved in essentials by the fact that a diagnosis of hysteria has been substituted for one of severe organic disease of the brain":

> Thus the recognition of the illness as hysteria makes little difference to
> the patient; but to the doctor quite the reverse. It is noticeable that his
> attitude towards hysterical patients is quite other than towards sufferers
> from organic diseases. He does not have the same sympathy for the
> former as for the latter. Through his studies the doctor has learned
> many things that remain a sealed book to the layman . . . But all his
> knowledge—his training in anatomy, in physiology and in pathology—

14

leaves him in the lurch when he is confronted by the details of hysterical phenomena. He cannot understand hysteria, and in the face of it he is himself a layman. This is not a pleasant situation for anyone who as a rule sets so much store by his knowledge. So it comes about that hysterical patients forfeit his sympathy. He regards them as people who are transgressing the laws of his science—like heretics in the eyes of the orthodox. He attributes every kind of wickedness to them, accuses them of exaggeration, of deliberate deceit, of malingering. And he punishes them by withdrawing his interest from them."[10]

In contrast, it is by stepping in his turn into the position of the patient, and by acknowledging an interchangeability between doctor and patient (a fact which the Irma dream dramatizes by Freud's own arthritic shoulder pain, echoing the pain of his patient Irma), that Freud creates the revolutionized clinical dimension of the *psychoanalytic dialogue*, an unprecedented kind of dialogue in which the doctor's testimony does not substitute itself for the patient's testimony, but *resonates with it*, because, as Freud discovers, *it takes two to witness the unconscious.*

In presenting his own testimony of the Irma dream as a correlative both to the dreams and to the symptoms of his patients, Freud makes a scientific statement of his discovery that there *is* in effect such a thing as an *unconscious testimony*, and that this unconscious, unintended, unintentional testimony has, as such, an incomparable heuristic and investigative value. Psychoanalysis, in this way, profoundly rethinks and radically renews the very concept of the testimony, by submitting, and by recognizing for the first time in the history of culture, that one does not have to *possess* or *own* the truth, in order to effectively *bear witness* to it; that speech as such is unwittingly testimonial; and that the speaking subject constantly bears witness to a truth that nonetheless continues to escape him, a truth that is, essentially, *not available* to its own speaker.

In the underground of language, Freud encounters Dostoevsky. Psychoanalysis and literature have come both to contaminate and to enrich each other. Both, henceforth, will be considered as primarily *events of speech*, and their testimony, in both cases, will be understood as a mode of *truth's realization* beyond what is available as statement, beyond what is available, that is, as a truth transparent to itself and

---

[10]First lecture, *Five Lectures on Psychoanalysis*, 1909 in *The Standard Edition of the Complete Psychological Works of Sigmund Freud*, Vol. XI (1910), pp 11–12. Consequent references to Freud's works (other than *The Interpretation of Dreams*) will refer to this edition under the abbreviation *Standard*, followed by volume number (in Roman numbers) and page number (in Arabic numbers).

entirely known, given, in advance, prior to the very process of its utterance. The testimony will thereby be understood, in other words, not as a mode of *statement of*, but rather as a mode of *access to*, that truth. In literature as well as in psychoanalysis, and conceivably in history as well, the witness might be—as the term suggests and as Freud knew only too well (as is evidenced by his insistence on "der Zeuge")—the one who (in fact) *witnesses*, but also, the one who *begets*, the truth, through the speech process of the testimony. This begetting of the truth is also what Freud does, precisely, through his witness and his testimony to the Irma dream, out of which he will *give birth* to the entire theory of dreams, and to its undreamt of implications.

Freud's whole attempt, henceforth, will be to bring the *evidence materialized* by the unconscious testimony into the realm of cognition. Through the material process of the act of *writing down* (which itself in some ways implicates the relevance, and the participation, in the psychoanalytic testimonial process, of the *literary act*): through a detailed recording and deciphering of the dream's associations, the Irma dream *bears witness* to the *unconscious* testimony of the dream in such a way as to transform it into the most reflective and most pointed *conscious* testimony, a conscious testimony which itself can only be grasped in the movement of its own production, and which increasingly embraces not just what is *witnessed*, but what is *begotten* by the unconscious testimony of the dream. The stupendous conscious testimony which the dream gives birth to will consist, therefore, not merely in the actual interpretation and elucidation of the dream, but in the transformation of this one particular event and of this one particular interpretation into a paradigmatic model not just of interpretation but of the very principle of psychoanalytical discovery, a model, that is, of the very birth of knowledge through the testimonial process. The unconscious testimony of one dream—through its conflation with the testimonies of other dreams—is transmuted into the pathbreaking conscious testimony of a universal *theory of dreams* which itself, in turn, founds the entire *theory of psychoanalysis.* Psychoanalytic theory, however, is nothing other than a finally available *statement* (or approximation) of a truth that, at the outset, was unknown but that was gradually *accessed* through the practice and the process of the testimony. In this sense, the whole *Interpretation of Dreams* can be viewed, indeed, as Freud's most revolutionary testimonial work: a universal testimonial work which at the same time dramatizes—to return once again to Canneti's terms with respect to Kafka's correspondence—a particular *life-testimony*, which, in this case, happens to be Freud's. In the preface to the second edition of *The Interpretation of Dreams*, written ten years after the original publication, Freud thus writes:

> The essence of what I have written about dreams and their interpretation, as well as about the psychological theorems to be deduced from them—all this remains unaltered: subjectively at all events, it has stood the test of time. Anyone who is acquainted with my other writings . . . will know that I have never put forward inconclusive opinions as though they were established facts, and that I have always sought to modify my statements so that they may keep in step with my advancing knowledge. In the sphere of my dream-life I have been able to leave my original assertions unchanged. During the long years in which I have been working at the problems of the neuroses I have often been in doubt and sometimes been shaken in my convictions. At such times it has always been *The Interpretation of Dreams* that has given me back my certainty.[11]

Much like Kafka's novel or Kafka's correspondence, much like Dostoevsky's underground or Camus' plague, Freud's dream narrative is equally, indeed, *the story of a trial*: a trial symbolized by the dramatic, anecdotal way in which Freud sees himself, within the dream, both tried and judged by his colleagues; an oneiric trial which, however, is itself the emblem of a larger, more decisive trial, encompassing the ways in which the revolutionary theory of psychoanalysis is being put to trial by the contemporary world. In this way, the very idiosyncrasy of Freud's autobiographical and clinical confession, the very triviality of the oneiric story of the trial, unwittingly emerges into the dimension of the truth of a ground breaking *theoretical event*. As the first dream Freud submitted not just to his own endeavor of detailed interpretation, not just to the further work of his own conscious understanding, but to the conscious witnessing of the whole world, the story of the Irma dream unsettlingly becomes, thus, a *generic* testimonial story.

The curious thing about this stunning theoretical event is the way in which its very generality hinges, paradoxically, on its accidental nature: on the contingency of a particular, idiosyncratic, symptomatic dream. In the symptomatic and yet theoretical illumination of this radically new kind of intelligibility, psychoanalysis can be viewed as a momentously felicitous, and a momentously creative, *testimony to an accident*.

[11]Freud, "Preface to the Second Edition," in *The Interpretation of Dreams, Standard*, Vol. IV (1900), pp. xxv–xxvi.

V

Poetry and Testimony: Stéphane Mallarmé, or An Accident of Verse

Curiously enough, it is also in such unexpected terms—those precisely of the testimony to an accident—that Mallarmé, the nineteenth-century French Symbolist and perhaps the greatest poet France has given to the world, speaks about contemporary poetry.

Having been invited to give a talk at Cambridge and at Oxford universities on new trends in French poetry—on the poetic revolution taking place around him in France—Mallarmé announces to his English audience:

> In effect I am bringing news, and the most surprising. Such a case has never been seen.
> They have done violence to verse . . .
> It is appropriate to relieve myself of that news right away—to talk about it now already—much like an invited traveler who, without delay, in breathless gasps, discharges himself of the testimony of an accident known, and pursuing him.[12]

The conjunction of the testimony and the accident that seemed at once to redefine the testimony in the psychoanalytical perspective and to pinpoint the newness of psychoanalysis, thus also describes, surprisingly enough, the altogether different realm of poetry in Mallarmé's perspective. Coincidentally, Mallarmé's and Freud's conceptual discoveries occur in the same year: Mallarmé's lecture in England is published in 1895, the very year in which Freud comes across the theory of dreams through the pivotal analysis of his Irma dream. I would suggest, indeed, that this remote conceptual and chronological encounter between Freud's and Mallarmé's juxtapositions of the testimony and the accident is not due purely to coincidence but that, in fact, in spite of the all-too-apparent differences between the two endeavors, something crucial in the depth of their conceptions and in the innovative thrust of their perceptions indeed resonates. What makes Mallarmé, therefore, at once perceive and in his turn convey

---

[12]"J'apporte en effet des nouvelles. Les plus surprenantes. Même cas ne se vit encore. Ils ont touché au vers. Il convient d'en parler déjà, ainsi qu'un invité voyageur tout de suite se décharge par traits haletants du témoignage d'un accident su et le poursuivant." "La Musique et les lettres," in Mallarmé, *Oeuvres complètes*, Paris: Gallimard (Bibliothèque de la Pléiade), 1945, pp. 643–644. Subsequent quotations from Mallarmé will refer to this French edition, indicated by page number. The English version of all cited texts from Mallarmé is here in my translation.

the very newness in French poetry as *testimony to an accident*? What is the nature of the accident referred to here by Mallarmé?

What the poetic revolution basically consists of is the introduction of "free verse" into French poetry, a change of form or a loosening of the poetic rules which entails a destitution or disintegration of the classical Alexandrine, the official French verse whose traditional twelve syllables and symmetric rhymes and rhythms had imposed themselves for centuries as the only possible mould—and as the only formal stamp—of French poetic writing.

If poetry can be essentially defined as an art of rhythm, Mallarmé redefines rhythm and thus radically rethinks the event of poetry as such through the rhythmical unpredictability of free verse which, in unsettling the predictibility—the formal structure of anticipation—of the Alexandrine, reaches out for what precisely *cannot be anticipated*: "they have done violence to verse." In opposition to the forms of traditional verse, poetry with Mallarmé becomes an *art of accident* in that it is an art of rhythmical surprises, an art, precisely, of unsettling rhythmical, syntactic and semantic expectations.

What is crucially important is, however, Mallarmé's acute and singular perception of the celebration of free verse as the violent experience of linguistic rupture, as the historical advent of a linguistic fragmentation in which the verse is violently and deliberately "broken," in what Mallarmé describes as a "fundamental crisis" which he calls, precisely, in a text so-titled *Crise de vers*, "Crisis of Verse."[13] As the testimony to an accident which is materially embodied in an *accidenting of the verse*, poetry henceforth speaks with the very power—with the very unanticipated impact—of its own explosion of its medium.

Apparently, the poetic revolution is purely aesthetic, purely formal. And yet, in Mallarmé's perception the *formal* change is crucially, implicitly endowed with a *political* dimension:

> In effect I am bringing news, and the most surprising.
> Such a case has never been seen. They have done violence to verse.
> Governments change: but always prosody remains intact: either, in the revolutions, it passes unnoticed, or the violent attempt upon it does not impose itself because of the opinion that this ultimate dogma can never vary. [643 – 644][14]

Mallarmé implicitly compares the effects of the poetic revolution to the ground-shaking processes unleashed by the French Revolution.

[13]Mallarmé, "Crise de vers," in "Variations sur un sujet," op. cit., p. 360.

[14]"Les gouvernements changent: toujours la prosodie reste intacte: soit que, dans les révolutions, elle passe inaperçue ou que l'attentat ne s'impose pas avec l'opinion que ce dogme dernier puisse varier."

Paradoxically enough, the political upheaval and the civil shaking of foundations brought about by the fall of governments and the collapse of institutions may not be in fact as profound and as radical a change as the one accomplished by a linguistic or by a poetic transformation. Insofar as the accidenting of the verse narrates the drama of the accidenting—the disruption and the shattering—of "this ultimate dogma," insofar as the resistance of tradition is now finally and formally dissolved and that traditional hierarchical divisions between poetry and prose—between *classes* in language—are now disposed of and inherently unsettled,[15] the breaking of the verse becomes itself a symptom and an emblem of the historical breaking of political and cultural grounds, and the freeing, or the *liberation* of the verse— through its decanonization—implicates the process of a vaster desacralization, of a vaster liberation taking place in social consciousness and in culture at large. "In effect, I am bringing news, and the most surprising." What is profoundly surprising, Mallarmé implies, is not simply that the verse is broken, but that the breaking of the verse picks up on something that the political dimensions of the French Revolution have inaugurated in their accidenting both of classes and of dogmas, but failed to consummate, failed to achieve completely. The revolution in poetic form testifies, in other words, to political and cultural changes whose historical manifestation, and its revolutionary aspect, is now noticed accidentally—accidentally breaks into awareness—through an *accident of verse.* The poetic revolution is thus both a replica and a sequence, an effect of, the French Revolution. What free verse by accident picks up on, therefore, is not merely former poetry which it now modifies, but the formerly unseen, ill-understood relationship which the accident reveals between culture and language, *between poetry and politics.*

The seeming triviality of the formal *location* of the accident in free verse—in a literal transgression of the rules of prosody and in a rupture of the Alexandrine—is thus fundamentally misleading. In much the same way as in Freud, the trivial story of the trial—in testifying to an *accident of dream*—amounts to a ground-breaking revolution in perception and in human understanding, Mallarmé's

---

[15]Free verse, in effect, has both declassified and mingled poetry and prose, both of which are henceforth equally infused with poetic inspiration. Prose, in Mallarmé's perspective, is essentially *poeticized* through the accidenting of the verse, and is thus no longer separate, no longer formally distinct from poetry. "Verse is all there is [le vers est tout]," says Mallarmé, "from the moment there is writing. There is style, versification, wherever there is rhythm, and this is why every prose . . . has the weight of a ruptured verse . . . This is indeed, the crowning of what was formerly entitled *prose poem*" ("La Musique et les lettres," *op. cit.*, p. 644).

accident of verse in effect bears witness to far-reaching transforma-
tions in the rhythm of life and to momentous cultural, political, and
historical processes of change.

Mallarmé's subject—his poetic testimony or the news he brings
about the accident—is, therefore, by no means trivial, nor is it, in
fact, what it appears to be: the scope of the accident is vaster, more
profound and more difficult to grasp than the sheer formality of the
concerns which convey it and which are its vehicle. Half way through
his Oxford lecture, Mallarmé acknowledges this *otherness* of his own
subject, which he himself does not entirely possess:

> In effect I am bringing news, and the most surprising . . .
> They have done violence to verse . . .
> It is appropriate to relieve myself of that news right away—to talk
> about it now already—much like an invited traveler who, without delay,
> in breathless gasps, discharges himself of the testimony of an accident
> known and pursuing him . . .
> Should I stop here, and where do I get the feeling that *I have come
> relatively to a subject vaster and to myself unknown*—vaster than this
> or that innovation of rites or rhymes; in order to *attempt to reach* this
> subject, if not to treat it . . .
> Consciousness in us is lacking of what, above, explodes or splits.[16]
> [643–647; emphasis mine]

In a way, Mallarmé suggests that he speaks too soon, before he is
quite ready, before he quite knows what his subject is about. And yet,
since he has been a witness to "an accident known," since he does
know that an accident has taken place, and since the accident "pursues
him," he has got to speak "*already*," almost compulsively, even though
he has not had as yet the time to catch his breath. He thus speaks in
advance of the control of consciousness; his testimony is delivered
"in breathless gasps": in essence, it is a *precocious testimony.*

Such precocious testimony in effect becomes, with Mallarmé, the
very principle of poetic insight and the very core of the event of
poetry, which makes precisely language—through its breathless
gasps—speak ahead of knowledge and awareness and break through
the limits of its own conscious understanding. By its very innovative
definition, poetry will henceforth speak *beyond its means, to testify*—
precociously—to the ill-understood effects and to the impact of an
accident whose origin cannot precisely be located but whose reper-

[16]"Faut-il s'arrêter là et d'où ai-je le sentiment que je suis venu relativement à un
sujet plus vaste peut-être à moi-même inconnu, que telle rénovation de rites et de
rimes; pour y atteindre, sinon le traiter . . .
Le conscient manque chez nous de ce qui là-haut éclate."

Stéphane Mallarmé, by Edouard Manet. Paris, Louvre.

cussions, in their very uncontrollable and unanticipated nature, still continue to evolve even in the very process of the testimony.

The accident is therefore "known," paradoxically enough, at once precociously but only through its aftermath, through its effects.[17] The accident is known, in other words, both to the extent that *it "pursues"* the witness and that *the witness is, in turn, in pursuit of it.* Indeed, the syntax of the French expression "ainsi qu'un invité voyageur se décharge du témoignage d'un accident su et le poursuivant" is radically ambiguous. As Barbara Johnson has pointed out, Mallarmé's unique poetic style—in its play on this syntactic ambiguity—leaves in suspension the question of who is pursuing whom, whether it is the accident that pursues the witness-traveler or whether it is the traveler, the witness, who pursues the accident:

> Is is the accident [—writes Johnson—] which pursues the traveler, or rather, the traveler who . . . pursues the accident? Where is the accident

[17]On the belated knowledge of "the accident," and the significance of this belatedness for an understanding of the relation between trauma and history, see Cathy Caruth, "Unclaimed Experience: Trauma and the Possibility of History" (in Freud), in *Yale French Studies*, "Literature and the Ethical Question," ed. Claire Nouvet, January 1991.

situated? . . . Is the witness the one who *sees*, the one who *undergoes*, or the one who *propagates*, the accident to which he bears witness?[18]

What difference does this ambiguity make in our understanding of the accident and of the testimony?

If it is the accident which *pursues the witness*, it is the compulsive character of the testimony which is brought into relief: the witness is "pursued," that is, at once compelled and bound by what, in the unexpected impact of the accident, is both incomprehensible and unforgettable. The accident does not let go: it is an accident from which the witness can no longer free himself.

But if, in a still less expected manner, it is the witness who *pursues the accident*, it is perhaps because the witness, on the contrary, has understood that from the accident a *liberation* can proceed and that *the accidenting*, unexpectedly, is also in some ways *a freeing.*

Mallarmé thus pursues the accident of *free verse* in the same way Freud pursues, after an accident of dream, the path of *free association.* Both *free verse* and *free association* undergo the process of a fragmentation—a breaking down, a disruption and a dislocation—of the dream, of verse, of language, of the apparent but misleading unities of syntax and of meaning. The passage through this fragmentation is a passage through a radical obscurity. "One does not write," Mallarmé says, "luminously, on an obscure field . . . ; man pursues black on white":[19]

To write—
The inkwell, crystal as a consciousness, with its drop of darkness at the bottom, . . . casts the lamp aside.[20]

"Hitherto," says Freud, ". . . all the paths along which we have traveled have led us toward the light—toward elucidation and fuller understanding":

But as soon as we endeavor to penetrate more deeply into the mental process involved in dreaming, *every path will end in darkness.* There is no possibility of explaining dreams since to explain a thing means to trace it back to something already known.[21]

---

[18]*Défigurations du langage poétique*, Paris: Flammarion, 1979, pp. 169–170; my translation.

[19]"Tu remarquas, on n'écrit pas, lumineusement, sur champ obscur . . . ; l'homme poursuit noir sur blanc." "L'Action restreinte," in Mallarmé, op. cit., p. 370.

[20]"Ecrire—L'encrier, cristal comme une conscience, avec sa goutte, au fond, des ténèbres . . . écarte la lampe." *Ibid.*, p. 370.

[21]Freud, *The Interpretation of Dreams*, in *Standard*, Vol. V, pp. 509–511.

Mallarmé's handwriting and signature (in a dedication of a book of poems)

In Mallarmé's as well as in Freud's case, what constitutes the specificity of the innovative figure of the witness is, indeed, not the mere telling, not the mere fact of *reporting* of the accident, but the witness's readiness to become himself a *medium of the testimony*—and a *medium of the accident*—in his unshakable conviction that the accident, formal or clinical, carries historical significance which goes beyond the individual and is thus, in effect, in spite of its idiosyncrasy, *not trivial.* What makes the newness and the radicality of the poetic—and the psychoanalytical—performance of a testimony which is both "surprising" and momentous is, in other words, not just the inescapability of the vocation of the witness insofar as the accident pursues him, but the witness's readiness, precisely, to *pursue the accident*, to actively pursue its path and its direction through obscurity, through darkness, and through fragmentation, without quite grasping the full scope and meaning of its implications, without entirely foreseeing where the journey leads and what is the precise nature of its final destination.

24

Poetry and Testimony: Paul Celan, or The Accidenting of Aesthetics

Half a century after Mallarmé, another poet will proceed to write in Paris (though this time in German) poetry that dramatizes yet another, more acute and more severe crisis of verse which, in its turn, sets out to *pursue* an "accidenting," to explore another kind of historic cataclysm and bear witness to another "fundamental crisis"—a fundamental shift in thinking and in being—proceeding this time not from the renewal triggered by a revolution, but from the destruction and the devastation which the Second World War and, in particular, the Holocaust, have set in motion. In exploding, once again—in the footsteps of the lesson taught by Mallarmé—its own poetic medium, in dislocating its own language and in breaking its own verse, the poetry of Paul Celan gives testimony, in effect, no longer simply to what Mallarmé refers to as an undefined, generic "accident," but to a more specific, more particularly crushing and more recent, cultural and historical breakdown, to the individual and the communal, massive trauma of a catastrophic loss and a disastrous fate in which nothing any more can be construed as *accident* except, perhaps, for *the poet's own survival.* Mallarmé's crisis of verse has come now to express, concretely and specifically, Celan's particular historical reality and his literally shattering experience as a Holocaust survivor. *The breakage of the verse enacts the breakage of the world.*

Like Mallarmé, the witness to the accident, Celan, the witness to catastrophe, is in turn a traveler, a witness-traveler whose poetry precisely is researching, through its testimony, the obscure direction and the unknown destination of his journey. "I have written poems," says Celan, "so as to speak, to orient myself, to explore where I was and was meant to go, to sketch out reality for myself."[22] Unlike Mallarmé, however, who brings "surprising news" to England as an "invited traveller," ("an invited traveller who, without delay, in breathless gasps, discharges himself of the testimony of an accident known and pursuing him"), Celan's witness is not that of an "invited," but rather that of an evicted, traveler: one whose journey has originated in the constraint of deportation, in the throes of an *ejection* from his native country.

[22]Paul Celan, *Bremen Speech*, address given on acceptance of the Literature Prize of the Free Hanseatic City of Bremen, in 1958. Here and elsewhere in this chapter, the Bremen speech is quoted in John Felstiner's translation, cited in John Felstiner, "Translating Celan's Last Poem," in *The American Poetry Review*, July/August 1982, p. 23.

Paul Ancel, who will after the War rename himself—anagrammati-
cally—Celan, was born to German-Jewish parents in 1920 in Czernowitz, Bukovina, a northern province of Romania. In July 1941 an *S.S.
Einsazgruppe*, aided by Romanian troops, began destroying Czernowitz's Jewish community. In 1942, Celan's parents were deported to a
concentration camp. Paul Celan managed to escape, but was sent to
a forced labor camp, in which he hauled debris and shoveled rocks
for eighteen months. The only letter Paul received from his mother
informed him that his father, totally spent, had been killed by the S.S.
A few months later, Paul learned from an escaped cousin that his
mother was in turn murdered, shot through the back of the neck. A
story published in a German newspaper in the late seventies suggests
that Celan (uncannily not unlike Dostoevsky) faced and in turn escaped execution in the camp, by crossing over a dividing line, by
switching places *in extremis* from a formation marked for death to
one designated for the fate of slave labor.

In 1944, Celan returns to Czernowitz, which has been liberated by
Soviet troops. After the war, he moves to Bucharest, then to Vienna,
and finally settles in Paris in 1948. His poetic translations from French,
English and Russian into German, accompany the publication of his
own poetic works, which win him both prestigious literary prizes and
immediate critical acclaim in the German-speaking world.

In April 1970, at the age of forty-nine, Paul Celan commits suicide
by drowning himself in the Seine.

In spite of his mastery of many languages and of his fluency in many
literatures, in spite of his own choice to live in Paris and to be
conversant with French culture, Celan could not give up writing in
German. "I do not believe in bilingualness in poetry," he said, in reply
to a question about his linguistic choices. "Poetry—that is the fateful
uniqueness of language."[23] To his biographer, Israel Chalfen, Celan
explained his loyalty to German: "Only in one's mother tongue can
one express one's own truth. In a foreign language the poet lies."[24]
Yet, this bonding to the mother tongue, this intimate connection to
the spoken legacy of his lost mother as the only language to which
truth—his own unique truth—can be *native*, is also, quite unbearably,

[23]Paul Celan, *Gesammelte Werke*, Frankfurt am Main: 1968, Vol. II, p. 20. John
Felstiner's translation. Quoted in John Felstiner, in "Mother Tongue, Holy Tongue: On
"Translating and Not Translating Paul Celan," in *Comparative Literature* 38, no. 2, Spring
1986, p. 122.

[24]Israel Chalfen, *Eine Biographie seiner Jugend, 1979*. Quoted in Katharine Washburn's introduction to *Paul Celan: Last Poems*, San Francisco: North Point Press, 1986,
p. vii.

Paul Ancel in Czernowitz, 1936, age sixteen

an indissoluble connection to the language of the murderers of his own parents, a subjugation to the very language from which death, humiliation, torture and destruction issued, in a verdict of his own annihilation. Celan's poetic writing therefore struggles with the German to annihilate his own annihilation in it, to reappropriate the language which has marked his own exclusion: the poems dislocate the language so as to remould it, to radically shift its semantic and grammatical assumptions and remake—creatively and critically—a new poetic language entirely Celan's own. Mallarmé's crisis of language here becomes the vital effort—and the critical endeavor—to

27

reclaim and repossess the very language in which *testimony* must—and cannot simply and uncritically—be given. This radical, exacting working through of language and of memory at once, takes place through a desperate poetic and linguistic struggle to, precisely, reappropriate the very language of one's own expropriation, to reclaim the German from its Nazi past and to retrieve the mother tongue—the sole possession of the dispossessed—from the Holocaust it has inflicted. "These," says Celan, "are the efforts of someone . . . shelterless in a sense undreamt of till now . . . , who goes with his very being to language, stricken by and seeking reality":

> Within reach, close and not lost, there remained, in the midst of the losses, this one thing: language.
>
> This, the language, was not lost but remained, yes, in spite of everything. But it had to pass through its own answerlessness, pass through a frightful falling mute, pass through the thousand darknesses of death-bringing speech. It passed through and yielded no words for what was happening—but it went through those happenings. Went through and could come into the light of day again, "enriched" by all that.
>
> In this language I have sought, then and in the years since then, to write poems—so as to speak, to orient myself, to explore where I was and was meant to go, to sketch out reality for myself.
>
> This, you see, was event, movement, a being underway, an attempt to gain direction. And if I ask about its meaning, I think I must say that this question also involves the clockhand's meaning.
>
> . . . These are the efforts of someone coursed over by the stars of human handiwork, someone also shelterless in a sense undreamt-of till now and thus most uncannily out in the open, who goes with his very being to language, stricken by and seeking reality [wirklichkeitswund und Wirklichkeit suchend].[25]

To *seek* reality is both to set out to explore the injury inflicted by it—to turn back on, and to try to penetrate, the state of being *stricken, wounded* by reality [wirklichkeitswund]—and to attempt, at the same time, to reemerge from the paralysis of this state, to engage reality [Wirklichkeit suchend] as an advent, a movement, and as a vital, critical necessity of *moving on.* It is beyond the shock of being stricken, but nonetheless within the wound and from within the woundedness that the event, incomprehensible though it may be, becomes accessible. The wound gives access to the darkness which the language had to go through and traverse in the very process of its "frightful falling-mute." To seek reality through language "with one's very being," to seek in language what the language had precisely to

[25]*Bremen Speech.*

pass through, is thus to make of one's own "shelterlessness"—of the openness and the accessibility of one's own wounds—an unexpected and unprecedented means of *accessing reality*, the radical condition for a wrenching exploration of the testimonial function, and the testimonial power, of the language: it is to give reality one's own vulnerability, as a condition of exceptional availability and of exceptionally sensitized, tuned in attention to the *relation between language and events*.

One such poem which attempts to probe precisely this relation between language and events is "Todesfuge" ("Death Fugue"), Celan's first published poem, written toward the end of 1944, immediately upon the poet's own emergence from his devastating war experience. The poem dramatizes and evokes a concentration camp experience, not directly and explicitly, however, not through linear narrative, through personal confession or through testimonial reportage, but elliptically and circularly, through the polyphonic but ironically disjointed art of counterpoint, and through the obsessional, compulsive repetitions and the vertiginous explosion of a mad song whose lament—half blasphemy, half prayer—bursts at once into a speechless, voiceless crying and into the dancing tumult of a drunken celebration. Amazingly enough, the poem which depicts the most unthinkable complexities of horror and the most outrageously degrading depths of suffering is not a poem about killing, but, primarily, a poem about *drinking*, and about the relation (and the nonrelation) between "drinking" and "writing."

> Black milk of daybreak we drink it at sundown
> we drink it at noon in the morning we drink it at night
> we drink and we drink it
> we dig a grave in the breezes there one lies unconfined
> A man lives in the house he plays with the serpents he writes
> he writes when dusk falls to Germany your golden hair
>   Margarete
> he writes it and steps out of doors and the stars are flashing he
>   whistles his pack out
> he whistles his Jews out in earth has them dig for a grave
> he commands us strike up for the dance
>
> . . . .
> he writes when dusk falls to Germany your golden hair
>   Margarete
> your ashen hair Shulamith we dig a grave in the breezes
>   there one lies unconfined.[26]

[26]"Death Fugue," Michael Hamburger's translation, in Paul Celan, *Poems*, selected, translated and introduced by Michael Hamburger, New York: Persea Books, 1980, p. 51.

The performance of the act of drinking, traditionally a poetic metaphor for yearning, for romantic thirst and for desire, is here transformed into the surprisingly abusive figure of an endless torture and a limitless exposure, a figure for the impotent predicament and the unbearable ordeal of having to endure, absorb, continue to *take in* with no end and no limit. This image of the drunkenness of torture ironically perverts, and ironically demystifies, on the one hand, the Hellenic-mythic connotation of libidinal, euphoric Dionysiac drinking of both wine and poetry, and on the other hand, the Christian connotation of ritual religious consecration and of Eucharistic, sacred drinking of Christ's blood—and of Christ's virtue. The prominent underlying Eucharistic image suggests, however, that the enigmatic drinking which the poem repetitiously invokes is, indeed, essentially drinking of blood.

The perversion of the metaphor of drinking is further aggravated by the enigmatic image of the "black milk," which, in its obsessive repetitions, suggests the further underlying—though unspeakable and inarticulated—image of a child striving to drink from the mother's breast. But the denatured "black milk," tainted possibly by blackened, burnt ashes, springs not from the mother's breast but from the dark-ness of murder and death, from the blackness of the night and of the "dusk" that "falls to Germany" when death uncannily becomes a "master." Ingesting through the liquefied black milk at once dark blood and burnt ashes, the drinking takes place not at the maternal source but at the deadly source, precisely, of the wound, at the bleeding site of reality as stigma.

The Christian figure of the wound, traditionally viewed as the mythic vehicle and as the metaphoric means for a *historical transcen-dence*—for the erasure of Christ's death in the advent of Resurrec-tion—is reinvested by the poem with the literal concreteness of the death camp blood and ashes, and is made thus to include, within the wound, not resurrection and historical transcendence, but the specificity of history—of the concrete historical reality of massacre and race annihilation—as unerasable and untranscendable. What Celan does, in this way, is to force the language of the Christian metaphorics to *witness* in effect the Holocaust, and be in turn wit-nessed by it.

The entire poem is, indeed, not simply about violence but about the relation between violence and language, about the passage of the language through the violence and the passage of the violence through

Quotations from Celan's poetry in Hamburger's translation will subsequently be cited as Hamburger, followed by page number.

language. The violence enacted by the poem is in the *speech acts* of the German master, the commandant who directs the orchestra of the camp inmates to musically accompany their own grave digging and to celebrate, in an ecstatic death fugue, at once the wounding of the earth and their own destruction and annihilation. But it is already in the very practice of his language that the commandant in effect annihilates the Jews, by actively denying them as *subjects*, by reducing their subjective individuality to a mass of indistinct, debased, inhuman *objects*, playthings of his whims, marionettes of his own pleasure of destruction and musical instruments of his own sadistic passion.

> he whistles his Jews out in earth has them dig for a grave
> he commands us strike up for the dance
>
> . . . .
>
> He calls out jab deeper into the earth you lot you others sing
> > now and play
>
> . . . .
>
> jab deeper you lot with your spades you others play on for the
> > dance
>
> He calls out more sweetly play death death is a master from
> > Germany
> he calls out more darkly now stroke your strings then as
> > smoke you will rise into air
> than a grave you will have in the clouds there one lies
> > unconfined

The violence is all the more obscene by being thus *aestheticized* and by aestheticizing its own dehumanization, by transforming its own murderous perversity into the cultural sophistication and the cultivated trances of a hedonistic art performance. But the poem works specifically and contrapuntally to dislocate this masquerade of cruelty as art, and to exhibit the obscenity of this aesthetization, by opposing the melodious ecstasy of the aesthetic pleasure to the dissonance of the commandant's speech acts and to the violence of his verbal abuse, and by reintroducing into the amnesia of the "fugue"—into the obliviousness of the *artistic drunkenness*—the drinking of black milk as *the impossibility of forgetting* and of getting a reprieve from suffering and memory, and as the sinister, insistent, *unforgettable return of what the aesthetic pleasure has forgotten.*

> we drink and we drink you
> A man lives in the house he plays with the serpents he writes
> he writes when dusk falls to Germany your golden hair
> > Margarete

> your ashen hair Shulamith we dig a grave in the breezes there
> > one lies unconfined
>
> Black milk of daybreak we drink you at night
> we drink you at noon . . .
> > . . . we drink and we drink you
>
> death is a master from Germany his eyes are blue
> he strikes you with leaden bullets his aim is true
> a man lives in the house your golden hair Margarete
> he sets his pack on to us he grants us a grave in the air
> he plays with the serpents and daydreams death is a master
> > from Germany
>
> Your golden hair Margarete
> your ashen hair Shulamith

The entire poem is contingent upon various forms of apostrophe and of address. The dehumanizing and annihilating interjections of the murderous address—"you lot, you others"—the address which institutes the other not as *subject* but as *target* ("He strikes you with leaden bullets his aim is true"), meets and clashes with the dreamy yearnings of the desiring address, the address that institutes the other as a *subject of desire* and, as such, a *subject of response*, of a called for *answer*:

> Your golden hair Margarete
> your ashen hair Shulamith

Marguerite, Faust's object of desire and Goethe's incarnation of romantic love, evokes at once the general tradition of German literary yearning and the actual longing—possibly of the commandant—for his German beloved. Shulamith, a female emblem of both beauty and desire celebrated and admired in *The Song of Songs*, evokes the Jewish biblical and literary yearning and the longing for the Jewish beloved. The invocation of the cherished name is traversed by the same depth of joy and sadness, charged with the same energy of human longing and desire. The yearnings, as such, resonate with one another. And yet, a bitter difference and a shocking irony resound from within this echoing resemblance. In contrast to the golden hair of Marguerite, the ashen hair of Shulamith connotes not just a mark of racial difference between the fair-haired maiden of the Aryan ideal and the ashen pallor of the Semitic beauty, but the hair reduced to ashes, the burnt hair of one race as opposed to the aesthetic idealization and self-idealization of the other race. Like the light of "daybreak" turned into night and into darkness, the dissonance of golden and of ashen thus produces, once again, only "black milk" as an answer to one's thirst, one's longing, one's desire. The call to Shulamith—beauty reduced to smoke—is bound to remain unanswered.

Black milk of daybreak we drink you at night

. . . .

we drink and we drink you
A man lives in the house he plays with the serpents he writes
he writes when dusk falls to Germany your golden hair
Margarete
your ashen hair Shulamith we dig a grave in the breezes there
one lies unconfined

The wound within the culture opens up in the discrepancy, the muteness, the abrupt disjunction, not only between "Marguerite" and "Shulamith," but, primarily, between "*we drink*," "*we dig*" and "*he writes*." The open wound is marked within the language by the incapacity of "*we*" to *address*, precisely, in this poem of apostrophe and of address, the "*he*." It is in this radical disruption of address between the "*we*" (who "drink" and "dig") and the "*he*" (who "writes" and who "commands") that Celan locates the very essence of the violence, and the very essence of the Holocaust.

If "death is a master from Germany," it is a "master" not just in the sense that it brings death and that it totally controls its slaves, nor even merely, in addition, in the sense that it plays the *maestro*, the musician or the meistersinger, *master of arts* who strives, ironically enough, to produce death as artistic *masterpiece*, but in the sense that Germany, unwittingly, has instituted death as Meister, as a *master-teacher*. Death has taught a lesson that can henceforth never be forgotten. If art is to survive the Holocaust—to survive death as a master—it will have to break, in art, this mastery, which insidiously pervades the whole of culture and the whole of the aesthetic project.

The necessity for art to *de-aestheticize* itself and to justify henceforth its own existence, has been forcefully articulated by the German critic Theodor Adorno, in a famous dictum which defines, indeed, Celan's predicament but which has become itself (perhaps too readily) a critical cliché, too hastily consumed and too hastily reduced to a summary dismissal of Celan's troubling poetic efficacity in poems like "Death Fugue": "After Auschwitz, it is no longer possible to write poems."[27] "The aesthetic principle of stylization," writes Adorno, " . . .

[27]"After Auschwitz" (1949), "Meditations on Metaphysics," in *Negative Dialectics*, trans. E. B. Ashton, New York: Continuum, 1973, p. 362.

make[s] an unthinkable fate appear to have had some meaning; it is transfigured, something of its horror is removed. This alone does an injustice to the victims . . . [Some] works . . . are even willingly absorbed as contributions to clearing up the past."[28] In Adorno's radical conception, it is, however, not just these specific works, nor simply lyric poetry as genre, but all of thinking, all of writing that has now to think, to write *against itself*:

> If thinking is to be true—if it is to be true today, in any case—it must be thinking against itself. If thought is not measured by the extremity that eludes the concept, it is from the outset in the nature of the musical accompaniment with which the SS liked to drown out the screams of its victims.[29]

Adorno himself, however, will return to his statement about poetry and Auschwitz in a later essay, to redefine its emphasis, to underscore the aporetic, and not simply negative, intention of his radical pronouncement, and to emphasize the fact (less known and more complex) that, paradoxically enough, it is only art that can henceforth be equal to its own historical impossibility, that art alone can live up to the task of contemporary thinking and of meeting the incredible demands of suffering, of politics and of contemporary consciousness, and yet escape the subtly omnipresent and the almost unavoidable cultural betrayal both of history and of the victims.

> I have no wish to soften the saying that to write lyric poetry after Auschwitz is barbaric . . . But Enzensberger's retort also remains true, that *literature must resist this verdict* . . . It is now virtually in art alone that suffering can still find its own voice, consolation, without immediately being betrayed by it.
>
> Today, every phenomenon of culture, even if a model of integrity, is liable to be suffocated in the cultivation of kitsch. Yet paradoxically in the same epoch it is to works of art that has fallen the burden of wordlessly asserting what is barred to politics.[30]

The whole endeavor of Celan's poetic work can be defined, precisely, in Adorno's terms, as poetry's creative and self-critical *resistance to the verdict* that it is barbaric, henceforth, to write lyrically, poetically; a verdict which the poetry receives, however, not from the outside but from inside itself; a verdict which "Death Fugue" encompasses

[28]Adorno, "Commitment" (1962), in *The Essential Frankfurt School Reader*, ed. Andrew Arato and Eike Gebhardt, introduction by Paul Ricoeur, New York: Continuum, 1982, p. 313.

[29]"After Auschwitz", op. cit., p. 365.

[30]"Commitment," *op. cit.*, pp. 312, 318.

already, and in fact enacts and sets in motion through the master's usurpation of the singing of the inmates.

*

Something of that usurpation has, however, inadvertently reproduced itself even in the very destiny of "Todesfuge," whose immense success and frequent anthologization in the German-speaking world had soon turned Celan into something like another celebrated "master." Celan himself, in later years, thus turned against his early poem, refused to allow its reprinting in further anthologies, and changed his writing style into a less explicit, less melodious, more disrupted and disruptively elliptical verse.

> **NO MORE SAND ART,** no sand book, no masters.
>
> Nothing won by dicing. How many
> dumb ones?
> Seventeen.
>
> Your question—your answer.
> Your song, what does it know?
>
> Deepinsnow,
>   Eepinnow,
>   Ee–i–o.

To prevent the possibility of an aesthetic, drunken infatuation with its own verse, the later poetry rejects, within the language, not its music and its singing—which continue to define the essence of poetic language for Celan—but a certain predetermined kind of recognizably *melodious* musicality. In Celan's own words, the verse henceforth "distrusts the beautiful, . . . insists on having its 'musicality' placed in a region where it no longer has anything in common with that 'melodious sound' which more or less undisturbed sounded side by side with the greatest horror. The concern of this language is, in all the unalterable multivalence of the expression, *precision.* It doesn't transfigure, doesn't 'poeticize, it names and places."[31]

> Deep in Time's crevasse
> by the alveolate
> waits, a crystal of breath,
> your irreversible
> witness.[32]

[31]"Reply to an Inquiry Held by the Librairie Flinker, Paris," (The Paper Castle), p. 23; emphasis mine.

[32]"Etched Away," in Hamburger, p. 189.

Paul Celan, 1947/48, age twenty-seven

The quest for musical precision—which shuns melody and which refrains, above all, from "poeticizing"—is, however, coupled with a tendency toward silence. "Tendency toward silence," notes Celan, "—this, too, can't be said just so. We mustn't create new fetishes. Even the anti-fetish can become a fetish."[33]

NO MORE SAND ART, no sand book, no masters.

[33]Paul Celan, "Conversational Statements on Poetry," in *Prose Writings and Selected Poems*, trans. Walter Billeter, The Paper Castle, p. 45.

"One of the truths hardest to demonstrate"—writes Pierre Boulez in an analysis of contemporary music that could apply as well to Celan's revised poetic musicality—"one of the truths hardest to demonstrate is that music is not just the 'Art of sound'—that it must be defined rather as a counterpoint of sound and silence. [Contemporary music's] rhythmic innovation is this conception whereby sound and silence are linked in a precise organization directed toward the exhaustive exploitation of our powers of hearing."[34]

By introducing silence as a rhythmic *breakdown* and as a displacing *counterpoint* to sound not just *in between* his stanzas and his verses, but even *in the very midst* of the phonetic flow and the poetic diction of his *words* ("You my words being crippled / together with me . . . / with the hu, with the man, with the human being."),[35] Celan strives to defetishize his language and to dislocate his own aesthetic mastery, by breaking down any self-possessed control of sense and by disrupting any unity, integrity or continuity of conscious meaning. Through their very breakdown, the sounds testify, henceforth, precisely to a knowledge they do not possess, by unleashing, and by drifting into, their own buried depths of silence.

> Your question—your answer.
> Your song, what does it know?
>
> Deepinsnow,
>   Eepinnow,
>   Ee–i–o.

But this breakdown of the word, this drift of music and of sound of the song which resists recuperation and which does not know, and cannot own, its meaning, nonetheless reaches a *you*, attains the hearing—and perhaps the question, or the answer, of an Other: "*Your question—your* answer / *Your* song." The poem strives toward the *Du*, the *you*, the listener, over the historical abyss from which the singing has originated and across the violence and the unending, shattered resonances of the breakage of the word. "A poem," writes Celan, "as a manifest form of language and thus inherently dialogue, can be a message in a bottle, sent out in the (not always greatly hopeful) belief that it may somewhere and sometime wash up on land, on heartland perhaps":

---

[34]Pierre Boulez, *The Threshold*, quoted by Katharine Washburn in her introduction to Paul Celan, *Last Poems*, San Francisco: North Point Press, 1986, p. xxv.

[35]". . . Plashes the Fountain," in Hamburger, p. 151.

Poems in this sense are always under way, they are making toward something.

Toward what? Toward something standing open, occupiable, perhaps toward a "thou" that can be *addressed*, an *addressable* reality.[36]

As an event directed toward the recreation of a "thou," poetry becomes, precisely, the event of *creating an address* for the specificity of a historical experience which annihilated any possibility of address. If the lesson of death ("Todesfuge's" *executioner, commandant* and *maestro*)—the lesson of the master—was precisely that a master is the one who *cannot be addressed*, the one to whom one cannot say "*you*," Celan's poetry now strives not simply, as is often said, to seek out the responsive *you*, to recreate the listener, the hearer, but to subvert, to dislocate and to displace the very essence of aesthetics as a *project of artistic mastery* by transforming poetry—as breakage of the word and as drifting testimony—into an inherent and unprecedented, testimonial *project of address*.

> As one speaks to stone, like
> you,
> from the chasm, from
> a home become a sister to me, hurled
> towards me, you,
> you that long ago
> you in the nothingness of a night,
> you in the multi-night en-
> countered, you
> multi-you—.[37]
>
> and at times when
> only the void stood between us we got
> all the way to each other.[38]

Crossing the Void, or Poetry as Setting Free

Along with the above-sketched journey of the various writers, theorists and poets, the class traveled its own path. Opened up to the diversity and touched by the concrete peculiarities of literary, clinical, historical and poetic testimonies; captivated and surprised by the unexpected ways in which the very different texts nonetheless unwit-

[36]*Bremen Speech.* Emphasis mine.
[37]"Radix, Matrix," in Hamburger, p. 153.
[38]"So many constellations," in Hamburger, p. 135.

tingly evolved into each other, came to engage each other's depth and put each other in an increasingly complex perspective, the students reemerged from each textual encounter somewhat changed. The formal and historical vicissitudes of Celan's poetry found them ready: ready to receive the silent counterpoints of the breakage of the words and of the poem's broken sounds; ready to be solicited by the namelessness of Celan's experience; ready, in other words, to assume the position of the "thou," to become the "you" that "in the nothingness of the night" the poetry was seeking. Through its responsive yet subdued, contained vibrations (vibrations evident both in the students' writing and in the keenness of attention in the class discussions), the class became, in fact, this responsive "you," this deeply attentive addressee, prepared to accompany the poet into the very place—the very night, the very silence—from which his poems had originated.

As Celan's drifting musicality became, indeed, the rhythm of the class, the class seemed to experience also, curiously enough, something like a liberation, the process of a freeing up. "Whoever has art before his eyes and on his mind," Celan said in his famous speech entitled "The Meridian," ". . . has forgotten himself. Art produces a distance from the I":

> Perhaps—I'm just asking—perhaps literature, in the company of the I which has forgotten itself, travels the same path as art, toward that which is mysterious and alien. And once again—but where? but in what place? but how? but as what?—it *sets itself free* . . .

> Can we now, perhaps, find the place where strangeness was present, the place where a person succeeded in setting himself free, as an— estranged—I? Can we find such a place, such a step? . . .
> *Is perhaps at this point, along with the I—with the estranged I, set free . . .—is perhaps at this point an Other set free?*[39]

Through Celan's poetry the class, in fact, felt strangely and obscurely freed up—freed from form, from rhythm, from melodiousness, from words, freed in sum from the "aesthetic project" and thus ready to become the addressee to the "message in the bottle" thrust into the sea "in the (not always greatly hopeful) belief that it may somewhere and sometime wash up on land, on heartland perhaps." The class became the inadvertent, unexpected heartland, on which Celan's po-

[39]"The Meridian," speech given by Celan in 1960, on the occasion of receiving the prestigious Georg Büchner Prize (by the German Academy for Language and Literature). English translation by Jerry Glenn, published in *The Chicago Review*, Winter 1978, Vol. 29, no. 3, pp. 29–40; citation from pp. 33–35. Emphasis mine.

Handwriting of Celan, in a translation into German of a French
poem by Jean Daive.

etic bottle did indeed—by chance—wash up. Opened to the risks
incorporated by the chance—and the necessity—of the encounter
with the drifting testimony, ready to receive, and resonate to, the
obscurity, the suffering, the uncertainty—and yet the absoluteness—
of the message in the bottle, the class was now prepared for the next
step.

VI

Life Testimonies

The next and final stage of the course itinerary was the screening
of two testimonial videotapes borrowed from the Video Archive for
Holocaust Testimonies at Yale, an archival collection of filmed testi-

monies—of autobiographical life accounts given by Holocaust survivors to volunteer, professionally trained interviewers, most of whom are psychoanalysts or psychotherapists. Within the context of these dialogic interviews, many of these Holocaust survivors in fact narrate their story *in its entirety* for the first time in their lives, awoken to their memories and to their past both by the public purpose of the enterprise (the collection and the preservation of first-hand, live testimonial evidence about the Holocaust), and, more concretely, by the presence and involvement of the interviewers, who enable them for the first time to believe that it is possible, indeed, against all odds and against their past experience, to tell the story and *be heard*, to in fact *address* the significance of their biography—to *address*, that is, the suffering, the truth, and the necessity of this impossible narration— to a hearing "you," and to a listening community. In the spirit of Celan's poetical endeavor, though on an altogether different level, the Video Archive for Holocaust Testimonies at Yale is thus, in turn, the endeavor of *creating* (recreating) *an address*, specifically, for a historical experience which annihilated the very possibility of address.

The Encounter with the Real: A Convergence of Historical, Poetical and Clinical Dimensions

In the context of the course we have previously explored in sequence, one after the other, the historical (Camus/Dostoevsky), the clinical (Camus/Dostoevsky/Freud), and the poetical (Mallarmé/ Celan) dimensions of the testimony. Neither dimension taken in itself, however, truly captures the complexity of what the testimony is, since this complexity, as we have seen, always implies, in one way or another, the coexistence of all three dimensions and their mutual interaction. The Holocaust testimonies in themselves are definitely, at least on their manifest level, as foreign to "poetry" as anything can be, both in their substance and in their intent. Yet many of them attain, surprisingly, in the very structure of their occurrence, the dimension of discovery and of advent and the power of significance and impact of a true *event* of language—an event which can unwittingly resemble a poetic, or a literary, act. The very real, overwhelming and as such, traumatic aspect of these narratives engages, on the other hand, both the clinical and the historical dimensions of the testimony. The clinical and the historical dimensions are implied, as well, by Celan's poetry. What makes Celan's poetry crucially poetic (even in its post-aesthetic, antipoetic stage) is, as we have seen, its formal insistence on the unpredictibility of its own rhythm. In thus insisting on the unpredictability of its own music and its "turns of breath,"[40] Celan's poetry insisted, in effect (as did Mallarmé's), on the risky unpredictibility of the endeavor of the witness, who does not master—and does not possess—his testimony or his "message in the bottle," which may or may not reach a "you." I would suggest, indeed, that both the mystery and the complexity of the endeavor of the testimony and of its compelling power derive, precisely, from this element of unpredictibility, from what is unpredictible, specifically, in the effects of the exchange and the degree of interaction between the historical, the clinical and the poetical dimensions of the testimony.

For the first time in the history of my teaching, I decided, therefore, to have recourse to the archive—to move on, as it were, from poetry into reality and to study in a literary class something which is *a priori* not defined as literary, but is rather of the order raw documents—historical and autobiographical. It seemed to me that this added dimension of *the real* was, at this point, both relevant and necessary to the insight we were gaining into testimony. Intuitively, I also knew that the transference, the shift in medium from text to video—from the literary to the real and from the textual to the visual—would have an impact that would somehow be illuminating, and that the interpenetration of historical and literary testaments would turn out to be quite crucial to the understanding—and the process—of this class.

The Determination to Survive

I watched a number of testimonies at the Video Archive for Holocaust Testimonies at Yale, and I selected, for the purpose of the class, two videotapes whose singular historical narration seemed to contain the added power of a figure, and the unfolding of a self-discovery: the testimonies of one woman and one man.

The woman's story is the story of a catastrophic, overwhelming *loss* which leads, however, to an insight into the joint mystery of *life* and of the need for *testimony.* The testimony is, precisely, to the experience of the narrator's repetitious crossing of the line dividing

---

[40]Cf. Celan in "The Meridian": "Literature: that can signify a turn-of-breath. Who knows, perhaps literature travels its path—which is also the path of art—for the sake of such a breath-turning?" (*op. cit.*, p. 35).

life from death. Starting at age fifteen, the testifier had to live through the successive deaths of nearly all the members of her family—her father, her mother, her youngest brother, her sister-in-law, and a baby (the last three dying in her presence, in her arms). The sole survivor of her family is her newly wedded husband, himself lost during the war but miraculously refound after liberation. Each one of them is, in turn, the only one to survive his or her own family. Although estranged at the time of their reunion, they stay together after the war because, she says, "he knew who I was":

> The man I married and the man he was after the war were not the same person. And I'm sure I was not the same person either . . . but somehow we had a need for each other because, he knew who I was, *he was the only person who knew* . . . He knew who I was, and I knew who he was . . . And we're here, we're here to tell you the story.[41]

What is unique about the story of this woman is her conscious determination to survive precisely at the most abysmal and most devastating moment of her confrontation with death. Her determination to survive, her decision to live, paradoxically springs out of her most intimate and close attendance of the actual dying of her youngest brother, a boy of thirteen who, asphyxiated in the transport wagon, literally expires in her arms:

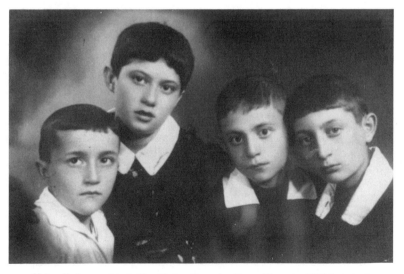

Helen K. (second to left) with her three brothers. Warsaw, 1935 (age ten)

[41]Fortunoff Video Archive for Holocaust Testimonies, Yale University, T 58, Helen K.

He was going to be thirteen . . . And you know, when my brother died in my arms, I said to myself, 'I'm going to live.' I made up my mind to defy Hitler. I'm not going to give in. Because he wants me to die, I'm going to live. This was our way of fighting back.[42] After I was liberated, . . . a Russian doctor examined me and said, "Under normal circumstances you would not have survived . . . It's just a medical miracle that you survived." But I told you, I really wanted to live, I said to myself, 'I want to live one day after Hitler, one day after the end of the war' . . . And we are here to tell you the story.[43]

The woman's testimony is, therefore, a testament to how she survived in order to give her testimony. The story of survival is, in fact, the incredible narration of the survival of the story, at the crossroads between life and death.

Liberation from Silence

The second videotaped testimony screened to the class narrates the story of a man who was a child survivor, one of the two children to remain alive of the four thousand children incarcerated in the Plashow concentration camp. In 1942, his parents decided to smuggle him out of the camp because they learned that all the children would shortly be rounded up for extermination. At the age of four he was thus instructed by his parents to leave them, to run away and head toward a refuge place, which at the time he took to be a hospital, but which turned out to have been—as he later learned—a high-class brothel, hospitable to marginal people like himself. As his stay there became in turn risky, he had to leave and make it on his own as a member of a gang of children of the streets, who stayed alive by begging and by stealing. In moments of distress, he would turn to—and pray to—a student ID picture of his mother, given to him by her at the time of his escape, with the promise that she and his father will come to look for him after the war and will find him wherever he will be. The promise of the picture and his trust in their future reunion gave him both the strength and the resourcefulness to endure and to survive the war.

In effect, after the war he did miraculously find his parents, but the people who returned from the camp—dressed in prison garb, emaciated and disfigured—bore no resemblance either to the moth-

---

[42]*Ibid.*
[43]*Ibid.*

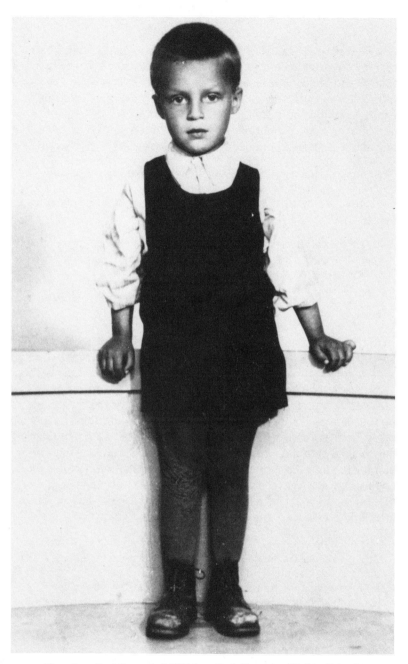

Menachem S. at the end of 1944 (age five). Brnowice Wielkie, Poland.

er's picture or to the parents he had been waiting for and dreaming of. He could not accept these strangers, could not address them as "Mom" and "Dad," but instead insisted upon calling them "Mr." and "Mrs." It was during the years that followed the war, when he was finally safe, that he disintegrated, could not sleep, developed fears, and started having nightmares. Haunted, he nonetheless could not talk about the war experience. For thirty five years he kept his silence:

> This was not a subject brought up in my father's household. It was always . . . something you have to forget . . .
> I was unable to read any books . . . I didn't read a word about the Holocaust . . . It just wasn't there.[44]

> For the past thirty five years I've been trying to convince myself that it never happened, that . . . maybe it happened, but I wasn't affected. I walked under the rain without getting wet.[45]

> But I never realized that I never talked about it, neither with my wife nor with my children.[46]

It is not without dread nor without conflict that he decides to give his testimony, after having first refused to do so. Once he resolves to testify, however, his own dreams—which he recounts—bear witness to the fact that he experiences his own decision to speak up as profoundly *freeing*: his own sudden realization of the magnitude of his burden of silence and its dead weight on himself and on his loved ones comes to him, surprisingly, at once as an exhilarating, unexpected liberation from his nightmares—a liberation which allows him for the first time to experience feelings both of mourning and of hope—and as a transfiguring illumination, a transforming insight into the extent to which this burden—and this silence—has in fact affected, and reshaped, his whole life:

> The thing that troubles me right now is the following: if we don't deal with our feelings, if we don't understand our experience, what are we doing to our children? . . .
> We are what we are, . . . we can change some, but we will never be able to eradicate . . . what happened . . . The big question is: Are we transferring our anxieties, our fears, our problems, to the generations to come? And this is why I feel that we are talking here not only of *the lost generation*—like the term they coined after World War I—this time

[44]Fortunoff Video Archive for Holocaust Testimonies, T. 152, Menachem S.
[45]*Ibid.*
[46]*Ibid.*

we are dealing with *lost generations.* It's not only us. It's the generations to come. And I think this is the biggest tragedy of those who survived.[47]

VII

The Class in Crisis

These reflections of the child survivor on the liberating, although frightening, effects of his own rebirth to speech in the testimonial process, on the value of his own emergence from a life of silence not just for himself, but for his children, for the conscious and unconscious legacy that history and memory—unwittingly or lucidly—leave for the forthcoming generations, were meant, in this way, to conclude the course with the very eloquence of life, with a striking, vivid and extreme *real example* of the *liberating, vital function of the testimony.*

But the eloquence of life—coupled with the eloquence of literature (with the testimonial eloquence of Albert Camus, Fyodor Dostoevsky, Sigmund Freud, Stéphane Mallarmé and Paul Celan)—carried the class beyond a limit that I could foresee and had envisioned. The unpredictibility of the events that took place at this point in the class indeed confirmed, once more, in an unanticipated manner, the unpredictability of testimony. Something happened, toward the conclusion of the class, which took me completely by surprise. The class itself broke out into a crisis. And it was this crisis which made this class unique in my experience, this crisis which determined me to write about it, and which contained, in fact, the germ—and the germination—of this book.

That turn of events took place after the screening of the first Holocaust videotape, recounting the story of the woman. The tapes were screened in the informal privacy of an apartment, with the students sitting on the carpet, all over the floor. During the screening some were crying, but that in itself is not an unusual phenomenon. When the film was over, I purposely left the floor to them. But even though this class, throughout the course, had been particularly literate and eloquent, they remained, after the screening, inarticulate and speechless. They looked subdued and kept their silence even as they left. That in itself is not unusual either. What was unusual was that the experience did not *end* in silence, but instead, fermented into endless and relentless talking in the days and weeks to come; a talking which

[47]*Ibid.*

47

could not take place, however, within the confines of the classroom but which somehow had to *break the very framework of the class* (and thus emerge outside it), in much the same way as the writers we examined somehow all *broke through the framework* of what they had initially set out to write.

I realized that something strange was going on when I started getting phone calls from the students at my home at all odd hours, in a manifest wish to talk about the session, although they did not quite know what to say. As I later learned from my colleagues, the students of my class who met in other classes could only talk about the session and could focus on no other subject. Friends and roommates of my students later wrote me letters, to tell me of the interest they had developed in my class, by virtue of their having become, as one letter puts it, the "coerced listeners" to these outside proceedings of the class and to the frantic talking of my students, who apparently could talk of nothing else no matter where they were, in other classes, study rooms or dorms. They were set apart and set themselves apart from others who had not gone through the same experience. They were obsessed. They felt apart, and yet not quite together. They sought out each other and yet felt they could not reach each other. They kept turning to each other and to me. They felt alone, suddenly deprived of their bonding to the world and to one another. As I listened to their outpour, I realized the class was entirely at a loss, disoriented and uprooted.

I was myself in turn taken by surprise, and worried by the critical dimensions of this crisis which the class was obviously going through, and which was gathering momentum. I realized, at the same time, that the unpredicted outcome of the screening was itself a psychoanalytical enhancement of the way in which the class felt actively *addressed* not only by the videotape but by the intensity and intimacy of the testimonial encounter throughout the course. Since the class viewing of the archive films had been in effect planned in the presence of the psychoanalyst who was, specifically, the interviewer of the two Holocaust survivors and the conceiver of the very idea of the archive—the coauthor of this book, Dr. Dori Laub—I turned to him for counsel.

After we discussed the turn of events, we concluded that what was called for was for me to reassume authority as the teacher of the class, and bring the students back into significance. I therefore called the students who had failed to contact me, to discuss with each one his or her reactions to the "crisis-session." Next I prepared a half-hour lecture as an introduction to the second screening in the form of an address to the class which opened, in effect, the next and final session. This address was divided into two parts: the first part summarized, and returned to the students, in their own words, the importance and significance of their reactions; the second part attempted to articulate for them *an integrated view* of the literary texts and of the video-tapes—of the significance of all the texts together, in relation to their own reactions.

The following are excerpts from this introduction.[48]

The Address to the Class

"We have in this second screening session quite a task before us: the task of surviving the first session. I would like to begin by reviewing with you your responses to the first Holocaust testimony. Your reactions helped me, started in me a process of thinking in dialogue with your responses.

"What your responses most of all conveyed to me was something like an *anxiety of fragmentation*. People talked of having the feeling of being "cut off" at the end of the session. Some felt very lonely. It struck me that Celan's words were very accurate to describe the feelings of the class:

A strange lostness
Was palpably present.[49]

There was a sort of *panic* that consisted in both emotional and intellectual disorientation, *loss of direction*. One person told me that he literally "lost the whole class," that the emotion of the first videotape was so overwhelming, that everything he thought he had acquired in the previous classes got somehow "*disconnected.*"

On the other hand, a number of people said that they suddenly realized how much this class counted for them, and the way in which it counted seemed crucially important, though unsettling. The videotape viewing was described as "a shattering experience"; it was felt that the last session "was not just painful, but very powerful," so powerful that it was "hard to think about it analytically without trivializing it." Most people said that they were much more affected twenty-four hours after the session, and as time went on, than on the spot. Some felt a need to write down their reflections and emotions. They kept diaries of every word thought or said. Some kept diaries of their dreams.

There was a great *need to talk* about the class experience, and everybody mentioned that. People frantically looked for interlocutors, but expressed their frustration at the fact that everything that they

---

[48]Given and tape recorded on December 4, 1984, and consequently transcribed.
[49]"Dumb Autumn Smells," in Hamburger, p. 139.

could say to an outsider to convey a sense of the event was just fragments: they could not convey the whole experience. "I was compelled," said one student, "to speak about the Holocaust testimonies, the class, etc., to friends who were not disinterested but who were perhaps a bit surprised. This speaking was at best fragmentary, dissolving into silence: at moments, lapsing into long, obsessive monologues. It was absolutely necessary to speak of it, however incoherently. It was the most fragmented of testimonies. At times, I felt that I would simply have to abduct someone and lock them up in my room and tell them about the *'whole'* thing."

One person suggested an analytic view of the whole situation. "Until now and throughout the texts we have been studying," he said, "we have been talking (to borrow Mallarmé's terms) about *'the testimony of an accident.'* We have been *talking* about the accident—and here all of a sudden *the accident happened* in the class, happened *to* the class. The accident *passed through* the class."

In trying to address the fragmentation in the class and bring it back into significance, I first *reread* to them an excerpt from Celan's "Bremen Speech" about what happened to the act of speaking, and to language, after the Holocaust. In setting out, however, to re-cite this text again, I now referred it to the resonances of what happened in the class:

"I will suggest that the significance of the event of your viewing of the first Holocaust videotape was, not unlike Celan's own Holocaust experience, something akin to *a loss of language*; and even though you came out of it with a deep need to talk about it and to talk it out, you also felt that language was somehow incommensurate with it. What you felt as a *"disconnection"* with the class was, precisely, an experience of *suspension*: a *suspension*, that is, *of the knowledge* that had been acquired in the class: you feel that you have lost it. But you are going to find it again. I will suggest it is this *loss* Celan precisely talks about, this loss that we have all been somehow made to live. You can now, perhaps, relate to this loss more immediately, more viscerally, when you hear the poet say that *language was "all that remained."* Here again is Celan's language, that remains: lost and regained again through the videotape experience.

Within reach, close and not lost, there remained, in the midst of the losses, this one thing: language.

This, the language, was not lost but remained, yes, in spite of everything. But it had to *pass through its own answerlessness*, pass through a frightful falling-mute, pass through the thousand darknesses of death-bringing speech. It passed through and yielded no words for what was happening—*but it went through*

those happenings. Went through and could come into the light of
day again, 'enriched' by all that. (Bremen Speech)
This, I would suggest, is also what has happened now to the language
of the class: it *passed through its own answerlessness.*

"Another possible response to the answerlessness through which
the class is passing now, can be given in the context of our thought
about the *significance of testimony.* You remember the very impressive
moment in the first videotape, where the woman-survivor speaks about
her husband whom she lost during the war, but with whom she reunited
after liberation. As if to explain the necessity—and the significance—
of this miraculous and improbable reunion, she says: *"He knew who I
was."* But *who she was was precisely her testimony.* "Who she was," in
other words, is here implicitly expressed by the survivor as a radical
and irretrievable *loss,* one of the most devastating losses—disposses-
sions—inflicted by the Holocaust, one of those "answerlessnesses," of
those answerless questions, through which the Holocaust inexorably
made one pass. The narrator herself does not know any longer who she
was, except *through her testimony.* This knowledge or self-knowledge
is neither a given before the testimony nor a residual substantial knowledge consequential to it. In itself, this knowledge *does not exist,* it can
only *happen* through the testimony: it cannot be separated from it. It
can only unfold itself in the process of testifying, but it can never
become a substance that can be possessed by either speaker or listener,
outside of this dialogic process. In its performative aspect, the testimony, in this way, can be thought of as a sort of signature.

"As the next step in the course, I want to ask you to write a paper
for next week. I would like you to think about this paper in relation
with, and as a function of, the *timing* of this act of writing. The writing
is designed to be, in other words, an essential element of your working
through of this experience. And as such, it needs precisely to encroach
on your reactions to the first screening session. Many of you, indeed,
quite literally said that they felt they *did not count* after the first session,
that, had they been there in the camps, they are certain that they would
have died. And I am inviting you now to testify to that experience, so
as to accept the obligation—and the right—to repossess yourselves, to
take, in other words, the *chance to sign,* the *chance to count.*

I invite you thus to write a paper on *your* experience of the testimony,
and on your experience of the class. To do that, you need to think of
the Holocaust videotapes in the context of the significance of the entire
course, and in relation to the other texts we studied. I want you to work
on precisely what you said was so difficult for you to achieve: you
felt a disconnection, and I want you to look, on the contrary, *for the
connections.* What has this experience taught you in the end? What did

it change in your perception of those other texts? *What difference* did it make in your global perception of the class?

What I am suggesting is that you view this paper as *your testimony to this course.* I admit that it would be a *precocious testimony*: I know you feel you are not ready. But perhaps the testimony *has* to be precocious, perhaps there is no other way. I wish to remind you of the fact that the writers we have read also, and quite often, give expression to the feeling that their testimony is precocious. Mallarmé, you will remember, says: "Il convient d'en parler déjà," "It is appropriate to talk about it *now already"*—

> It is appropriate to talk about it *now already*, much like an invited traveller who, without delay, in breathless gasps, discharges himself of the testimony of an accident known and pursuing him . . .

Celan in turn puts an emphasis on the precocity of testimony:

> I have gotten ahead of myself (not far enough, I know).[50]

> But after all, literature, too, often shoots ahead of us. *La poésie, elle aussi, brûle nos étapes.*[51]

I am inviting *you*, in turn, to "shoot ahead of yourselves" precisely in this way and to give, in turn, *your* precocious testimony."

Upon reading the final paper submitted by the students a few weeks later, I realized that the crisis, in effect, had been worked through and overcome and that a resolution had been reached, both on an intellectual and on a vital level. The written work the class had finally submitted turned out to be an amazingly articulate, reflective and profound statement of the trauma they had gone through and of the significance of their assuming the position of the witness.

IX

Pedagogical Transvaluation

I have since had the occasion—and the time—to reflect upon the nature of what took me then so completely by surprise. Because what happened then happened as an accident—an unpredictable vicissitude of teaching—I am recounting it (to borrow Mallarmé's words once again), as my own *testimony to an accident.* And yet, I would submit that the very singularity, the very idiosyncrasy both of the accident and of my testimony to it (like the idiosyncratic and yet archetypal status of the Irma dream) comprises a generic story, and

---

[50]"The Meridian," p. 33.

[51]*Ibid.*, p. 34.

52

the validity of a generic pedagogical event and thus of a generic lesson.

I would venture to propose, today, that teaching in itself, teaching as such, takes place precisely only through a crisis: if teaching does not hit upon some sort of crisis, if it does not encounter either the vulnerability or the explosiveness of a (explicit or implicit) critical and unpredictable dimension, it has perhaps *not truly taught*: it has perhaps passed on some facts, passed on some information and some documents, with which the students or the audience—the recipients—can for instance do what people during the occurrence of the Holocaust precisely did with information that kept coming forth but that no one could *recognize*, and that no one could therefore truly *learn, read* or *put to use.*

Looking back at the experience of that class, I therefore think that my job as teacher, paradoxical as it may sound, was that of creating in the class the highest state of crisis that it could withstand, without "driving the students crazy"—without compromising the students' bounds.

The Event of Teaching

In the era of the Holocaust, of Hiroshima, of Vietnam—in the age of testimony—teaching, I would venture to suggest, must in turn *testify*, make something *happen*, and not just transmit a passive knowledge, pass on information that is preconceived, substantified, believed to be known in advance, misguidedly believed, that is, to be (exclusively) a *given.*

There is a parallel between this kind of teaching (in its reliance on the testimonial process) and psychoanalysis (in its reliance on the psychoanalytic process), insofar as both this teaching and psychoanalysis have, in fact, to *live through a crisis.* Both are called upon to be *performative*, and not just *cognitive*, insofar as they both strive to produce, and to enable, *change.* Both this kind of teaching and psychoanalysis are interested not merely in new information, but, primarily, in the capacity of their recipients to *transform themselves* in function of the newness of that information.

In the age of testimony, and in view of contemporary history, I want my students to be able to receive information that is *dissonant*, and not just *congruent*, with everything that they have learned beforehand. Testimonial teaching fosters the capacity to witness something that may be surprising, cognitively dissonant. The surprise implies the crisis. Testimony cannot be authentic without that crisis, which has to break and to transvaluate previous categories and previous frames of reference. "The poem," writes Celan, "takes its position at the edge of itself."[52] In a post-traumatic age, I would suggest that teaching, equally, should take position at the edge of itself, at the edge of its conventional conception.

As far as the great literary subjects are concerned, teaching must itself be viewed not merely as *transmitting*, but as *accessing*: as accessing the crisis or the critical dimension which, I will propose, is inherent in the literary subjects. Each great subject has a turning point contained within it, and that turning point has to be met. The question for the teacher is, then , on the one hand, how to access, how *not to foreclose* the crisis, and, on the other hand, how to *contain it*, how much crisis can the class sustain.

It is the teacher's task to recontextualize the crisis and to put it back into perspective, to relate the present to the past and to the future and to thus reintegrate the crisis in a *transformed* frame of meaning.

Teaching as Testimony

In much the same way as psychoanalysts, in their practice of dream interpretation, will register as literally as they can the manifest dream content and the incoherent flow of dream associations, so did I take down, word by word, the emotional upheaval of my students' statements and the spectrum both of their responses and of their literal expressions. This documentation and this written record served as the material basis upon which interpretation—in the guise of a returned testimony—could indeed begin to be articulated.

In much the same way as the psychoanalyst serves as witness to the story of the patient, which he then interprets and puts together, so did I return to the students—in their own words—the narrative I had compiled and formed of their own reactions. When the story of the class—the story I am telling now—was for the first time, thus, narrated to the class itself in its final session, its very telling was a "crisis intervention." I lived the crisis with them, testified to it and made them testify to it. My own testimony to the class, which echoed their reactions, returning to them the expressions of their shock, their trauma and their disarray, bore witness nonetheless to the important

[52]*Ibid.*, p. 36.

fact that their experience, incoherent though it seemed, *made sense*, and that *it mattered.* My testimony was thus both an echo and a *return of significance*, both a repetition and an affirmation of the double fact that their response was *meaningful*, and that it *counted.*

In working through the crisis which broke the framework of the course, the dynamics of the class and the practice of my teaching exceeded, thus, the mere concept of the testimony as I had initially devised it and set out to teach it. What was first conceived as a *theory* of testimony got unwittingly *enacted*, had become itself not theory, but an *event* of life: of life itself as the perpetual necessity—and the perpetual predicament—of a learning that in fact can never end.

Epilogue

In conclusion, I would like to quote two excerpts from two papers that were written as the last assignment of the class.

The first excerpt, written by a Chinese woman, reflects on the testimony of the child survivor.

> The testifier seemed to be a man of great compassion. He wondered aloud what sorts of testimony one leaves to one's children, when one does not confront the past. I thought at first, what sorts of burdens will I pass on to *my* children, in the unlikely event that I have any. And then, I thought of my father, who lived through the Chinese Civil War, and four years of incarceration as a political prisoner on the Island of Taiwan. What sorts of burdens has he passed on to me? . . .
>
> In an odd sort of way, I feel a strange sort of collectivity has been formed in the class. This, of course, is a most frightening thing. As I mentioned above, my mode of interaction with those whom I do not know, has always been one of radical differentiation, rather than of collectivization. My autonomy has been rendered precarious, even fragile. Somehow, though, I have managed to survive, whole and a bit fragmented at the same time; the same, but decidedly altered. Perhaps this final paper can only be testimony to that simple fact, that simple event.

The second paper was, in contrast, written by a man (a man who—I might mention in parenthesis—was not Jewish).

> Viewing the Holocaust testimony was not for me initially catastrophic—so much of the historical coverage of it functions to empty it from its horror. Yet, in the week that followed the first screening, and throughout the remainder of the class, I felt increasingly implicated in the pain of

55

the testimony, which found a particular reverberation in my own life
. . .

Literature has become for me the site of my own stammering. Literature, as that which can sensitively bear witness to the Holocaust, gives me a voice, a right, and a necessity to survive. Yet, I cannot discount the literature which in the dark awakens the screams, which opens the wounds, and which makes me want to fall silent. Caught by two contradictory wishes at once, to speak or not to speak, I can only stammer. Literature, for me, in these moments, has had a performative value: my life has suffered a burden, undergone a transference of pain. If I am to continue reading, I must, like David Copperfield, read *as if for life*.

TWO

Bearing Witness
or the Vicissitudes of Listening

DORI LAUB, M.D.

I

A Record That Has Yet to Be Made

The listener to the narrative of extreme human pain, of massive psychic trauma, faces a unique situation. In spite of the presence of ample documents, of searing artifacts and of fragmentary memoirs of anguish, he comes to look for something that is in fact nonexistent; a record that has yet to be made. Massive trauma precludes its registration; the observing and recording mechanisms of the human mind are temporarily knocked out, malfunction. The victim's narrative—the very process of bearing witness to massive trauma—does indeed begin with someone who testifies to an absence, to an event that has not yet come into existence, in spite of the overwhelming and compelling nature of the reality of its occurrence. While historical evidence to the event which constitutes the trauma may be abundant and documents in vast supply, the trauma—as a known event and not simply as an overwhelming shock—has not been truly witnessed yet, not been taken cognizance of. The emergence of the narrative which is being listened to—and heard—is, therefore, the process and the place wherein the cognizance, the "knowing" of the event is given birth to. The listener, therefore, is a party to the creation of knowledge *de novo*. The testimony to the trauma thus includes its hearer, who is, so to speak, the blank screen on which the event comes to be inscribed for the first time.

By extension, the listener to trauma comes to be a participant and a co-owner of the traumatic event: through his very listening, he comes to partially experience trauma in himself. The relation of the victim to the event of the trauma, therefore, impacts on the relation

57

of the listener to it, and the latter comes to feel the bewilderment, injury, confusion, dread and conflicts that the trauma victim feels. He has to address all these, if he is to carry out his function as a listener, and if trauma is to emerge, so that its henceforth impossible witnessing can indeed take place. The listener, therefore, by definition partakes of the struggle of the victim with the memories and residues of his or her traumatic past. The listener has to feel the victim's victories, defeats and silences, know them from within, so that they can assume the form of testimony.

The listener, however, is also a separate human being and will experience hazards and struggles of his own, while carrying out his function of a witness to the trauma witness. While overlapping, to a degree, with the experience of the victim, he nonetheless does not become the victim—he preserves his own separate place, position and perspective; a battleground for forces raging in himself, to which he has to pay attention and respect if he is to properly carry out his task.

The listener, therefore, has to be at the same time a witness to the trauma witness and a witness to himself. It is only in this way, through his simultaneous awareness of the continuous flow of those inner hazards both in the trauma witness and in himself, that he can become the enabler of the testimony—the one who triggers its initiation, as well as the guardian of its process and of its momentum.

The listener to trauma, therefore, needs to know "the lay of the land"—the landmarks, the undercurrents, and the pitfalls in the witness and in himself. He needs to know that the trauma survivor who is bearing witness has no prior knowledge, no comprehension and no memory of what happened. That he or she profoundly fears such knowledge, shrinks away from it and is apt to close off at any moment, when facing it. He needs to know that such knowledge dissolves all barriers, breaks all boundaries of time and place, of self and subjectivity. That the speakers about trauma on some level prefer silence so as to protect themselves from the fear of being listened to—and of listening to themselves. That while silence is defeat, it serves them both as a sanctuary and as a place of bondage. Silence is for them a fated exile, yet also a home, a destination, and a binding oath. To *not* return from this silence is rule rather than exception.

The listener must know all this and more. He or she must *listen to and hear the silence*, speaking mutely both in silence and in speech, both from behind and from within the speech. He or she must recognize, acknowledge and address that silence, even if this simply means respect—and knowing how to wait. The listener to trauma needs to know all this, so as to be a guide and an explorer, a companion in a journey onto an uncharted land, a journey the survivor cannot traverse or return from alone.

Testimony and Historical Truth

A woman in her late sixties was narrating her Auschwitz experience to interviewers from the Video Archive for Holocaust Testimonies at Yale. She was slight, self-effacing, almost talking in whispers, mostly to herself. Her presence was indeed barely noteworthy in spite of the overwhelming magnitude of the catastrophy she was addressing. She tread lightly, leaving hardly a trace.

She was relating her memories as an eyewitness of the Auschwitz uprising; a sudden intensity, passion and color were infused into the narrative. She was fully there. "All of sudden," she said, "we saw four chimneys going up in flames, exploding. The flames shot into the sky, people were running. It was unbelievable." There was a silence in the room, a fixed silence against which the woman's words reverberated loudly, as though carrying along an echo of the jubilant sounds exploding from behind barbed wires, a stampede of people breaking loose, screams, shots, battle cries, explosions. It was no longer the deadly timelessness of Auschwitz. A dazzling, brilliant moment from the past swept through the frozen stillness of the muted, grave-like landscape with dashing meteoric speed, exploding it into a shower of sights and sounds. Yet the meteor from the past kept moving on. The woman fell silent and the tumults of the moment faded. She became subdued again and her voice resumed the uneventful, almost monotonous and lamenting tone. The gates of Auschwitz closed and the veil of obliteration and of silence, at once oppressive and repressive, descended once again. The comet of intensity and of aliveness, the explosion of vitality and of resistance faded and receded into the distance.

Many months later, a conference of historians, psychoanalysts, and artists, gathered to reflect on the relation of education to the Holocaust, watched the videotaped testimony of the woman, in an attempt to better understand the era. A lively debate ensued. The testimony was not accurate, historians claimed. The number of chimneys was misrepresented. Historically, only one chimney was blown up, not all four. Since the memory of the testifying woman turned out to be, in this way, fallible, one could not accept—nor give credence to—her whole account of the events. It was utterly important to remain accurate, least the revisionists in history discredit everything.

A psychoanalyst who had been one of the interviewers of this woman, profoundly disagreed. "The woman was testifying," he insisted, "not to the number of the chimneys blown up, but to something else, more radical, more crucial: the reality of an unimaginable occurrence. One chimney blown up in Auschwitz was as incredible as four. The number mattered less than the fact of the occurrence. The event itself was almost inconceivable. The woman testified to an event that broke the all compelling frame of Auschwitz, where Jewish armed revolts just did not happen, and had no place. She testified to the breakage of a framework. That was historical truth."

The psychoanalyst who had interviewed that woman happened to have been myself, and though my attitude vis-à-vis her testimony was different than the attitude of the historians, I had myself the opportunity of encountering—during the very process of the interviewing—questions similar in nature to those that the historians were now raising. And yet I had to deal with those objections and those questions in a different manner.

I figured from the woman's testimony that in Auschwitz she had been a member of what is known as "the Canada commando," a group of inmates chosen to sort out the belongings of those who had been gassed, so that those belongings could be recuperated by the Nazis and sent back to Germany. The testifying woman spoke indeed at length of her work in a commando that would leave each morning, separately from the others, and return every night with various items of clothes and shoes in excellent condition. She emphasized with pride the way in which, upon returning, she would supply these items to her fellow inmates, thus saving the lives of some of them who literally had no shoes to walk in and no clothes to protect them from the frost. She was perking up again as she described these almost breathtaking exploits of rescue. I asked her if she knew of the name of the commando she was serving on. She did not. Does the term "Canada commando" mean anything to her? I followed up. "No," she said, taken aback, as though startled by my question. I asked nothing more about her work. I had probed the limits of her knowledge and decided to back off; to respect, that is, the silence out of which this testimony spoke. We did not talk of the sorting out of the belongings of the dead. She did not think of them as the remainings of the thousands who were gassed. She did not ask herself where they had come from. The presents she brought back to her fellow inmates, the better, newer clothes and shoes, had for her no origin.

My attempt as interviewer and as listener was precisely to respect—not to upset, not to trespass—the subtle balance between
what the woman *knew* and what she *did not*, or *could not, know*. It
was only at the price of this respect, I felt, this respect of the con-
straints and of the boundaries of silence, that what the woman *did
know* in a way that none of us did—what she came to testify about—
could come forth and could receive, indeed, a hearing. The historians'
stance, however, differed from my way of listening, in their firm conviction that the limits of the woman's knowledge in effect called into
question the validity of her whole testimony.

"Don't you see," one historian passionately exclaimed, "that the
woman's eyewitness account of the uprising that took place at Auschwitz is hopelessly misleading in its incompleteness? She had no idea
what was going on. She ascribes importance to an attempt that,
historically, made no difference. Not only was the revolt put down and
all the inmates executed; the Jewish underground was, furthermore,
betrayed by the Polish resistance, which had promised to assist in the
rebellion, but failed to do so. When the attempt to break out of the
camps began, the Jewish inmates found themselves completely alone.
No one joined their ranks. They flung themselves into their death,
alone and in desperation."

When I interviewed the woman, I knew, of course, that the Auschwitz uprising was put down, but I myself did not know the specific
contribution of the Polish underground to the defeat: I did not know
of the extent of the betrayal.

Had I known, however, would I have questioned her about it?
Probably not, since such questions might have in effect suppressed
her message, suppressed what she was there to tell me.

Had I known, moreover, I might have had an agenda of my own
that might have interferred with my ability to listen, and to hear. I
might have felt driven to confirm my knowledge, by asking questions
that could have derailed the testimony, and by proceeding to hear
everything she had to say in light of what I knew already. And whether
my agenda would have been historical or psychoanalytical, it might
unwittingly have interfered with the process of the testimony. In this
respect, it might be useful, sometimes, not to know too much.

Of course, it is by no means ignorance that I espouse. The listener
must be quite well informed if he is to be able to hear—to be able to
pick up the cues. Yet knowledge should not hinder or obstruct the
listening with foregone conclusions and preconceived dismissals,
should not be an obstacle or a foreclosure to new, diverging, unexpected information.

In the process of the testimony to a trauma, as in psychoanalytic practice, in effect, you often do not want to know anything except what the patient tells you, because what is important is the situation of *discovery* of knowledge—its evolution, and its very *happening.* Knowledge in the testimony is, in other words, not simply a factual given that is reproduced and replicated by the testifier, but a genuine advent, an event in its own right. In a case such as this witness, for example, I had to be particularly careful that what I knew would not affect—would not obstruct, coerce, or overshadow—what she was there to tell me. I had, in fact, to be all the more cautious because this testifying woman did not simply come to convey knowledge that was already safely, and exhaustively, in her possession. On the contrary, it was her very talk to me, the very process of her bearing witness to the trauma she had lived through, that helped her now to come to know of the event. And it was through my listening to her that I in turn came to understand not merely her subjective truth, but the very historicity of the event, in an entirely new dimension.

She was testifying not simply to empirical historical facts, but to the very secret of survival and of resistance to extermination. The historians could not hear, I thought, the way in which her silence was itself part of her testimony, an essential part of the historical truth she was precisely bearing witness to. She saw four chimneys blowing up in Auschwitz: she saw, in other words, the unimaginable taking place right in front of her own eyes. And she came to testify to the unbelievability, precisely, of what she had eyewitnessed—this bursting open of the very frame of Auschwitz. The historians' testifying to the fact that only one chimney was blown up in Auschwitz, as well as to the fact of the betrayal of the Polish underground, does not break the frame. The woman's testimony, on the other hand, is breaking the frame of the concentration camp by and through her very testimony: she is breaking out of Auschwitz even by her very talking. She had come, indeed, to testify, not to the empirical number of the chimneys, but to resistance, to the affirmation of survival, to the breakage of the frame of death; in the same way, she had come to testify not to betrayal, nor to her actual removal of the belongings of the dead, but to her vital memory of helping people, to her effective rescuing of lives. This was her way of being, of surviving, of resisting. It is not merely her speech, but the very boundaries of silence which surround it, which attest, today as well as in the past, to this assertion of resistance.

There is thus a subtle dialectic between what the survivor did not know and what she knew; between what I as interviewer did not know and what I knew; between what the historians knew and what they did not know. Because the testifier did not know the number of the chimneys that blew up; because she did not know of the betrayal of the Polish underground and of the violent and desperate defeat of the rebellion of the Auschwitz inmates, the historians said that she knew nothing. I thought that she knew more, since she knew about the breakage of the frame, that her very testimony was now reenacting.

Setting Witnessing in Motion: The Password

It has happened to me many times that thinking back to a psychoanalytic session with a patient, I suddenly realize that I have understood it. Everything falls into place and comes together; the patient's life, the issues that s/he was addressing and the ones that were on my mind. Yet hardly anything of all this gets explicitly said in words. We part at the end of the session with an ostensible understanding of what went on, an understanding, however, that barely touches on what it is really all about. Such sudden illuminations are not rare. They often do not last, however. I do forget them before the next appointment, and my patient and I sink back into the routine of everyday quabble. It is as though two simultaneous dialogues proceed and the ordinary one, the one that is commonplace, prevails.

Occasionally, I am aware of both dialogues during the clinical encounter. It seems to me that in addition to what is manifestly said, associated to, dreamt about and elaborated, there is another, a more subtle melody. A cue is dropped, barely heard. "Do I really hear something?" I ask myself. Can I lock in on it, take hold of it? Is it not too esoteric? Is it not simply originating from the deep recesses of my own unconscious? At times, when I lose myself in such deliberations, the melody is gone and "work proceeds" in its empty track—a stylized dance—a minuet of empty postures. At other times, I seize upon it and echo it in my response. I simply indicate that I know it, and thus *make myself known as one who knows.* The patient may dismiss it or pass over it in silence; yet there are times in which it is as though a cord is struck and an internal chorus, a thousand voices are set free. The other melody, that subtler music, then emerges, suddenly resounding loud and clear. It has always been there, center-stage, waiting to be liberated from its captivity of silence. It is as though a secret password has been uttered, in the expectation that it be passed over once again; a word by which the patient names himself and asks against all odds for a reciprocal identification. Only this time I responded. And only this time, when I was present enough to recognize and hear the password, could the door be opened and the hidden voice emerge and be released. I had to hear it first, acknowledge that I spoke its language, identify myself to it, acknowledge both to myself and to my patient, who I really was, so that it would be possible for him or her to really speak.

Nowhere in my work with patients have I found this to be more true than in my listening to victims of trauma and particularly to survivors of the Holocaust and to their children, when such secret password comes to be a signal that we both share the knowledge of the trauma, the knowledge of what facing it and living in its shadow are really all about.

The Black Hole

In thus acknowledging the password and in hearing it as a signal of this mutual recognition of a shared knowledge, the analyst identifies himself as a listener who can precisely recognize, and *meet* the victim's silence; a listener who can recognize, in other words, and meet, "the gaping, vertiginous black hole" of the experience of the trauma. It is in these words that Nadine Fresco describes, indeed, on the basis of her interviews with children of Holocaust survivors,[1] the silence that has swallowed up their past:

> The gaping, vertiginous black hole of the unmentionable years . . . The silence formed like a heavy pall that weighed down on everyone. Parents explained nothing, children asked nothing. The forbidden memory of death manifested itself only in the form of incomprehensible attacks of pain . . . The silence was all the more implacable in that it was often concealed behind a screen of words, again, always the same words, an unchanging story, a tale repeated over and over again, made up of selections from the war.

> It was a silence that swallowed up the past, all the past, the past before death, before destruction. To speak up and thus to realize the grip of death, which was the grip of silence, seems to have represented for these parents too grave a danger for such an action to seem possible.

It is thus that the place of the greatest density of silence—the place of concentration where death took place—paradoxically becomes, for those children of survivors, the only place which can provide an

---

[1]Nadine Fresco, "Remembering the Unknown," in *International Review of Psychoanalysis* 1984, no. 11, pp. 417–427.

access to the *life* that existed before their birth. "It is," notes Fresco, "a concentration of death, but it is also the ultimate concentration of life." As a site which marks, and is marked, by a massive trauma I would suggest, then, that the figure of " the concentration" is, in turn, a black hole. Concentrating at once life and death, the black hole in effect collapses, in this way, both the gaping hole of genocide and the gaping hole of silence. The impossibility of speaking and, in fact of listening, otherwise than through this silence, otherwise than through this black hole both of knowledge and of words, corresponds to the impossibility of remembering and of forgetting, otherwise than through the genocide, otherwise than through this "hole of memory." As Nadine Fresco puts it:

> As if one gave oneself the right to remember only with genocide as one's memory. As if the very faculty of remembering and forgetting derived from the genocide. As if the genocide alone had made you a being of memory and forgetting.

It is thus genocide, and genocide alone, that one can give oneself the right to feel as *real* and as *lasting*, making it in this way both the nidus of one's actual life and the driving force that shapes the meaning of one's destiny. The continued power of the silenced memory of genocide as an overriding, structuring and shaping force, may be, however, neither truly known by the survivors, nor recognized as representing, in effect, memory of trauma. It finds its way into their lives, unwittingly, through an uncanny repetition of events that duplicate—in structure and in impact—the traumatic past.

Second Holocausts, or the Return of the Trauma

Survivors will experience tragic life events not as mere catastrophes, but rather as a second Holocaust, the ultimate victory of their cruel fate, which they have failed to turn around, and the final corroboration of the defeat of their powers to survive and to rebuild.

Such was the experience of French author Martin Gray, who, in spite of his unyielding struggle and thirst for life, was forced to witness the destruction of his entire family in the flames of Warsaw and Treblinka. He rebounds from it, builds a new family, a new castle for himself in the South of France, until a forest fire, momentarily, destroys it all again.

In Martin Gray's own words:[2]

At that time too, I could save nothing but my naked life. I escaped from fields of ruins, I fled from sewers and from Treblinka, and not one of those that had been mine remained alive . . .

Later, it seemed that after all my lonesomeness, the time had come for me to find my peace: my wife, the children. But then that blaze, Tanneron in flames, the crackling of the fire, that smell, that heat—just like Warsaw. Once again everything was taken away from me, everything that seemed to have been given to me as a present: a wife, children, a life. For the second time I remained alone, with nothing but my life . . .

I speak, I try to comprehend. Their death has reopened all the graves. In those graves, my people, my parents, my siblings, my friends were coming back to life; my people, my family, died in them a second death.

And such was the experience of another man who came to live the tragic loss of his second family as yet another Holocaust. Like Martin Gray, this man in turn had lost all his family in Auschwitz and married another survivor in the DP camp. The couple had two children, a girl and then a boy. Two years after the boy was born, the wife suddenly died of a severe internal hemorrhage, a late sequela of the pregnancies she should not have had, because of persecution-related health damage. This loss was more than the survivor could bear, and he gave in. He promptly gave up the baby for adoption, married an American-born woman from the neighborhood, and after insisting that the daughter call his new wife "mother," disappeared for a whole year—ostensibly hospitalized for a mysterious illness. The dead mother's name was banned in this new family—her existence was denied.

When the daughter grew up, she carried on her father's legacy. She left the husband she had married and aborted the baby she had conceived, and embarked instead on a mission of repair: to refind and to regain her younger brother—the son her father has lost of his own volition. When her biological brother, meanwhile estranged and raised by other parents, failed to return, she proceeded to have a baby—a little boy—of her own and on her own, without the encumbrance of a husband. To her surprise, her father, although saddened that she did not have a conventional family, was totally delighted with the newborn baby.

As in Martin Gray's case, it was the second, reiterated loss of the survivor's family—of his first wife and consequently, of their newborn baby—which was experienced by the camp survivor as a *second*

[2]Martin Gray, *Der Schrei nach Leben*, Der Goldman Verlag, Munich: 1988.

holocaust, an inescapable fate he could neither prevent nor fight, and a devastating blow to which he had no choice but to succumb. It was the child, his daughter, whose life unwittingly bore witness to the trauma of this second holocaust which her father was attempting to repress and to forget, by acting out and living out the lessons learned from him—not to love, not to dare fate, not to risk having a family of her own (for such family and such loved ones were only destined to be taken away again)—and by setting out at the same time to refind, rebuild and recreate the family the father had relinquished. Both the father and the daughter shied away from *knowing* and from grieving, a loss they could henceforth only *relive* as haunting memory in real life, at once through the actual return of the trauma and through its inadvertent repetition, or transmission, from one generation to another.

The "second holocaust" thus turns out to be itself a testimony to a history of repetition. Through its uncanny reoccurrence, the trauma of the second holocaust bears witness not just to a history that has not ended, but, specifically, to the historical occurrence of an event that, in effect, *does not end.*

The Dread of the Return

The fear that fate will strike again is crucial to the memory of trauma, and to the inability to talk about it. On breaking the internal silence, the Holocaust from which one had been hiding, may come to life and once more be relived; only this time around, one might not be spared nor have the power to endure.

The act of telling might itself become severely traumatizing, if the price of speaking is *re-living*; not relief, but further retraumatization. Poets and writers who have broken their silence may have indeed paid with their life for that deed (Celan, Améry, Borowski, Levi, Bettelheim).

Moreover: if one talks about the trauma without being truly heard or truly listened to, the telling might itself be lived as a return of the trauma—a *re-experiencing of the event itself.* Primo Levi narrates a recurring nightmare in Auschwitz.

> They are all listening to me and it is this very story that I am telling: the whistle of three notes, the hard bed, my neighbour whom I would like to move, but whom I am afraid to wake as he is stronger than me. I also speak diffusely of our hunger and of the lice-control, and of the Kapo who hit me on the nose and then sent me to wash myself as I was bleeding. It is an intense pleasure, physical, inexpressible, to be at home, among friendly people and to have so many things to recount:

but I cannot help noticing that my listeners do not follow me. In fact, they are completely indifferent: they speak confusedly of other things among themselves, as if I was not there. My sister looks at me, gets up and goes away without a word.

A desolating grief is now born in me, like certain barely remembered pains of one's early infancy. It is pain in its pure state, not tempered by a sense of reality and by the intrusion of extraneous circumstances, a pain like that which makes children cry; and it is better for me to swim once again up to the surface, but this time I deliberately open my eyes to have a guarantee in front of me of being effectively awake . . .

My dream stands in front of me, still warm, and although awake I am still full of its anguish: and then I remember that it is not a haphazard dream, but that I have dreamed it not once but many times since I arrived here, with hardly any variations of environment or details. I am now quite awake and I remember that I have recounted it to Alberto and that he confided to me, to my amazement, that it is also his dream and the dream of many others, perhaps of everyone. Why does it happen? Why is the pain of every day translated so constantly into our dreams, in the ever-repeated scene of the unlistened-to story?"[3]

Similarly, Chaim Guri, in his film *The Eighty-first Blow,* portrays the image of a man who narrates the story of his sufferings in the camps only to hear his audience say: "All this cannot be true, it could not have happened. You must have made it up." This denial by the listener inflicts, according to the film, the ultimately fateful blow, beyond the eighty blows that a man, in Jewish tradition, can sustain and survive. The absence of an empathic listener, or more radically, the absence of an *addressable other,* an other who can hear the anguish of one's memories and thus affirm and recognize their realness, annihilates the story. And it is, precisely, this ultimate annihilation of a narrative that, fundamentally, *cannot be heard* and of a story that *cannot be witnessed,* which constitutes the mortal eighty-first blow.

III

Undoing the Entrapment: Psychoanalytic Work with Trauma

"The real," says Lacan, is that which always comes back to the same place."[4] While the trauma uncannily returns in actual life, its

[3]Primo Levi, *Survival in Auschwitz,* trans. Stuart Woolf, New York: Macmillan/Collier, 1961, pp. 52–53.

[4]*Jacques Lacan: The Four Fundamental Concepts of Psychoanalysis,* ed. Jacques-Alain Miller, trans. Alan Sheridan, New York: Norton, 1978, p. 42.

reality continues to elude the subject who lives in its grip and unwittingly undergoes its ceaseless repetitions and reenactments. The traumatic event, although real, took place outside the parameters of "normal" reality, such as causality, sequence, place and time. The trauma is thus an event that has no beginning, no ending, no before, no during and no after. This absence of categories that define it lends it a quality of "otherness," a salience, a timelessness and a ubiquity that puts it outside the range of associatively linked experiences, outside the range of comprehension, of recounting and of mastery. Trauma survivors live not with memories of the past, but with an event that could not and did not proceed through to its completion, has no ending, attained no closure, and therefore, as far as its survivors are concerned, continues into the present and is current in every respect. The survivor, indeed, is not truly in touch either with the core of his traumatic reality or with the fatedness of its reenactments, and thereby remains entrapped in both.

To undo this entrapment in a fate that cannot be known, cannot be told, but can only be repeated, a therapeutic process—a process of constructing a narrative, of reconstructing a history and essentially, of *re-externalizating the event*—has to be set in motion. This re-externalization of the event can occur and take effect only when one can articulate and *transmit* the story, literally transfer it to another outside oneself and then take it back again, inside. Telling thus entails a reassertion of the hegemony of reality and a re-externalization of the evil that affected and contaminated the trauma victim.

The psychoanalytic reconstruction of the history of trauma is uniquely suited for this process to take place. In psychoanalytic work with survivors, indeed, historical reality has to be reconstructed and reaffirmed before any other work can start. This primary stage of the psychoanalytic work has been described as "the phase of joint acceptance of the Holocaust reality" by both analyst and patient.[5] The analyst must often be there first, ahead of his patient, and, once having acquired factual information, must wait with patience and with readiness for the latter to join him in that place. To allow the psychoanalytic process of evolving knowledge to be set in motion, a place that is safe and safeguarded by human presence has to be created. During this joint endeavor of the psychoanalytic encounter, both parties have to pass a mutual test of safety: they have to prove to each other that they are stable and strong enough to affirm the

---

[5]Ilse Grubrich-Simitis, "From Concretism to Metaphor," in *The Psychoanalytic Study of the Child*, New Haven: Yale University Press, 1984, vol. 39, pp. 301–19.

reality of the terror of the extermination camps in actual *nonmeta-phorical statements.* It is only when and if this task is accomplished, that the survivor is enabled to surrender himself to the psychoanalytic process and to reclaim both his life and his past.

Undoing the Entrapment:
The Testimonial Process

Autobiographical accounts of trauma such as the historical testimonies recorded by the Video Archive for Holocaust Testimonies at Yale, in turn set in motion a testimonial process similar in nature to the psychoanalytic process, in that it is yet another medium which provides a listener to trauma, another medium of re-externalization—and thus historicization—of the event. As such the testimonial enterprise is yet another mode of struggle against the victims' entrapment in trauma repetition, against their enslavement to the fate of their victimization.

My personal experience comprises both these perspectives of listening to trauma: that of the analyst in my practice with patients and that of the historical witness—of the testimonial interviewer—in recorded interviews with Holocaust survivors. With all the obvious and perhaps irreconcilable differences between these two perspectives, I find the process that is set in motion by psychoanalytic practice and by the testimony to be essentially the same, both in the narrator and in myself as listener (analyst or interviewer).

From a clinical perspective, we can try to understand what is happening in the testimonial interviews in the technical, metaphorically approximate terms of "a brief treatment contract": a contract between two people, one of whom is going to engage in a narration of her trauma, through the unfolding of her life account. Implicitly, the listener says to the testifier: "For this limited time, throughout the duration of the testimony, I'll be with you all the way, as much as I can. I want to go wherever you go, and I'll hold and protect you along this journey. Then, at the end of the journey, I shall leave you."

Bearing witness to a trauma is, in fact, a process that includes the listener. For the testimonial process to take place, there needs to be a bonding, the intimate and total presence of an *other*—in the position of one who hears. Testimonies are not monologues; they cannot take place in solitude. The witnesses are talking *to somebody*: to somebody they have been waiting for for a long time.

The Listening Position: The Interviewer's Task

The task of the listener is to be *unobtrusively present*, throughout the testimony; even when and if at moments the narrator becomes absent, reaches an almost detached state. The listener has to respond very subtly to cues the narrator is giving that s/he wants to come back, to resume contact, or that s/he wishes to remain alone, a wish for aloneness that sometimes coincides with the emergence of a creative testifying self. Survivors beginning to remember often desire to be alone, although very much in someone's presence; the listener has to be exquisitely responsive to these cues. For lack of a better term, I will propose that there is a need for a tremendous libidinal investment in those interview situations: there is so much destruction recounted, so much death, so much loss, so much hopelessness, that there has to be an abundance of holding and of emotional investment in the encounter, to keep alive the witnessing narration; otherwise the whole experience of the testimony can end up in silence, in complete withholding.

Paradoxically enough, the interviewer has to be, thus, both unobtrusive, nondirective, and yet imminently present, active, in the lead. Because trauma returns in disjointed fragments in the memory of the survivor, the listener has to let these trauma fragments make their impact both on him and on the witness. Testimony is the narrative's address to hearing; for only when the survivor knows he is being heard, will he stop to hear—and listen to—himself. Thus, when the flow of fragments falters, the listener has to enhance them and induce their free expression. When the trauma fragments, on the contrary, accelerate, threaten to get too intense, too tumultuous and out of hand, he has to reign them in, to modulate their flow. And he has to see and hear beyond the trauma fragments, to wider circles of reflections.

Where such circles of associations and reflections intersect, converge, a latent and forgotten memory might suddenly emerge—come back to life—establishing a further link in the testimonial chain. The listener must firmly be there to confirm it, assist in its full deliverance. He has to move quietly and decisively in bringing things together, yet not succumb to the temptation and the danger of a premature foreclosure, which might be reached, alternatively, through a cognitive suppression, through an emotional catharsis, or through a crushed surrender to the ubiquity of silence.

The Hazards of Listening

For the listener who enters the contract of the testimony, a journey fraught with dangers lies ahead. There are hazards to the listening to trauma. Trauma—and its impact on the hearer—leaves, indeed, no hiding place intact. As one comes to know the survivor, one really comes to know oneself; and that is not a simple task. The survival experience, or the Holocaust experience, is a very condensed version of most of what life is all about: it contains a great many existential questions, that we manage to avoid in our daily living, often through preoccupation with trivia. The Holocaust experience is an inexorable and, henceforth, an unavoidable confrontation with those questions. The listener can no longer ignore the question of facing death; of facing time and its passage; of the meaning and purpose of living; of the limits of one's omnipotence; of losing the ones that are close to us; the great question of our ultimate aloneness; our otherness from any other; our responsibility to and for our destiny; the question of loving and its limits; of parents and children; and so on.

To maintain a sense of safety in the face of the upheaval of such questions and the onslaught of the images of trauma, the listener experiences a range of defensive feelings, which he needs to control and of which he needs to be aware if he is to carry out his task. These listening defenses may include the following:

- A sense of total paralysis, brought about by the threat of flooding—by the fear of merger with the atrocities being recounted.
- A sense of outrage and of anger, unwittingly directed at the victim—the narrator. When we meet a friend who has a malignant disease, we often feel angry at that person. We are torn apart by the inadequacy of our ability to properly respond, and inadvertently wish for the illness to be the patient's responsibility and wrongdoing.
- A sense of total withdrawal and numbness.
- A flood of awe and fear; we endow the survivor with a kind of sanctity, both to pay our tribute to him and to keep him at a distance, to avoid the intimacy entailed in knowing.

72

- Foreclosure through facts, through an obsession with factfinding; an absorbing interest in the factual details of the account which serve to circumvent the human experience. Another version of this foreclosure, of this obsession with factfinding is a listener who already "knows it all," ahead of time, leaving little space for the survivor's story.
- Hyperemotionally which superficially looks like compassion and caring. The testifier is simply flooded, drowned and lost in the listener's defensive affectivity.

These are some of the ways in which the listener feels the need to protect himself from the offshoots of the trauma and from the intensity of the flood of affect that, through the testimony, comes to be directed toward him.

A Cultural Transvaluation

Sometimes the defenses in the listener are engendered, consciously or not, in response to the defensive life activities the listener observes or senses in trauma survivors. Most Holocaust survivors have, by any measure, rebuilt their lives, and the thrust of this rebuilding covers the widest spectrum of activities and the highest levels of accomplishment. Survivors have, in fact, rebuilt new friendships, new careers, new families, and have kept the careers highly successful and the families intensely bonded and cohesive. Yet in the center of this massive, dedicated effort remains a danger, a nightmare, a fragility, a woundedness that defies all healing. Around and against this woundedness survivors keep amassing fortunes, keep erecting castles. They cannot help but keep up this relentless, driven productivity, this fierce undoing of destruction. They cannot stop, cannot divert their gaze. The notion of a life cycle which comprises a diversity of rhythms and of phases, a cycle in which one can sometimes take pause and decide to change direction, is radically alien to their self-perception and does not pertain to their life scheme.

Before the defensive fierceness of this relentless productivity, ceaselessly erecting fortresses against the danger of its own annihilation, the listener in turn experiences a need, an urgency to pull back, to withdraw into a safer place, a place where he can in turn protect himself.

Insofar as they remind us of a horrible, traumatic past, insofar as they bear witness to our own historical disfiguration, survivors frighten us. They pose for us a riddle and a threat from which we cannot turn away. We are indeed profoundly terrified to truly face the traumas of our history, much like the survivor and the listener are.

What can we learn from the realization of our fear? What can we learn from the trauma, from the testimony and from the very process of our listening?

In the wake of the atrocities and of the trauma that took place in the Second World War, cultural values, political conventions, social mores, national identities, investments, families and institutions have lost their meaning, have lost their context. As a watershed event, the Holocaust entailed an implicit revolution in all values, a reevaluation or, to use a Nietzschean term, a "transvaluation" of which we have not yet measured the array of cultural implications for the future. Within today's "culture of narcissism,"[6] which may itself be explained as a historical diversion, a trivialization, a philosophical escape from, and a psychological denial of, the depth and the subversive power of the Holocaust experience, the survivors, as *asserters of life out of the very disintegration and deflation of the old culture*, unwittingly embody a *cultural shock value* that has not yet been assimilated. Their very life-assertion, paradoxically enough, constitutes as yet another threat in that it is the vehicle of an inexorable historical transvaluation, the implications of which we have yet to understand.

[6]Cf. Christopher Lasch, *The Culture of Narcissism*, New York: Norton, 1978.

THREE

An Event Without a Witness: Truth, Testimony and Survival

DORI LAUB, M.D.

I would like to propose some reflections on the relation of witnessing to truth, in reference to the historical experience of the Holocaust. For a long time now, and from a variety of perspectives,[1] I have been concretely involved in the quest of testifying and of witnessing—and have come to conceive of the process of the testimony as, essentially, a ceaseless struggle, which I would like here to attempt to sketch out.

I

My Position as a Witness

I recognize three separate, distinct levels of witnessing in relation to the Holocaust experience: the level of being a witness to oneself within the experience; the level of being a witness to the testimonies of others; and the level of being a witness to the process of witnessing itself.

The first level, that of being a witness to oneself, proceeds from my autobiographical awareness as a child survivor. I have distinct memories of my deportation, arrival in the camp, and the subsequent life my family and I led there. I remember both these events and the feelings and thoughts they provoked, in minute detail. They are not facts that were gleaned from somebody else's telling me about them. The explicit details (including names of places and people), which I so vividly remember, are a constant source of amazement to my

---

[1]As the cofounder of the Fortunoff Video Archive for Holocaust Testimonies at Yale: as an interviewer of the survivors who give testimony; as a psychoanalyst who treats Holocaust survivors and their children, and as a child survivor myself.

75

mother in their accuracy and general comprehension of all that was happening.

But these are the memories of an adult. Curiously enough, the events are remembered and seem to have been experienced in a way that was far beyond the normal capacity for recall in a young child of my age. It is as though this process of witnessing is of an event that happened on another level, and was not part of the mainstream of the conscious life of a little boy. Rather, these memories are like discrete islands of precocious thinking and feel almost like the remembrances of another child, removed, yet connected to me in a complex way.

This essay will be based in part on this enigma of one child's memory of trauma. The remembrances of yet another child survivor, known to me quite intimately (from having been his later interviewer and friend) and therefore subtly related to my own in the quality of their precociousness, will serve as a connecting, reemerging thread in the latter part of the essay.

The second level of my involvement in the process of witnessing is my participation, not in the events, but in the account given of them, in my role as the interviewer of survivors who give testimony to the archive[2], that is, as the immediate receiver of these testimonies. My function in this setting is that of a companion on the eerie journey of the testimony. As an interviewer, I am present as someone who actually participates in the reliving and reexperiencing of the event. I also become part of the struggle to go beyond the event and not be submerged and lost in it.

The third level is one in which the process of witnessing is itself being witnessed. I observe how the narrator, and myself as listener, alternate between moving closer and then retreating from the experience—with the sense that there is a truth that we are both trying to reach, and this sense serves as a beacon we both try to follow. The traumatic experience has normally long been submerged and has become distorted in its submersion. The horror of the historical experience is maintained in the testimony only as an elusive memory that feels as if it no longer resembles any reality. The horror is, indeed, compelling not only in its reality, but even more so, in its flagrant distortion and subversion of reality. Realizing its dimensions becomes a process that demands retreat. The narrator and I need to halt and reflect on these memories as they are spoken, so as to reassert the veracity of the past and to build anew its linkage to, and assimilation into, present-day life.

---

[2]The Fortunoff Video Archive for Holocaust Testimonies at Yale, founded in 1981.

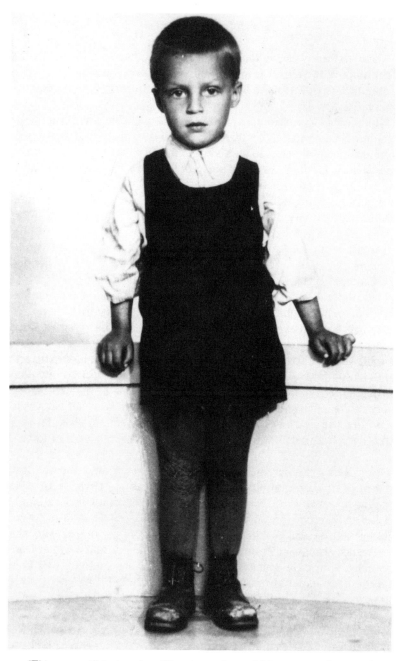

"This essay will be based on this enigma of one child's memory of trauma."

The Imperative to Tell

Toward the end of her testimony at the Video Archive for Holocaust Testimonies at Yale, one woman survivor made the statement: "We wanted to survive so as to live one day after Hitler, in order to be able to tell our story."

In listening to testimonies, and in working with survivors and their children, I came to believe the opposite to be equally true. The survivors did not only need to survive so that they could tell their story; they also needed to tell their story in order to survive. There is, in each survivor, an imperative need to *tell* and thus to come to *know* one's story, unimpeded by ghosts from the past against which one has to protect oneself. One has to know one's buried truth in order to be able to live one's life.

This imperative to tell and to be heard can become itself an all-consuming life task. Yet no amount of telling seems ever to do justice to this inner compulsion. There are never enough words or the right words, there is never enough time or the right time, and never enough listening or the right listening to articulate the story that cannot be fully captured in *thought, memory* and *speech*. The pressure thus continues unremittingly, and if words are not trustworthy or adequate, the life that is chosen can become the vehicle by which the struggle to tell continues. The above-mentioned survivor did so by constructing her life in such a fated way, that it came to be a testimony to her loneliness and bereavement in spite of the fact that her world was filled with loving people and in spite of her remarkable gifts—her creativity, her warmth, her generosity, her eloquence and her love of life.

Hers was a life in which the new family she created, the children she bore, had to give continuance and meaning, perhaps provide healing and restitution, to the so suddenly and brutally broken family of her childhood—parents, brothers and children, several of whom died while she was holding them in her arms. In her present life, she relentlessly holds on to, and searches, for what is familiar to her from her past, with only a dim awareness of what she is doing. Her own children she experiences with deep disappointment as unempathic strangers because of the "otherness" she senses in them, because of their refusal to substitute for, and completely fit into, the world of parents, brothers and children that was so abruptly destroyed.

Yet hers is a story that could never be told in the way she chose to tell it, that is by structuring her whole life as a substitution for the mourned past, because there could not be an audience (even in her family) that was generous, sensitive and self-effacing enough to obliterate its own existence, and be nothing but the substitutive actors of her unexplicated memory. Her specific attempt to tell her story by the very conduct of her life led to an unavoidable dead end, in which the fight against the obliteration of the story could only be at the cost of the obliteration of the audience.

The Impossibility of Telling

In this case as in many others, the imperative to tell the story of the Holocaust is inhabited by the impossibility of telling and, therefore, silence about the truth commonly prevails. Many of the survivors interviewed at the Yale Video Archive realize that they have only begun the long process of witnessing now—forty years after the event. Some have hardly spoken of it, but even those who have talked incessantly feel that they managed to say very little that was heard. None find peace in silence, even when it is their choice to remain silent. Moreover, survivors who do not tell their story become victims of a distorted memory, that is, of a forcibly imposed "external evil," which causes an endless struggle with and over a delusion.[3] The "not telling" of the story serves as a perpetuation of its tyranny. The events become more and more distorted in their silent retention and pervasively invade and contaminate the survivor's daily life. The longer the story remains untold, the more distorted it becomes in the survivor's conception of it, so much so that the survivor doubts the reality of the actual events.

This power of distortion in present-day life is demonstrated by the loss of a sense of human *relatedness* experienced by one woman survivor I interviewed. She described herself as "someone who had never known feelings of love." This feeling of *lack* encompassed all the people in her life. Her family, including her children, were never able to thaw her heart, or penetrate the bars of her "self-imprisonment." Because of this self-inflicted emotional imprisonment, she found herself surrounded by hatred and disdain for and by all those closest to her. Ironically, throughout those years she spent all her free time, and still does, caring for the terminally sick and old. But these anguished people she cares for make her feel precisely that she cannot love them enough.

[3]As an example for the core of this delusion, I shall quote the interpretation made by a psychoanalyst to a survivor patient. "Hitler's crime was not only the killing of the Jews, but getting the Jews to believe that they deserved it."

As a teenager during the war, she had lost most of her family and witnessed many awesome events. Among them was the choking to death of a small baby who had cried too loudly, as well as the burning alive of several of her close relatives. These relatives had been put into a boarded up wooden shack that was set afire. Toward the end of the war, she participated as a partisan in the hunting down and killing of local collaborators. During this period, her fellow partisans captured and turned over a seventeen-year-old German youth to her. She was given free hand to take revenge. After all that she had witnessed and lived through, this woman bandaged the German's wounds and turned him over to the POW group. When asked why she had done this, she replied: "How could I kill him—he looked into my face and I looked into his."

Had she been fully able to grasp the truth about herself, and not perceived herself as someone "with a heart of stone" but as a compassionate, loving person, she might have lived her life differently. Her previous inability to tell her story had marred her perception of herself. The untold events had become so distorted in her unconscious memory as to make her believe that she herself, and not the perpetrator, was responsible for the atrocities she witnessed. If she could not stop them, rescue or comfort the victims, *she* bore the responsibility for their pain. In other words, in her memory of her Holocaust experience, as well as in the distorted way in which her present life proceeded from this memory, she failed to be an authentic witness to herself. This collapse of witnessing is precisely, in my view, what is central to the Holocaust experience.

II

An Event Without a Witness

On the basis of the many Holocaust testimonies I have listened to, I would like to suggest a certain way of looking at the Holocaust that would reside in the following theoretical perspective: that what precisely made a Holocaust out of the event is the unique way in which, during its historical occurrence, *the event produced no witnesses*. Not only, in effect, did the Nazis try to exterminate the physical witnesses of their crime; but the inherently incomprehensible *and* deceptive psychological structure of the event precluded its own witnessing, even by its very victims.

A witness is a witness to the truth of what happens during an event.

During the era of the Nazi persecution of the Jews, the truth of the event could have been recorded in perception and in memory, either from within or from without, by Jews, or any one of a number of "outsiders." Outsider-witnesses could have been, for instance, the next-door neighbor, a friend, a business partner, community institutions including the police and the courts of law, as well as bystanders and potential rescuers and allies from other countries.

Jews from all over the world, especially from Palestine and the United States, could have been such possible outside witnesses. Even the executioner, who was totally oblivious to the plea for life, was potentially such an "outside" witness. Ultimately, God himself could be the witness. As the event of the Jewish genocide unfolded, however, most actual or potential witnesses failed one-by-one to occupy their position as a witness, and at a certain point it seemed as if there was no one left to witness what was taking place.

In addition, it was inconceivable that any historical insider could remove herself sufficiently from the contaminating power of the event so as to remain a fully lucid, unaffected witness, that is, to be sufficiently detached from the inside, so as to stay entirely *outside* of the trapping roles, and the consequent identities, either of the victim or of the executioner. No observer could remain untainted, that is, maintain an integrity—a wholeness and a separateness—that could keep itself uncompromised, unharmed, by his or her very witnessing. The perpetrators, in their attempt to rationalize the unprecedented scope of the destructiveness, brutally imposed upon their victims a delusional ideology whose grandiose coercive pressure totally excluded and eliminated the possibility of an unviolated, unencumbered, and thus sane, point of reference in the witness.

What I feel is therefore crucial to emphasize is the following: it was not only the reality of the situation and the lack of responsiveness of bystanders or the world that accounts for the fact that history was taking place with no witness: it was also the very circumstance of *being inside the event* that made unthinkable the very notion that a witness could exist, that is, someone who could step outside of the coercively totalitarian and dehumanizing frame of reference in which the event was taking place, and provide an independent frame of reference through which the event could be observed. One might say that there was, thus, historically no witness to the Holocaust, either from outside or from inside the event.

What do I mean by the notion of a witness from inside? To understand it one has to conceive of the world of the Holocaust as a world in which the very imagination of the *Other* was no longer possible.

There was no longer an other to which one could say "Thou"[4] in the hope of being heard, of being recognized as a subject, of being answered. The historical reality of the Holocaust became, thus, a reality which extinguished philosophically the very possibility of address, the possibility of appealing, or of turning to, another. But when one cannot turn to a "you" one cannot say "thou" even to oneself. The Holocaust created in this way a world in which one *could not bear witness to oneself.* The Nazi system turned out therefore to be foolproof, not only in the sense that there were in theory no outside witnesses but also in the sense that it convinced its victims, the potential witnesses from the inside, that what was affirmed about their "otherness" and their inhumanity was correct and that their experiences were no longer communicable even to themselves, and therefore perhaps never took place. This loss of the capacity to be a witness to oneself and thus to witness from the inside is perhaps the true meaning of annihilation, for when one's history is abolished, one's identity ceases to exist as well.

The Secret Order

Survivors often claim that they experience the feeling of belonging to a "secret order" that is sworn to silence. Because of their "participation" in the Holocaust they have become the "bearers of a secret" (*Geheimnisstraeger*) never to be divulged. The implications of this imaginary complicity and of this conviction of their having been chosen for a secret mission are that they believe, out of loyalty, that their persecution and execution by the Nazis was actually warranted. This burdensome secret belief in the Nazi propagated "truth" of Jewish subhumanity compels them to maintain silence. As "subhumans," a position they have accepted and assumed as their identity by virtue of their contamination by the "secret order," they have no right to speak up or protest. Moreover, by never divulging their stories, they feel that the rest of the world will never come to know the *real* truth, the one that involved the destruction of their humanity. The difficulty that prevents these victims from speaking out about their victimization emphasizes even more the delusional quality of the Holocaust. This delusion, fostered by the Holocaust, is actually lived as an uncon-

---

[4]See Martin Buber, *The I and the Thou* Edinburgh: T. and T. Clark, 1953. See also the discussion of Paul Celan's poetry as "an event directed toward the recreation of a you" in chapter 1.

scious alternate truth, by executioners, victims and bystanders alike. How can such deadlock be broken?

The Emperor's New Clothes

It is in children's stories that we often find the wisdom of the old. "The Emperor's New Clothes" is an example of one such story about the secret sharing of a collective delusion. The emperor, though naked, is deluded, duped into believing that he is seated before his audience in his splendid new clothes. The entire audience participates in this delusion by expressing wonderment at his spectacular new suit. There is no one in the audience who dares remove himself from the crowd and become an outcast, by pointing out that the new clothes are nonexistent. It takes a young, innocent child, whose eyes are not veiled by conventionality, to declare the emperor naked. In much the same way that the power of this delusion in the story is ubiquitous, the Nazi delusion was ubiquitously effective in Jewish communities as well. This is why those who were lucid enough to warn the Jewish communities about the forthcoming destruction either through information or through foresight, were dismissed as "prophets of doom" and labeled traitors or madmen. They were discredited because they were not conforming by staying within the confines of the delusion. It is in this way that the capability of a witness alone to stand out from the crowd and not be flooded and engulfed by the event itself, was precluded.

The silence about the Holocaust after the war might have been, in turn, a continuation of the power and the victory of that delusion. As in the story of "The Emperor's New Clothes," it has taken a new generation of "innocent children" removed enough from the experience, to be in a position to ask questions.

III

Across the Gap

Because the event that had no witness to its truth essentially did not exist, and thus signified its own death, its own reduction to silence, any instance of its survival inevitably implied the presence of some sort of informal discourse, of some degree of unconscious witnessing that could not find its voice or its expression during the event.

And indeed, against all odds, attempts at bearing witness did take place; chroniclers of course existed and the struggle to maintain the process of recording and of salvaging and safeguarding evidence was carried on relentlessly. Diaries were written and buried in the ground so as to be historically preserved, pictures were taken in secret, messengers and escapees tried to inform and to warn the world of what was taking place. However, these attempts to inform oneself and to inform others were doomed to fail. The historical imperative to bear witness could essentially *not be met during the actual occurrence*. The degree to which bearing witness was required, entailed such an outstanding measure of awareness and of comprehension of the event—of its dimensions, consequences, and above all, of its radical *otherness* to all known frames of reference—that it was beyond the limits of human ability (and willingness) to grasp, to transmit, or to imagine. There was therefore no concurrent "knowing" or assimilation of the history of the occurrence. The event could thus unimpededly proceed *as though* there were no witnessing whatsoever, *no witnessing that could decisively impact on it.*[5]

The experience of encountering today the abundance of the retrospective testimonies about the Holocaust is thus doubly significant and doubly moving. It is not by chance that these testimonies—even if they were engendered during the event—become receivable only *today*; it is not by chance that it is only now, *belatedly*, that the event begins to be historically grasped and seen. I wish to emphasize this *historical gap* which the event created in the collective witnessing. This emphasis does not invalidate in any way the power and the value of the individual testimonies, but it underscores the fact that these testimonies were not transmittable, and integratable, at the time. It is all the more imperative to recognize and to enhance today the value and the momentuous contributions of the testimonies and the witnesses who preserved evidence often by risking their lives. The ultimate historical transmission of the testimonies beyond and through the historical gap, indeed emphasizes the human will to live and the human will to know even in the most radical circumstances designed for its obliteration and destruction.

The perspective I propose tries to highlight, however, what was ultimately missing, not in the courage of the witnesses nor in the depth of their emotional responses, but in the human cognitive capacity to

[5]Had there been such effective, material witnessing, the event would have had to change its course and the "final solution" could not have been carried out to the extent that it was, in full view of the civilized world.

perceive and to assimilate the totality of what was really happening at the time.

Witnessing and Restoration

Yet it is essential for this narrative that *could not be articulated*, to be *told,* to be *transmitted,* to be *heard.* Hence the importance of historical endeavors like the Video Archive for Holocaust Testimonies at Yale, designed to enable the survivors to bear witness, to enable, that is, the act of bearing witness (which the Holocaust invalidated) to take place, belatedly, as though retroactively.

Such endeavors make up for the survivors' need for witnesses, as well as for the historical lack of witnessing, by setting the stage for a reliving, a reoccurrence of the event, in the presence of a witness. In fact, the listener (or the interviewer) becomes the Holocaust witness *before* the narrator does.

To a certain extent, the interviewer-listener takes on the responsibility for bearing witness that previously the narrator felt he bore alone, and therefore could not carry out. It is the encounter and the coming together between the survivor and the listener, which makes possible something like a repossession of the act of witnessing. This joint responsibility is the source of the reemerging truth.

The Video Archive might, therefore, be thought of as helping to create, after the fact, the missing Holocaust witness, in opening up the historical conceivability (the retrospective condition of possibility), of the Holocaust witness. The testimony constitutes in this way a conceptual breakthrough, as well as a historical event in its own right, a historical recovery which I tend to think of as a "historical retroaction."

What ultimately matters in all processes of witnessing, spasmodic and continuous, conscious and unconscious, is not simply the information, the establishment of the facts, but the experience itself of *living through* testimony, of giving testimony.

The testimony is, therefore, the process by which the narrator (the survivor) reclaims his position as a witness: reconstitutes the internal "thou," and thus the possibility of a witness or a listener inside himself.

In my experience, repossessing one's life story through giving testimony is itself a form of action, of change, which has to actually pass through, in order to continue and complete the process of survival after liberation. The event must be reclaimed because even if successfully repressed, it nevertheless invariably plays a decisive formative role in who one comes to be, and in how one comes to live one's life.

IV

The Icon

To illustrate the importance of the process of witnessing and of giving testimony and the struggle involved in it, I would like to relate the story of a man who is currently a high-ranking officer in the Israeli army and whom I interviewed during a sabbatical year he spent at Yale.

As a little boy of about five years old, he was placed with his parents in the Plashow labor camp, in the vicinity of Krakow city. A rumor, which eventually materialized, began spreading that all children were going to be rounded up for extermination. The parents started to make plans to devise ways to save their son by smuggling him out of the camp. They would talk about it at night when he should have been asleep, but he overheard them. One night, while the guards were being distracted, they indeed managed to get him out of the gate. His mother wrapped him up in a shawl and gave him a passport photograph of herself as a student. She told him to turn to the picture whenever he felt the need to do so. His parents both promised him that they would come and find him and bring him home after the war. With that, and with an address where to go, he was sent out into the streets. The address was a whorehouse, a marginal institution itself and therefore, more hospitable to the homeless. He was received with open arms. For years he used to speak of the whorehouse as a hospital, with the color white featuring predominantly in his memory, because the first thing he was given on arrival was a white glass of milk, and, in his imagination, the place could not be anything but a helping hospital. Eventually his hideout became too dangerous and he had to leave. He roamed the streets, joined other gangs of boys and found refuge in the homes of generous, gentile families who took him in for periods of time. The task of making it from day to day preoccupied him completely and in moments of solitude he would take out his mother's picture and talk to her.

In one of the gentile houses he stayed in (living on the papers of a child that had died), the family was in the habit of praying together every evening. When everybody knelt and prayed to the crucifix, the

Menachem S. and his mother, Krakow, 1940.

lady of the house, who may have suspected he was Jewish, was kind enough to allow him to pray to whomever he wished. The young boy would take out the photograph of his mother and pray to it, saying, "Mother, let this war be over and come and take me back as you promised." Mother indeed had promised to come and take him back after the war, and not for a moment did he doubt that promise.

In my interpretation, what this young vagabond was doing with the photograph of his mother was, precisely, creating his first witness, and the creation of that witness was what enabled him to survive his years on the streets of Krakow. This story exemplifies the process whereby survival takes place through the creative act of establishing and maintaining an internal witness who substitutes for the lack of witnessing in real life.

This early internal witness in turn played a crucial role not only in his actual physical survival but also in the later adult testimony the child survivor gave to himself and to others by augmenting his ability to create a cohesive, integrated narrative of the event. This testimony to himself came to be the story of the hidden truth of his life, with which he has to struggle incessantly in order to remain authentic to himself.

A Passage through Difference,
or the Broken Promise

Knowing one's real truth, however, can also be very costly, as is demonstrated by what happens to the little vagabond boy after liberation. He manages miraculously to find his parents, but when he and his parents are reunited, they are not the people he remembers: they no longer even resemble the image he has carried in his mind for so long. His mother does not look like the person in the photograph. His parents have come back as death camp survivors, haggard and emaciated, in striped uniforms, with teeth hanging loose in their gums. Their return does not bring back the lost safety of childhood the boy has so ardently prayed for. He finds that he can only address them as Mr. and Mrs., not as Mom and Dad. I read this story to mean that in regaining his real mother, he inevitably loses the internal witness he had found in her image. This loss of his internal witness to whom he has addressed his daily prayers causes the boy to fall apart. He begins to have a nightmare that will recur all his life. In it he finds himself on a conveyor belt moving relentlessly toward a metal compactor. Nothing he can do will stop that conveyor belt and he will be carried to his end, crushed to death by the machine. Every time he has this dream, he wakes up, totally disoriented and utterly terrified. Because he has lost the life-sustaining internal witness he found in his mother's image, after the war, he becomes, paradoxically enough, a mere "child victim" deprived of the holding presence of a witness. Many of the things he consequently does, as he grows up to be a man, are desperate attempts to subdue the abandoned child victim within himself. As a high-ranking officer in the Israeli army be becomes known for repeated acts of bravery, risking his life as he rescues wounded soldiers under heavy fire. In speaking about these brave acts, he will later state, however, that he did not consider them brave at all. They simply partook of his feeling of being invulnerable. He was convinced he could walk in a hail of bullets and not be hit. In my understanding, this conviction is part of a psychological construction which centered his life on the denial of the child victim within himself. He becomes instead an untouchable and self-sufficient hero. Because he had lost his inner witness and because he could not face his horrors without a witness, he was trapped. He could neither allow himself to experience the horrors nor could he move away from the position of the child victim, except by relentlessly attempting to deny them.

It was years later that I happened to meet him and invite him to

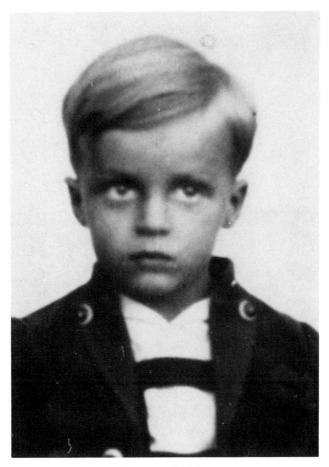

Menachem S., 1942

give his testimony to the archive at Yale. This provoked a crisis in him. At first he refused. A prolonged struggle with himself ensued.

My initial reaction was, "NO." My wife said, "Why don't you think it over? . . . What are you afraid of?" I said, "I'm scared that everything will come back, my nightmares, and so on . . . "She said, "You've been living with this thing for thirty-five years after the war, and you're still afraid. You never talked about it. Why don't you try the other way?" We spent a lot of time talking about it; I began to see the logic. This particular night we went to bed very early in the morning, because we had talked very far into the night, and the next night I had my nightmares

Col. Dr. Menachem S., 1988.

again. But this time it was different. It was again the conveyor belt, it was again the rolling presses; it was again the feeling of helplessness and of terrible anxiety. But for the first time in my life, I stopped the conveyor belt. I woke up, still feeling anxious, but the anxiety was turning into a wonderful sense of fulfillment and satisfaction. I got up; for the first time I wasn't disoriented. I knew where I was; I knew what happened . . . I feel strongly that it has to do with the fact that I decided to open up.[5-bis]

Once the link to the listener has been reestablished in his mind, once no longer along and without a witness, he is able to stop the death machine in his dream without having to wake up. Coincidentally he

[5-bis] Fortunoff Video Archive for Holocaust Testimonies, Yale University, T 152, Menachem S.

expresses the fact that for the first time in his life he was able to experience feelings of fear as well.

As is evident in the example of this child survivor, the act of bearing witness at the same time *makes* and *breaks* a promise: the promise of the testimony as a realization of the truth. On the one hand, the process of the testimony does in fact hold out the promise of truth as the return of a sane, normal and connected world. On the other hand, because of its very commitment to truth, the testimony enforces at least a partial breach, failure and relinquishment of this promise. The mother who comes back not only fails to make the world safe for the little boy as she promised, but she comes back different, disfigured, and not identical to herself. She no longer looks like the mother in the picture. There is no healing reunion with those who are, and continue to be, missing, no recapture or restoration of what has been lost, no resumption of an abruptly interrupted innocent childhood. The testimony aspires to recapture the lost truth of that reality, but the realization of the testimony is not the fulfillment of this promise. The testimony in its commitment to truth is a passage through, and an exploration of, differences, rather than an exploration of identity, just as the experience it testifies to—the Holocaust—is unassimilable, because it is a passage through the ultimate difference—the otherness of death.

Yet it is this very commitment to truth, in a dialogic context and with an authentic listener, which allows for a reconciliation with the broken promise, and which makes the resumption of life, in spite of the failed promise, at all possible. The testimony cannot efface the Holocaust. It cannot deny it. It cannot bring back the dead, undo the horror or reestablish the safety, the authenticity and the harmony of what was home. But neither does it succumb to death, nostalgia, memorializing, ongoing repetitious embattlements with the past, or flight to superficiality or to the seductive temptation of the illusion of substitutions. It is a dialogical process of exploration and reconciliation of two worlds—the one that was brutally destroyed and the one that is—that are different and will always remain so. The testimony is inherently a process of facing loss—of going through the pain of the act of witnessing, and of the ending of the act of witnessing—which entails yet another repetition of the experience of separation and loss. It reenacts the passage through difference in such a way, however, that it allows perhaps a certain repossession of it.

It is the realization that the lost ones are not coming back; the realization that what life is all about is precisely living with an unfulfilled hope; only this time with the sense that you are not alone any longer—that someone can be there as your companion—knowing you, living with you through the unfulfilled hope, someone saying: "I'll be with you in the very process of your losing me. I am your witness."

> To stand in the shadow
> of the scar up in the air.
>
> To stand-for-no-one-and nothing.
> Unrecognized,
> for you
> alone.
>
> With all there is room for in that,
> even without
> language.[6]

[6]Paul Celan, *Poems*, trans. Michael Hamburger, New York: Persea Books, 1980, p. 181.

FOUR

Camus' The Plague, *or a Monument to Witnessing*

SHOSHANA FELMAN

I

What we call history we usually conceive of as a discipline of inquiry and as a mode of knowledge. What we call narrative we usually conceive of as a mode of discourse and as a literary genre. The relationship between narrative and history has been posited, time and again, both in theories of narrative and in theories of history. I will define here narrative, along with Barbara Herrnstein Smith, as "verbal acts consisting of *someone telling someone else that something happened.* "[1] That "something happened" in itself is history; that "someone is telling someone else that something happened" is narrative. If narrative is basically a verbal act that functions as a historiographical report, history is, parallelly but conversely, the establishment of the facts of the past through their narrativization.

Between Narrative and History

"The term history," writes Hegel in his *Lectures on the Philosophy of History,* "unites the objective and the subjective side, and denotes . . . not less what *happened* than the *narration*[2] of what happened. This union of the two meanings we must regard as of a higher order than mere outward accident; we must suppose historical narrations to

---

[1] "Narrative Versions, Narrative Theories", in *On Narrative,* ed. N. J. T. Mitchell, Chicago and London: University of Chicago Press, 1980, 1981, p. 228.

[2] In the quoted passages, italics are mine unless otherwise indicated.

have appeared contemporaneously with historical deeds and events."[3] Although this classical philosophy of history, which claimed to unravel history, on the one hand, as the manifestation of a definite principle of progress and, on the other, as the materialization of a universal, overarching meaning, was, as one historian puts it, "consumed in the holocaust of two world wars,"[4] contemporary theorists of history still by and large subscribe, on different grounds, to the view of the necessity of historical narrativization and of the inherent relationship between history and narrative. "Historians," writes Louis Mink, "generally claim that they can give at least partial explanations of past events." But historical explanation requires a certain perspective. "The insistence on historical perspective seems to be more than a mere recommendation of the attitude of objectivity. . . . It is at least in part a claim that for the historical understanding of an event one must know its consequences as well as its antecedents; that the historians must look before *and* after . . . ; that in *some* sense we may understand a particular event by locating it correctly in a narrative sequence."[5] History is thus contingent on interpretive narrativization. "And it is these [*interpretive* hypotheses] which historians generally believe in some way distinguish history as *interpretive narrative* from chronology on the one hand and 'science' on the other"(36). "The major point of difficulty in attempting to transform history into a cumulative science," argues Mink, "is not one of the *logic of evidence* but one of the *meaning of conclusions*" (39). Detachable conclusions are possible in science, but not in history: "despite the fact that an historian may 'summarize' conclusions in the final chapter, it seems clear that these are seldom or never detachable conclusions; not merely their validity but their meaning refers back to the ordering of evidence in the total argument. The significant conclusions, one might say, are ingredient in the argument itself, . . . in the sense that they are *represented by the narrative order itself*" (39).

The question I would like to address in the present essay is the following: If narrative is defined by a claim to establish a certain history, and if history is defined by a claim to explain events through their narrativization, is the mode of operation of these mutual claims (from history to narrative and from narrative to history) itself subject to history? Has contemporary history—with its cataclysm of the Sec-

[3]G. W. F. Hegel, *The Philosophy of History*, trans. J. Sibree, New York: 1956, p. 60.

[4]Louis Mink, "The Autonomy of Historical Understanding", in *History and Theory*, vol. V, no. 1, Middletown, Conn., Wesleyan University Press, 1966, p. 24.

[5]*Ibid.*, p. 33. Hereafter, page references to this article will be given in parenthesis in the text.

ond World War and the Holocaust—left intact the traditional shuttle movement between narrative and history? If not, what is the impact of the Holocaust on the mutual claims of history and narrative and the manner in which they are implicated in each other? Can contemporary narrative historically bear witness, not simply to the impact of the Holocaust but to the way in which the impact of *history as holocaust* has modified, affected, shifted the very modes of the relationship between narrative and history?

Under Western Eyes, or the Contemporary Witness

As an initial textual approach, I will attempt to search for answers to these questions in the postwar narrative writings of Albert Camus. Why Camus?

Because Camus, I would maintain, exemplifies the way in which traditional relationships of narrative to history *have changed* through the historical necessity of involving literature in action, of creating a new form of *narrative as testimony* not merely to record, but to rethink and, in the act of its rethinking, in effect *transform history* by bearing literary witness to the Holocaust. I will argue that Camus does indeed exemplify this literary witness to the Holocaust and this new, transformational relationship between narrative and history,[5-bis] even though it is by no means clear or obvious that his texts in any way refer to, or claim to deal with, the Holocaust as such.

"There is no such thing as a literature of the Holocaust, nor can there be," writes Elie Wiesel.[6] The fact that the author of this statement is himself the best-known writer of the Holocaust adds sharpness to the paradox of its pronouncement. I would like, however, to take this statement of impossibility seriously, and to explore the implications of its paradox in a different sense. What if we did not know what a literature of the Holocaust is, or might be? What if we did not know what the Holocaust is, or might be? What if, by reading, we could only try to find out, leaving the space of such a question open?

Granting that it might well be that "there is no such thing as a literature of the Holocaust, nor can there be," I propose to test the

---

[5-bis]See also Chapter 1, III, "Narrative and Testimony: Albert Camus."

[6]In *Confronting the Holocaust*, ed. Alvin Rosenfeld and Irving Greenberg, Bloomington and London: Indiana University Press, p. 4.

impact of the Holocaust on narrative (on the relationship of narrative to history) precisely in a writer who *does not* present himself, and *is not officially identified as,* a writer of (about) the Holocaust.

I wish, moreover, to explore the meaning of the Holocaust for a specifically *non-Jewish* European writer, one who, in his fate as Frenchman, was nonetheless immediately implicated in the cataclysm of the Second World War.

Historically, Camus' artistic productivity extends from 1942 to 1960, that is, from the last phase of the Second World War through the decade and a half that form the war's immediate aftermath. During those postwar years, Camus held a position of intellectual leadership attested by the 1957 Nobel Prize for literature he was awarded (at the age of 43, three years before his accidental death in a car crash) for illuminating, as the prize citation goes, "the problems of the human conscience in our time." I will argue that, by virtue of his intellectual leadership and of the ethical stance he occupied throughout the war and after it, Camus' work indeed exemplifies "the problems of the human conscience in our time" as the problems of a radical and necessary transformation: the radical and necessary transformation of the very categories both of ethics and of history, in their relation to the function of the writer. "The writer's function," said Camus in his Nobel acceptance speech, "is not without its arduous duties. By definition, he cannot serve today those who make history; he must serve those who are subject to it." What does it mean to be subject to history? What is the historic specificity of our being subject to the history of our times? Why and how does the contemporary writer serve, not the making of, but the subjection to (the state of being subject to) history? I propose here to explore the impact of history as holocaust on those *subjects of history* who were, however, neither its perpetrators nor its most immediate and most devastated victims, but its historic *onlookers*: its *witnesses.*

In light of those concerns, I will study the relationship of narrative to history as it evolves in two novels by Camus, crucially situated at the beginning and at the end of his career as writer: *The Plague* (1947) and *The Fall* (1956). Both those novels, although separated by a nine-year interval (an interval whose historical and narrative significance I will try to ponder) were written subsequent to the trauma of the Second World War. Both, I would maintain, are endeavoring, each in its own way, to assimilate the trauma. Both are explicitly preoccupied by the very possibilities—and impossibilities—of dialogue between history and language.

The Historic Resonances of the Plague

Promptly after the war's end, Camus published *The Plague,* the story of a town stricken by a ravaging bubonic epidemic. I would like to start meditating on the book by listening, first, to the particular resonance of a few quotations. When the first signs of the Plague have been discovered in the city, the narrator of the novel, a doctor in his profession, tries to envision the forthcoming horror of the spread of the contagion.

> There have been as many plagues as wars in history; yet always plagues and wars take people by surprise. [35]

> Figures floated across his memory, and he recalled that some thirty or so great plagues known to history had accounted for nearly a hundred million deaths. But what was a hundred million deaths? When one has served in a war, one hardly knows what a dead man is, after a while. And since a dead man has no substance unless one has actually seen him dead, a hundred million corpses broadcast throughout history are no more than a puff of smoke in the imagination. [36–37]

It is obviously not any war that is here implicitly evoked by Camus' narrator, but one whose historical atrocities are quite specific. How is it possible, indeed, to read about a hundred million corpses in connection with the singularly chosen metaphor of "a puff of smoke" without immediately associating it with the millions of corpses that were literally transformed into smoke in the Nazi death camps' crematoria?

> The doctor remembered the plague in Constantinople that . . . caused ten thousand deaths in a single day. Ten thousand dead made about five times the audience in a biggish cinema. Yes, that was how it should be done. You should collect the people at the exits of five picture-houses, you should lead them to a city square and make them die in heaps if you wanted to get a clear notion of what it means. Then at least you could add some familiar faces to the anonymous mass. But naturally that was impossible to put into practice; moreover, what man knows ten thousand faces? [37]

It is not hard to understand why it has become, indeed, a commonplace to read the novel as an allegory of the Second World War: the horror of the epidemic constantly suggests that of the war through the Plague's potential for a massive killing. What the Plague, above all, means is a *mass murder* of such scope that it deprives the very loss of life of any tragic impact, reducing death itself to an anonymous, depersonalized experience, to a statistical *abstraction.*

> "No," Rambert said bitterly, "you can't understand. . . . You live in a world of abstractions.
>
> The doctor glanced up at the statue of the Republic, then said . . . he knew he was using the language of the facts as everybody could see them . . . but was [Rambert] right in reproaching him, Rieux, in living in a world of abstractions? Could that term "abstraction" really apply to those days he spent in his hospital while the Plague was battening on the town, raising the death-toll to five hundred victims a week? Yes, an element of abstraction, of a divorce from reality, entered into such calamities. Still when abstraction sets to killing you, you've got to get busy with it. [82–83]

If the Plague is as murderous, as dehumanizing as the war, the specific situation of the *town under quarantine* which, in its isolation from the outside world, is enclosed within its own contagious, deadly space and abandoned to its fear and desperation, is reminiscent of the situation of a concentration camp.

> There were other camps of much the same kind in the town, but the narrator, for lack of first-hand information and in deference to veracity, has nothing to add about them. This much, however, he can say: the mere existence of these camps, the smell of crowded humanity coming from them, the baying of their loud-speakers in the dusk, the air of mystery that clung about them, and the dread these forbidden places inspired told seriously on our fellow-citizens' morale and added to the general nervousness and apprehension. [226]

On the other hand, the organization of the "volunteers" who, at the risk of their lives, offer themselves as medical helpers in the desperate fight against the plague, evokes the struggle of European resistance movements throughout Europe against the overpowering forces of Nazism.

To recognize in the dramatic allegory of the epidemic the recent history of the struggle against Nazism, readers did not need to know that Camus was himself during the war a member of the French Resistance, that he edited the French underground newspaper *Combat,* and that a long extract of *The Plague* had appeared clandestinely in Occupied France in a collection of Resistance texts. But in the context of the question of the dialogue between history and narrative, it is instructive to take notice of the fact that the novel was initially produced as an underground testimony, as a verbal action of resistance which, as such, is not a simple *statement* or description of the

Camus at the underground newspaper "Combat".

historical conflict it narrates, but an actual intervention in this conflict. Camus' narrative intends to be not merely a historic witness, but a participant in the events it describes.

The Project of Recording History

Emerging out of the very urgency of history, *The Plague* nonetheless presents itself as a pure "chronicle," an objective reproduction of historical events. Thus, the opening chapter reads:

The unusual events described in this chronicle occurred in 194- at Oran.[3]

. . . Our fellow citizens had not the faintest reason to apprehend the incidents that took place in the spring of the year in question and were (as we subsequently realized) premonitory signs of the grave events

99

"The first non-clandestine issue of "Combat."

we are to chronicle. To some, these events will seem quite natural; to others, all but incredible. But obviously, a narrator cannot take account of these differences of outlook. *His business is only to say: this is what happened,* when he knows that it actually did happen, that it affected the life of a whole populace, and that there are *thousand of eyewitnesses* who can appraise in their hearts the truth of what he writes.

In any case the narrator . . . would have little claim to competence for a task like this, had not chance put him in the way of *gathering much information,* and had he not been, by the force of things, closely involved in all that he proposes to narrate. *This is his justification for playing the part of the historian.* Naturally, a historian, even an amateur, always has data, personal or at second hand, to guide him. The present narrator has *three kinds of data:* first, *what he saw himself;* secondly, *the accounts of other eyewitnesses* (thanks to the part he played, he was enabled to learn their personal impression from all those figuring in this chronicle); and lastly, *documents* that subsequently came into his hands. [6]

In this opening chapter of *The Plague,* the relationship of narrative to history seems to be direct and entirely unproblematic: if history is of the order of a "happening"—of an "acting" and a "seeing"—and if narrative is of the order of a "telling," the two orders are conflated in the discourse of the *testimony,* through which language is transmitting the direct experience of "eyewitnessing." As testimony, the account of *The Plague* is thus itself a first-hand document, situated at the level of primordial data, closely adhering to historical perception. Joining events to language, the narrator-as-eyewitness is the testimonial *bridge* which, mediating between narrative and history, guarantees their correspondence and adherence to each other. This bridging between narrative and history is possible since the narrator is both an *informed* and an *honest* witness ["témoin fidèle"]. Once endowed with language through the medium of the witness, *history speaks for itself.* All the witness has to do is to *efface himself,* and let the *literality of events* voice its own *self-evidence.* "His business is only to say: *this is what happened,* when he knows that it actually did happen." The "subject of history" can thus voice its presence to the history of which it was a part in articulating, in a single, unified and homogeneous utterance, history's presence to itself.

II

A Missing Literality, or an Event Without a Referent

If the narrative is testimony, a historiographical report whose sole function is to say "This is what happened," why, however, does Camus have recourse to the metaphor of the plague? If the *literality* of a historical event is what is here at stake, why not designate this historical event by its literal, referential name? Why not refer directly to the Second World War as the explicit subject of the testimony?

A superficial answer to this question could invoke the political necessity of disguise stemming from the initial underground testimonial status of the first published excerpt of the novel, that sees the light still under Nazi occupation. But beyond this circumstantial expla-

Camus at Oran.

nation, what is striking in Camus' choice of metaphor in lieu of the historic referent is that the Plague designates not simply a metaphorically substitutive event, but an event that is *historically impossible: an event without a referent.* "It is impossible," say the doctors at the first signs of the plague, "everybody knows that it has vanished from the Western world." [36, tm][6 - bis]

[6 - bis]My re-translation from the French original: here and elsewhere, the abbreviation *"tm"*—"translation modified"—indicates my alterations of the English version.

There is thus a certain tension, a certain aporia that inheres between the allegorical and the historical qualities of the event: the allegory seems to name the *vanishing of the event* as part of its *actual historical occurrence.* The literality of history includes something which, from inside the event, makes its literality vanish. Camus' testimony is not simply to the literality of history, but to its *unreality,* to the historical vanishing point of its unbelievability. In much the same way as the doctors think the Plague historically impossible because it does not fit into the frame of reference of their science (their knowledge of medical history), the victims of the plague do not believe in the foreshadowing disaster because it contradicts their "humanism," their ideological beliefs and expectations.

> In this respect our townsfolk were like everybody else, wrapped up in themselves; in other words they were humanists: they disbelieved in pestilences. A pestilence isn't a thing made to man's measure; therefore we tell ourselves that pestilence is a mere bogy of the mind, a bad dream that will pass away. But it doesn't always pass away and, from one bad dream to another, it is men who pass away, and the humanists first of all, because they have not taken their precautions. Our townsfolk . . . thought that everything still was possible for them; which presupposed that pestilences were impossible. [36]

The Plague (the Holocaust) is disbelieved because it does not enter, and cannot be framed by, any existing frame of reference (be it of knowledge or belief). Because our perception of reality is molded by frames of reference, what is outside them, however imminent and otherwise conspicuous, remains historically invisible, unreal, and can only be encountered by a systematic disbelief.

In much the same way as Camus' victims of the epidemic, the victims of the Holocaust in turn did not believe in the information that was forthcoming about the Nazis' final aims. "The majority of Jewish leaders in Eastern Europe did not yet realize that this was the beginning of a systematic campaign of destruction. The whole scheme was beyond human imagination; they thought the Nazis incapable of the murder of millions. . . . If the information about the "final solution" had been believed it would have reached every corner of Poland within a few days. But it was not believed. After July 1942 (the deportations from Warsaw) it is more and more difficult to understand that there still was widespread confusion about the Nazi designs among Jews in Poland, and that the rumors were not recognized for what they were—certainties. Any rational analysis of the situation would have shown that the Nazi aim was the destruction of all Jews. But the psychological pressures militated against rational analysis and created an atmosphere in which wishful thinking seemed to offer the only antidote to utter despair . . . Most Jews in Europe, and many non-Jews, had at the very least heard rumors about some horrible events in Western Europe . . . But they were either not believed or it was assumed that "it cannot happen here." Only a relatively small minority tried to hide or to escape, aware that deportation meant death."[7]

The unreality that strikes, thus, the event before and during its occurrence through the victims' own refusal to believe in its historic referentiality, is matched and reenacted on another level by the way in which the relief at the war's end is immediately accompanied by a denial and forgetfulness of the war's horrors. As soon as the quarantined town finds itself liberated from the Plague,

> these ecstatic couples, locked together . . . proclaimed in the midst of the tumult of rejoicing, with the proud egoism and injustice of happy people, that the plague was over, the reign of terror ended. Calmly they *denied, in the teeth of evidence, that we had ever known a crazy world* in which men were killed off like flies, or that precise savagery, that calculated frenzy of the plague . . . In short, they denied that we had ever been that hag-ridden populace a part of which was daily fed into a furnace and went up in oily fumes. [276–277]

Paradoxically enough, the event historically occurs through its disappearance as an historic actuality and as a referential possibility. It is as though the vanishing point of its literality ("Everybody knows that it has vanished from the Western world") is what constitutes, precisely, the historical particularity of the event before and after its occurrence. The event (the Plague—, the Holocaust) occurs, in other words, as what is not provided for by the conceptual framework we call "History," and as what, in general, has no place in, and therefore cannot be assimilated by or integrated into, any existing cultural frame of reference. Since we can literally witness only that which is within the reach of the conceptual frame of reference we inhabit, the Holocaust is testified to by *The Plague* as an event whose specificity resides, precisely, in the fact that *it cannot, historically, be witnessed.*

> One could not imagine plague or could imagine it only along misleading lines [La peste ne s'imaginait pas ou s'imaginait faussement]. [39, *TM*]

---

[7]Walter Laqueur, *The Terrible Secret*, New York, Penguin Books: 1983 (first edition Great Britain: 1980), pp. 198–199.

Literature as Testimonial Breakthrough

It is precisely because history as holocaust proceeds from a *failure to imagine,* that it takes an *imaginative* medium like the Plague to gain an insight into its historical *reality,* as well as into the attested historicity of its unimaginability.

What, however, is the nature of the failure to imagine and what is the imaginative breakthrough that Camus requires of the testimony for the act of witness to become truly historical, or historically insightful?

We may feel our way toward an answer to this question in the dialogue between Dr. Rieux, Camus' narrator, and Rambert, a visiting journalist to the town. Rambert's Parisian newspaper had commissioned him to make a report on the living conditions prevailing among the Arab population.

> Rieux replied that these conditions were not good. But, before he said any more, he wanted to know if the journalist could tell the truth.
> "Certainly," Rambert replied.
> "I mean," Rieux said, "would you be capable of pronouncing a *total condemnation* [pouvez-vous porter une condemnation totale]?
> "Total? Well, no, I must admit. But surely such a condemnation would be unfounded?"
> "Rieux said quietly that it would in effect be unfounded; but that he had put the question solely to find out if Rambert's *testimony* could or couldn't be an *unqualified* one *'I've no use for testimonies that are not unqualified,'* he added. [Je n'admets que les témoignages sans reserve] That is why I shall not support your testimony with my information. [11–12, *TM*]

Normally, it is the journalist who, by profession, is considered the historical *witness* of society and culture, the bearer of historic testimony. And yet, Camus' narrator is suggesting that the testimony he himself enacts by the very telling of *The Plague* (playing "the part of the historian") is by no means a journalistic testimony, but something else. If "his business is only to say: this is what happened," he does not say it in the manner of a journalist, because his is an *unqualified testimony* which, as such, implies "a total condemnation."

A Total Condemnation

What, however, does Rieux exactly mean by "unqualified testimony" and by "total condemnation," and in what way are the two

Francine and Albert Camus near Oran, in 1942 (*)

related? In the initial dialogue between the doctor and the journalist, both these concepts that Rieux states as his narrative and testimonial standards remain somewhat elliptical and enigmatic. They can be clarified, however, by the later dialogue between the two protagonists in their next encounter. Rambert seeks to leave the quarantined town so that he can rejoin a beloved women whom he had left behind in Paris. Since the gates of the town are locked by decree of the medical authorities, Rambert comes to plead with Rieux.

> He had explained that his presence in Oran was purely accidental, he had no connection with the town and no reasons for staying in it; that being so, he surely was entitled to leave ... The official told him he quite appreciated his position, but no exception could be made ...
>
> "But, counfound it," Rambert exclaimed, I'm not from here [je ne suis pas d'ici] ...

*Like Rambert, Albert Camus was separated from his wife Francine, because of the German military occupation, on November 11, 1942, of the Vichy-controlled Southern zone of France, where he was staying (in the town of Le Chambon-sur-Lignon) for medical treatment of his tuberculosis. Camus' plans to return to his North African homeland and to rejoin Francine were unsettled, ironically enough, because North Africa had been liberated by the surprise invasion of the Allied troops on November 7 1942. Consequently, mainland France and Algeria were now on opposite sides of the

"Quite so. Anyhow, let's hope the epidemic will soon be over". Finally, he tried to console Rambert by pointing out that, as a journalist he had an excellent subject to his hand in Oran . . .

Whereat Rambert had shrugged his shoulders . . .

When Rieux said nothing, [Rambert] continued: . . . "All I wanted to know was whether you couldn't possibly give me *a certificate stating that I haven't got this damned disease"* . . .

"Please don't doubt I understand you," Rieux said, "but you must see your argument doesn't hold water. *I can't give you that certificate, because I don't know whether you have the disease or not,* and even if I did, how could I certify that between the moment of leaving my consulting-room and your arrival at the Prefect's Office you wouldn't be *infected?* And even if . . . I gave you a certificate, it wouldn't help".

"Why not?"

"Because there are thousands of people placed as you are in this town, and there can't be any question of allowing them to leave it" . . .

"But *I'm not from here."*

"Unfortunately, *from now on you will be from here,* like everybody else." [80–82, *TM*]

This episode implicitly recalls the very first encounter between the journalist and the physician: the enigmatic "total condemnation" of which Rieux had spoken as the touchstone of an "unqualified" discursive (testimonial) truth—a "total condemnation" which Rambert, however, could perceive only as a theoretical, unreal question and which, in his capacity as witness (journalist), he therefore could not (would not) utter, here turns out to be, ironically, Rambert's own total condemnation—to the Plague and to the quarantine, his inescapable implication in a situation which condemns him absolutely to imprisonment and to contagion. The adjective *total*, which was precisely what Rambert could not conceive of, thus turns out to have two meanings: "total" in the sense that the condemnation is without the possibility of a remission or exception; "total," also, in the sense that the condemnation *implicates* its bearer, *contaminates* the witness, *includes* the onlooker. Rambert wishes to prevent precisely this inclusion: to testify as an outsider, to exclude himself both from the condemned and the condemning situation to which he testifies. This is why his testimony is not "unqualified."

But a "total condemnation" is a situation from which one cannot choose to exclude oneself, except by self deception. And it is precisely his attitude of self-exclusion from the condemnation which condemns

---

War and totally cut off from each other. Trapped in Le Chambon-sur-Lignon, Camus could neither rejoin, nor even get in touch with, his wife.

Rambert, in making him unwittingly participate in the historical death sentence inflicted upon others, while maintaining his own blindness with respect to his own situation as condemned.[8]

Rambert does not believe in the reality of a "total condemnation," as people failed to believe in the reality of gas chambers. This is why Camus' own testimony, as opposed to the journalist's, cannot be simply referential but, to be truly historical, must be *literary*. If the failure to imagine out of which history as holocaust proceeds stems, precisely, from the witnesses' failure to imagine their own implication and their own inclusion in the condemnation, Camus' own literary testimony must, above all, wrench the witnessing away from this historical failure of imagination. Literature bears testimony not just to duplicate or to record events, but to make history available to the imaginative act whose historical unavailability has prompted, and made possible, a holocaust.

Bearing Witness to the Body

The specific task of the literary testimony is, in other words, to open up in that belated witness, which the reader now historically becomes, the imaginative capability of perceiving history—what is happening to others—*in one's own body*, with the power of sight (of insight) usually afforded only by one's own immediate physical involvement.[9]

[8]In contrast to Rambert, Tarrou has no such blindness and, consequently, no illusions. That is why, however, he lives with no hope. "There can be no peace without hope, and Tarrou *denying as he did the right to condemn* anyone whomsoever—*though he knew well that no one can help condemning and it befalls even the victim to turn executioner*—Tarrou had lived a life riddled with contradictions." (*The Plague*, p. 271).

[9]The artist's role is to demolish the deceptive image of history as an *abstraction* (as an ideological and/or statistical, administrative picture in which death becomes invisible) by *bearing witness to the body*. "In a civilization where murder and violence are already doctrines in the process of becoming institutions," and "where the executioners have gained the right to become administrative managers," the artist, says Camus, is by vocation "Freedom's witness" [le Témoin de la liberté], in that he "testifies not to the Law, but to the body" [les artistes . . . sont les témoins de la chair, non de la loi] ["Le Témoin de la liberté" (1948), in Actuelles I, pp. 188 et 191; *Oeuvres complétes d'Albert Camus*, Vol. 5, Paris: Gallimard and Club de L'Honnête Homme, 1983; my translation].

"The work of art, by the mere fact of its existence, negates the conquests of ideology," affirms Camus (*Ibid.*, 189). Ideology partakes of theory: "When one wants to unify the world in the name of theory, there are no other means than rendering this world as *disembodied, blind* and *deaf* as theory itself" (188).

As a "witness to the body, not to the Law," the artist's role in history is, by inference (in my understanding both of what Camus *says* and of what he *does* both in *The Plague* and in this speech addressed to writers), not so much to witness *truth* (a theory) as to witness *freedom* (the bodys difference; the body's otherness to theory; the body's

It is thus that the literary testimony of *The Plague* offers its *historical eyewitnessing in the flesh*. Rambert has to learn on his body what a holocaust—a situation of "total condemnation"—is: a situation which does not—cannot—except the witness; an experience that requires one to live through one's own death, and paradoxically, bear witness to that living through one's dying; a death experience which can be truly comprehended, witnessed only from inside (from inside the witness' own annihilation); a radical experience to which no outsider can be witness, but to which no witness can be, or remain, outsider.

Having been an involuntary witness to the Plague, Rambert finds himself, in the course of time, radically transformed by the very process of his witnessing. Ultimately, he decides to stay in town of his own accord so as to join the medical volunteers:

> "Doctor," Rambert said, "I'm not going. I want to stay with you."
> . . . Rieux seemed unable to shake off his fatigue.
> "And what about her?" . . .
> Rambert said he'd thought it over very carefully, and his views hadn't changed, but if he went away, he would feel ashamed of himself, and that would embarrass his relations with the woman he loved.
> Showing more animation, Rieux told him that was sheer nonsense; there was nothing shameful in preferring happiness.
> "Certainly," Rambert replied. "But it may be shameful to be happy by oneself."
> Tarrou, who had not spoken so far, now remarked, without turning his head, that if Rambert wished to take a share in other people's unhappiness, he'd have no time left for happiness. So the choice had to be made.

Testimony as a Crisis

> "That's not it," Rambert rejoined. "Until now I always felt a stranger in this town, and that I'd no concern with you people. *But now that I have seen what I have seen, I know that I'm from here* [je sais que je suis d'ici], whether I want it or not. This business is everybody's business [cette histoire nous concerne tous] [174, *TM*]

Bearing witness to the way in which "this history concerns us all," *The Plague* partakes of an *apprenticeship in history* through an

---

physical *resistance to theory*). Witnessing itself becomes thus not a passive function, but an *act* (an *art*) partaking of the very physicality of Resistance. "And, in the end, it is not combat which makes us artists, but art which makes us combatants. By this very function, the artist is freedom's witness . . . True artists testify not to the law, but to the body" (190–191).

apprenticeship in witnessing. The relationship of narrative to history is not, however, as unproblematic as the opening chapter seemed to indicate, since the witness—or the witnessing—which joins the two is *not a given.* The historical apprenticeship takes place only through a *crisis in*, and a consequent *transformation of*, the witness. And it is only through the medium of that crisis that the event can speak, and that the narrative can lend its voice to history. If the narrative is truly *claimed* by history, it is by virtue of that radical discontinuity, that radical change the witness has undergone:

> If only he could put the clock back and be once more the man who, at the outbreak of the epidemic, had had only one thought and one desire: to escape and return to the woman he loved! But that, he knew, was out of the question now; he had changed too greatly. The plague had forced on him a detachment which, try as he might, he couldn't think away, and which like a formless fear haunted his mind. Almost he thought the plague had ended too abruptly, he hadn't had time to pull himself together. Happiness was bearing down on him full speed, the event outrunning expectation. [273–274]

"Almost he thought the event had ended too abruptly, he hadn't had time to pull himself together." The event outrunning expectation, history outruns the narrative, as though the narrative did not quite have the time to catch its breath and to catch up with history, to catch up with the full significance as well as the abruptness, the overwhelming aspect of the crisis and of the change that history has meant.

Knowledge and Memories

Nevertheless, the narrative is testimony to an apprenticeship of history and to an apprenticeship of witnessing insofar as this historical crisis of the witness brings about a certain form of *cognition.* "Now that I have seen what I have seen," said Rambert, "*I know* that I'm from here." However anguishing and ground shaking, seeing leads to knowing, a knowing that, in some ill-understood way, might be ground breaking. Rieux, in turn, in his double role as a doctor (involved witness) and as a narrator (a "historian," witness of the other witnesses), *learns something* from the witnessing and from the telling, and his testimony takes stock of this knowledge:

> Tarrou had "lost the match," as he put it. But what had he, Rieux, won? No more than the experience of *having known* plague and remembering

it, of *having known* friendship and remembering of, of *knowing* affection and being destined one day to remember it. So all a man could win in the conflict between plague and life was *knowledge* and memories . . .

Knowing meant that: a living warmth, and a picture of death [Une chaleur de vie et une image de mort, c'était cela la connaissance]. [270–271]

The task of the testimony is to impart that knowledge: a firsthand, carnal knowledge of victimization, of what it means to be "from here" (from quarantine), wherever one is from; a firsthand knowledge of a historical passage through death, and of the way life will forever be inhabited by that passage and by that death; knowledge of the way in which "this history concerns us all," in which "this business" of the Plague "is everybody's business"; knowledge of the way in which history is the body's business; knowledge of a "total condemnation."

To Speak for All

It is from this communal knowledge that the authority of the witness, that is, the truth claim of the narrative, proceeds, when Rieux finally emerges from his anonymity to name himself as the narrator. The maintained narrative veil of anonymity that only the end unveils embodies, on the one hand, the narrator's objectivity (his self-effacement) and, on the other hand, his shared vulnerability to death and to the Plague (in the course of the account, we do not know if Rieux, as others, will survive since we do not know until the very final pages who is the narrator, who is the survivor). And it is by virtue of this shared vulnerability, and on the grounds of his communal knowledge, that Rieux has earned his historical vocation, his obligation—and his right—to speak for all:

This chronicle is drawing to an end, and this seems to be the moment for Dr. Bernard Rieux to confess that he is the narrator . . . His profession put him in touch with a great many of our townspeople while plague was raging, and he had opportunities of hearing their various opinions. Thus he was well placed for giving a *true account* of all he saw and heard . . .

Summoned to give evidence [appelé à témoigner] regarding what was a sort of crime, he has exercised the restraint that behooves a *conscientious witness* [un témoin de bonne volonté]. All the same, following the dictates of his heart, *he has deliberately taken the victim's side* and tried to share with his fellow citizens the only certitudes they had in common—love, exile, and suffering. Thus he can *truly say* there was not one of their anxieties in which he did not share, no predicament of theirs that was not his.

To be an *honest witness* [témoin fidèle], it was for him to confine himself mainly to what people did or said and what could be gleaned from documents. Regarding his personal troubles and his long suspense, his duty was to hold his peace . . . *Thus, decidedly, it was up to him to speak for all.* [280–281].

The Physician's Witness

It is, of course, not a coincidence that the key-witness whose position appoints him to speak for all is a physician. Not only is the doctor's stance designated naturally and symbolically for the most insightful *body-witnessing* of history; but, by virtue of his job—his professional struggle against death—the doctor's testimonial stance is, of necessity, at once one of *resistance* (to the Plague) and one of *preservation* (of life, as well as of its memory): in much the same way the physician wishes to preserve life, the historian in Rieux wishes to preserve events. It is thus in the midst of the oblivious joy of liberation from the Plague—joy in which Rieux cannot fail but witness the crowd's immediate forgetfulness of history as holocaust—that Rieux decides to "compile his chronicle," so as to rescue from the death of an oblivion not just the evidence of the survival, but the evidence— the knowledge—of its cost. Mediating between life and death as well as between past and future, the testimonial stance of the physician incorporates, indeed, this further knowledge which the crowd does not possess, that the *cost* of the survival has not been paid once and for all, but will be paid again; that history might once again claim the price of such a testimony; that the experience of survival is by no means in itself immune to a future plague.

> He knew what those jubilant crowds did not know but could have learnt from books: that the plague bacillus never dies or disappears for good; that it can lie dormant for years and years . . . and that perhaps the day would come when, for the bane and the enlightenment of men, it would rouse up its rats again and send them forth to die in a happy city. [287]

> From the dark harbor soared the first rocket of the firework display organized by the municipality, and the town acclaimed it with a long-drawn sign of delight. Cottard, Tarrou, the men and the woman Rieux had loved and lost—all alike, dead or guilty, were forgotten . . . And it was in the midst of shouts rolling against the terrace wall in massive

Camus by Cartier-Bresson

waves that waxed in volume and duration, while cataracts of colored fire fell thicker through the darkness, that Dr. Rieux resolved to compile this chronicle, so that he should not be one of those who hold their peace but should bear witness in favor of those plague-stricken people; so that some memorial of the injustice and outrage done them might endure . . .

Nonetheless, he knew that the tale he had to tell could not be one of a final victory. It could be only the record of what had to be done, and what assuredly will have to be done again in the never-ending fight against terror and its relentless onslaughts, despite their personal afflictions, by all who, while unable to be saints but refusing to bow down to pestilences, strive their utmost to be healers. [286–287]

III

An Age of Testimony

The story of the Plague amounts, thus, to the historical determination to bear witness, a determination that is lived at once as an artistic and as a political decision, and that functions at the novel's end not as a true closure, but as a signature, of Camus' work. "If the Greeks invented tragedy, the Romans the epistle and the Renaissance the sonnet," as Elie Wiesel has put it, "our generation invented a new literature, that of testimony. We have all been witnesses and we

feel we have to bear testimony for the future."[10] Without quite yet
exhausting its significance, the ending of *The Plague* announces the
new awareness and the new moral and political imperative of an *Age
of Testimony*: an age whose writing task (and reading task) is to
confront the horror of its own destructiveness, to attest to the unthinkable disaster of culture's breakdown, and to attempt to assimilate the
massive trauma, and the cataclysmic shift in being that resulted,
within some reworked frame of culture or within some revolutionized
order of consciousness. "It is true that consciousness is always lagging
behind reality," writes Camus in one of his editorials in *Combat* (1948):
"History rushes onward while thought reflects. But this inevitable
backwardness becomes more pronounced the faster History speeds
up. The world has changed more in the past fifty years than it did in
the previous two hundred years."[11] The "literature of testimony" is
thus not an art of leisure but an art of urgency: it exists *in time* not
just as a memorial but as an artistic promissory note, as an attempt to
bring the "backwardness" of consciousness to the level of precipitant
events. "As everybody knows," writes Camus, "political thought today
lags more and more behind events. Thus the French fought the 1914
war with 1870 methods and the 1939 war with the methods of 1918."[12]
The literature of testimony, therefore, is not simply a statement (any
statement can but lag behind events), but a performative *engagement*
between consciousness and history, a struggling act of readjustment
between the integrative scope of words and the unintegrated impact
of events. This ceaseless engagement between consciousness and
history *obliges* artists, in Camus' conception, to transform words into
events and to make *an act* of every publication; it is what keeps art
in a state of *constant obligation*. "To tell the truth, it is not easy," says
Camus, "and I can understand why artists regret their former comfort":

> Indeed, history's amphitheater has always contained the martyr and
> the lion. The former relied on eternal consolations and the latter on
> raw historical meat. But until now the artist was on the sidelines. He
> used to sing purposely ... to encourage the martyr and make the
> lion forget his appetite. But now the artist is in the amphitheater. Of
> necessity, his voice is not quite the same; it is not nearly so firm.
> It is easy to see all that art can lose from such a *constant obligation*.

[10]"The Holocaust as a Literary Inspiration," in *Dimensions of the Holocaust*, Evanston,
Ill. Northwestern University Press, 1977, p. 9. See also Chapter 1, I, "Crisis of Truth".
  [11]Camus, *Neither Victims nor Executioners*, trans. Dwight McDonald, World Without
War Publications, San Francisco 1972, p. 44. ["Ni Victimes ni bourreaux," *Combat* 1948,
reprinted in *Actuelles, Erits politiques,* Paris: Gallimard, 1950.]
  [12]*Ibid.*, p. 43.

Ease, to begin with, and that divine liberty so apparent in the work of Mozart. It is easier to understand why our works of art have a drawn, set look and why they collapse so suddenly. It is obvious why we have more journalists than creative writers . . . The period of the revered master, of the artist with a camellia in his buttonhole, of the armchair genius, is over. To create today is to create dangerously. *Any publication is an act, and that act exposes one to the passions of an age that forgives nothing* . . .

The problem is more complex . . . as soon as it becomes apparent that the battle is waged within the artist himself . . . The doubt felt by the artists who preceded us concerned their own talent. The doubt felt by artists of today concerns the necessity of their art . . .

The questioning of art by the artist has many reasons . . . Among the best explanations is the feeling the contemporary artist has of lying or of indulging in useless words if he pays no attention to history's woes.[13]

A Debt of Silence

Contemporary writing is testimonial to the extent that it exists in a state of *referential debt*, of "constant obligation" to the "woes of history," and to its dead. Thus, Rieux must testify because Tarrou's death has entrusted him with the testimonial legacy of the latter's notebooks. The age of testimony is the age of the transferral of a writing debt:

> "And your colleague, doctor, how's he getting on?"
> "He's dead." Rieux was listening to his patient's rumbling chest.
> "Ah, really?" The old fellow sounded embarrassed.
> "Of plague," Rieux added.
> "Yes," the old man said after a moment's silence, "it's always the best who go. That's how life is. But he was a man who knew what he wanted."
> "Why do you say that?" The doctor was putting back his stethoscope.
> "Oh, for no particular reason. Only—well, *he never talked just for talking's sake* . . . All those folks are saying: 'It was plague. We've had the plague here.' You'd almost think they expected to be given medals for it. But what does that mean—'plague'? Just life, no more than that."
> [285]

If Rieux's writing is indebted to Tarrou's, it is to the extent that "Tarrou never talked just for talking's sake," never made of Plague a claim or

[13]Camus, "Create Dangerously," lecture given at the University of Uppsala in Dec. 1957; in *Resistance, Rebellion, and Death*, trans. Justin O'Brien, New York: Knopf, 1961, pp. 250–252.

an entitlement for moral or emotional profiteering. Thus, the writing debt is not so much a debt of words as it is a debt of silence.

And it is as much a debt of knowledge as of acknowledging the unpayability of the debt of knowledge. "And how, in effect, is it possible to accept not to know?" asks Maurice Blanchot in his contemporary meditation on the relationship between writing and disaster: "We read the books on Auschwitz. The vow of everybody there, the last vow: know what has happened, do not forget, and at the same time: you will never know."[14]

Thus, the literature of testimony is at once a performance of its obligation and a statement of its falling short of canceling its referential debt. "This is why I write certain things rather than others," says Elie Wiesel: "to remain faithful."

> Of course, there are times of doubt for the survivor, times when one would . . . long for comfort. I hear a voice within me telling me to stop mourning the past. I too want to sing of love and of its magic . . . I would like to shout, and shout loudly: 'Listen, listen well! I too am capable of victory, do you hear? I too am open to laughter and joy! I want to stride, head high, my face unguarded, without having to point to the ashes over there on the horizon . . . One feels like shouting this, but the shout changes into a murmur. One must make a choice; one must remain faithful . . . This sentiment moves all survivors: they owe nothing to anyone, but everything to the dead.
>
> I owe them my roots and memory. I am duty-bound to serve as their emissary, transmitting the history of their disappearance, even if it disturbs, even if it brings pain. Not to do so would be to betray them . . . And since I feel incapable of communicating their cry by shouting, I simply look at them. I see them and I write . . .
>
> All those children, those old people, I see them. I never stop seeing them. I belong to them.
>
> But they, to whom they belong?[15]

A Question of Belonging

The literature of testimony puts into effect, puts into action a question of belonging. To whom do the dead belong? And conse-

[14]Maurice Blanchot, *L'ecriture du désastre*, Paris: Gallimard, 1980, p. 131. My translation. Blanchot quotes Lewental, whose testimonial notes were hidden near a crematorium: "Truth was always more atrocious, more tragic than anything that might be said about it." What is ungraspable, indeed, is not the content of the statement, but the survival of its testimonial utterance: the fact that it is literally *spoken* from within the ashes of a crematorium.

[15]Elie Wiesel, "Why I Write," in *Confronting the Holocaust*, ed. Alvin Rosenfeld and Irving Greenberg, Bloomington and London: Indiana University Press, 1978, p. 202–203.

quently, on whose side must the living (the surviving) be? Is it possible to *belong with* Plague? "I'm not from here," says Rambert at first; but his experience as a witness to the Plague makes him cross the inner boundary of the very concept of belonging: "Now that I have seen what I have seen, I know that I'm from here." This is, as we have remarked, the thrust of Camus' radical concept of "total condemnation," in its correlation with the demand for "unqualified testimony." Neither the condemnation of contemporary history, nor the testimony of contemporary writing, is any longer bound by conventional limits of belonging, or by the commonsensical limits that insure the separation between life and death. But the purpose of the testimony is, precisely, to cross these lines in an opposite direction to the way the condemnation cancels them out: *to come out on the other side*—of death, of life, of the limits of belonging, of history as total condemnation. To come out on the other side of language: "the concentration camp language," writes Elie Wiesel, "negated all other language and took its place. Rather than link, it became wall. Can the reader be brought to the other side?"[16]

The Other Side

But to bring the reader to the other side of language, one must first come out on the other side of death: one must *survive* in order to bear witness, and one must bear witness in order to affirm one's survival, one's own crossing of the line of death. "Survival and bearing witness become reciprocal acts," notes profoundly Terrence Des Pres.[17] Tied up with survival, bearing witness is then not just a linguistic, but an existential[18] stance. "Rejected by mankind," writes Elie Wiesel, "the condemned . . . persist in surviving—not only to survive, but to testify. The victims elect to become witnesses." In Camus' testimonial work, it is also the reverse that could be said: the witnesses elect to become victims. Or rather, in the impossibility of being, in Camus' utopian terms, *Neither Executioners nor Victims*, and faced with the historical necessity of choosing between those two contemporary roles, Camus' witnesses elect to *side with* the targets of victimization. This is the

[16]*Ibid.*, p. 201.

[17]Terrence Des Pres, *The Survivor-An Anatomy of Life on the Death Camps*, New York: Pocket Books, 1977, p. 32.

[18]I mean by "existential" not "pertaining to existentialism" (a theory), but, pragmatically, "involving the whole of existence" (a practice).

quintessence of the historical, ethical and existential choice that constitutes their unqualified testimonial stance.

> Summoned to testify [appelé à témoigner] regarding what was a sort of crime, [Rieux] had exercised the restraint that behooves a conscientious witness. All the same, following the dictates of his heart, *he has deliberately taken the victims' side* and tried to share with his fellow citizens the only certitudes they had in common—love, exile and suffering. Thus he can truly say there was not one of their anxieties in which he did not share, no predicament of theirs that was not his . . . Thus, decidedly, it was up to him to speak for all.

The Sniper

> But there was at least one of our townsfolk for whom Dr. Rieux could not speak . . . It is fitting [il est juste] that this chronicle should end with some reference to that man, who had an ignorant, that is to say, lonely, heart.
> On turning out of the main thoroughfares where the rejoicings were in full swing . . . Dr. Rieux was held up by a police cordon . . .
> "Sorry, doctor," a policeman said, "but I can't let you through. There's a crazy fellow with a gun, shooting at everybody. But you'd better stay; we may need you" . . .
> "It's Cottard!" Grand's voice was shrill with excitement. "He's gone mad!" [281–285]

"It is fitting [*juste*, judicious] that this chronicle should end with some reference to that man." How to account for this residue of violence and madness? Even though *The Plague* ends with the healer's vow to testify—to do justice to history—it is *juste*, judicious, right, the narrator tells us, that the narrative should terminate with this incongruent episode of the sniper. Why is such an ending "*juste*"? There is more to justice, and more to doing justice to history, than the doctor's testimony can account for: "But there was at least one of our townsfolk for whom Dr. Rieux could not speak." Perhaps the most profound feature of Camus' testimony is that, in the very midst of its monumental effort to take the victims' side from the perspective of the healer, it acknowledges this residue, this failure of the healer's testimonial stance to encompass all of Plague, to "speak for all," to say all.

The Plague's testimony to the Holocaust, "unqualified" though it may be, nonetheless leaves out the "judicious" residue of a radical and self-subversive question:

In a holocaust, is a healer's testimony truly possible? Can a healer's testimony exhaust the lesson of history as plague?

It will take Camus nine years to be able to address—and to articulate—this question, which he will dramatize in his last novel. The sixth chapter will consider how *The Fall* (1956) revisits, in effect, the testimony borne by *The Plague* by dramatizing, paradoxically enough, the disintegration of the integrity (of the authority) of the witness. *The Fall* bears witness to the witness's fall, precisely, from the healer's testimonial stance.

FIVE

After the Apocalypse:
Paul de Man and the Fall to Silence

SHOSHANA FELMAN

In Herman Melville's famous novel *Moby-Dick,* which Paul de Man published in Belgium in his own translation into Flemish in 1945, at the conclusion of the Second World War and three years before his emigration to the United States, the narrator, on his way to board the ship on which he has arranged to sail, is accosted by a stranger who mysteriously insists that the narrator does not know all he should—or all there is to know—about the captain of the ship. Do we ever know all we should—or all there is to know—about the figures who have an impact on us, those who spontaneously stand out as metaphoric captains—leaders, mentors, or role models? " 'Look here, friend,' " says *Moby-Dick's* narrator to the unsolicited informer, " 'if you have anything important to tell us, out with it . . . Ah, my dear fellow, you can't fool us that way—you can't fool us. It is the easiest thing in the world for a man to look as if he had a great secret in him.' "[1]

It looks today as though Paul de Man himself—a controversial yet widely admired and highly influential thinker and literary critic, who died in 1983 as the Sterling Professor of Humanities at Yale—had such a secret. It was recently discovered that his formerly unknown youthful activities included writing, in 1941 and 1942, a literary column for *Le Soir,* a major Belgian newspaper that had been seized by the Nazis in 1940 and that functioned consequently under Nazi supervision as a pro-German, collaborationist journal. What are we to make of this discovery?

---

[1]Herman Melville, *Moby-Dick; or, The Whale,* vol. 6 of *The Writings of Herman Melville,* ed. Harrison Hayford, Hershel Parker, and G. Thomas Tanselle (Evanston and Chicago, 1988), p. 93; hereafter abbreviated *M-D.*

I

History and Ethics

The responses to this discovery, in the press and elsewhere, seem to focus on the act of passing judgment, a judgment that reopens with some urgency the question of the ethical implications of de Man's work and, by extension, of the whole school of critical approach known as "deconstruction."

The discourse of moral judgement takes as its target three distinct domains of apparent ethical misconduct:

1. the collaborationist political activities in themselves;
2. de Man's apparent erasure of their memory—his radical "forgetting" of his early past;
3. the silence that de Man chose to keep about his past: the absence of public confession and public declaration of remorse.

The question of ethics thus seems to be linked to the separate questions of the nature of political activities, of the nature of memory, and of the nature of silence. It is judged unethical, of course, to engage in acts that lent support to Germany's wartime position; but it is also judged unethical to forget; and unethical, furthermore, to keep silent in relation to the war and to the Holocaust. The silence is interpreted as a deliberate concealment, a suppression of accountability that can only mean a denial of responsibility on de Man's part.

I will here argue that de Man's silence has an altogether different personal and historical significance, and thus has much more profound and far-reaching implications than this simplistic psychological interpretation can either suspect or account for.

Although the question of ethics is indeed a fundamental and an urgent one, the hasty trials in the press are in danger of grossly oversimplifying matters, blinded as they are not only by the difficulty of understanding the experience of another, but also by the ease and the misleading comfort of a retrospective historical illusion. "It is easy," writes Edouard Colinet, one of de Man's colleagues from the Belgian period, "when you are not occupied by a foreign army, to tell how you should have behaved in those circumstances or, if you know the end of the story, to lay out a possible long-term policy. This was not our situation."[2] It is easy to pronounce lapidary judgments from within today's belated and anachronistic clarity, with the self-compla-

---

[2]Edouard Colinet, "Paul de Man and the Cercle du Libre Examen," in *Responses: On Paul de Man's Wartime Journalism,* ed. Werner Hamacher, Neil Hertz, and Thomas Keenan (Lincoln, Neb., 1989), p. 429; hereafter abbreviated "P."

cent self-assurance of history's hindsight. As Primo Levi puts it, "In countries in which the elementary needs are satisfied, today's young people experience freedom as a good that one must in no case renounce: one cannot do without it, it is a natural and obvious right, and furthermore, it is gratuitous, like health and the air one breathes. The times and places where this congenital right is denied are perceived as distant, foreign, and strange."[3]

In fact, the easy judgments made on de Man's historical misjudgments provide not insight but relief: in passing judgment on de Man, we distance and disown his dangerous closeness to us, in an attempt to distance history, the Holocaust, as past, *his* past, which, as such, remains foreign and exterior to our present. We blind ourselves to the historical reality of that past by reducing its obscurity to a paradigm of readability—an easily intelligible and safely remote Manichaean allegory of good and evil: "Yale Scholar Wrote for Pro-Nazi Newspaper" (*New York Times,* December 1, 1987 [New York edition]). "Popular history," writes Primo Levi, "and also the history taught in schools, is influenced by this Manichaean tendency, which shuns half-tints and complexities: it is prone to reduce the river of human occurrences to conflicts, and the conflicts to duels—we and they, . . . winners and losers, . . . the good guys and the bad guys, respectively, because the good must prevail, otherwise the world would be subverted" (*DS,* 37). De Man was "Nazi": in denouncing him as one of "them," we believe we place ourselves in a different zone of ethics and of temporality; "we," as opposed to "they," are on the right side of history—a side untouched, untainted by the evil of the Holocaust. But the very nature of the Holocaust was precisely to belie this opposition between "we" and "they." As Primo Levi testifies, "The world into which one was precipitated was terrible, yes, but also indecipherable: it did not conform to any model; the enemy was all around but also inside, the 'we' lost its limits, the contenders were not two, one could not discern a single frontier but rather many confused, perhaps innumerable frontiers, which stretched between each of us" (*DS,* 38).

Paradoxically, when we cast de Man as "Nazi" in a self-righteous bipartition of "the good guys" and "the bad guys," we profoundly *forget* what the Holocaust was like, while at the same time we accuse de Man, precisely, of *forgetting,* judging it unethical in his case. But to vindicate the necessity of remembering the Holocaust by deciding that we can henceforth dismiss or forget de Man is to limit our

[3]Primo Levi, *The Drowned and the Saved,* trans. Raymond Rosenthal (New York, 1988), p. 151; hereafter abbreviated *DS.*

remembering of recent history only to a screen memory. In reality, we are all implicated—and in more than one way—in de Man's forgetting, and in his silence. A certain noisiness about the Holocaust does not diffuse the silence but deepens it, while deafening us to the complexity of our implication in it. To talk about the Holocaust from a position of self-righteousness and rightness is to deny the very essence of the Holocaust, which was to render this position unavailable.

This is not to say that judgment is not necessary; but, in Primo Levi's words, "It is a judgment that we would like to entrust only to those who found themselves in similar circumstances and had the opportunity to test for themselves what it meant to act in a state of coercion . . . I know of no human tribunal to which one could delegate the judgment" (*DS,* 44). The moral implications of the Holocaust are such that our task today is to find ways, precisely, to *rearticulate* the question of ethics outside the problematic—and the comfort—of a judgment that can be delegated to no human tribunal.

The crucial ethical dimensions of a historical experience like de Man's need to be probed by being measured up against the incommensurability of that experience. No doubt, in being taken in by the seduction and deception exercised by Germany at the beginning of the Second World War, the twenty-year-old Paul de Man made a grave mistake in judgment, in failing to foresee and to assess the disastrous impact of the Nazis as soon as they took over Belgium. But the question is: given this fatal political mistake, given such a radical failure of vision, such a lapse of consciousness experienced early in one's life, how can one *wake up?* What would waking up mean? And what can one consequently do, for oneself and for another, not simply with the deadweight of the past but, specifically, with the mistake and with one's own awakening? I will suggest that de Man's writing is precisely motivated and informed by these central questions, and that the moral his writing implicitly propounds is that of an unyielding ethics, of a rigorous commitment to these questions in a constant intellectual and moral effort whose overriding concern is: how *not to compromise* a truth which, he now knows, no one can own but to which he can continue to wake up? How not to compromise the action and henceforth the process, the endeavor, of awakening?

As far as we as readers are concerned, the ethical question with respect to the information that has come forth therefore resides neither in a verdict nor in the trivializing academic wonder—could an evil man have propounded wise ideas?—but in an attempt at understanding how precisely de Man's writings *do* in fact relate to the moral implications of contemporary history. The reductive notion of the writing as a "cover-up" or as a psychological defense against the past paradoxically situates *us* outside these moral and historical implications. It thus fails to grasp what is essentially at stake: how de Man articulates *our silence;* how today we are all implicated in de Man's ordeal and in his incapacity to tell us more about it; how, having faced what he faced, de Man chose an inevitable syntax and an inevitable understated (silent) language. The question that should be addressed in light of de Man's history is, therefore, not how we can dismiss or forget de Man, but why we *must* relate—why we cannot escape from— de Man's writings: how his later writing, the mature work, is inextricably tied up with a historical event that, whether we like it or not, whether we have forgotten it or not, is still a crucial and immediate part of our present; how both de Man's silence and his speech articulate, and thus can help us understand, the ways in which we are still wounded by the Holocaust, and the ways in which we harbor the unfinished business of this recent history within us.

To try to shed light on the way in which de Man's work does address the trauma of contemporary history, let me first review the facts of de Man's wartime experience. What is the particular historical and biographical context of de Man's position at the beginning of the Second World War?

II

The Seduction of Apocalypse

A series of disasters preceded, in de Man's life, the outbreak of the war. When he was seventeen years old, his brother Hendrik died in a bicycle accident at a railroad crossing; a year later his mother committed suicide on the anniversary of his brother's death. Consequently, Paul de Man's uncle, also named Hendrik, became a sort of adoptive father to his nephew, meeting him weekly for lunch with his own son, Jan de Man.

Now this uncle was a charismatic intellectual and political authority in Belgium, the author of a number of influential books on Marxism and on socialist theory. He had also been a successful politician and a minister in several Belgian governments. On the eve of the war, a number of factors conspired to sway this prominent politician in a pro-German direction. Having been a veteran of the first World War and having consequently become a zealous pacifist; having studied in Germany and been an admirer of German culture and philosophy; on the other hand, having been all his life a Marxist militant in favor of a socialist revolution, Hendrik de Man was led to believe that this social revolution, which the Western democracies had failed to achieve, could be brought about by means of the strong leadership of German National Socialism, under whose hegemony a unified Europe, in which Belgium would keep its independence and neutrality, would allow for the implementation of a radical social reform and renewal. After Belgium's invasion by the German army in 1940, Hendrik de Man, as president of the Belgian Workers' Party, issued a public manifesto urging his followers to cooperate with the Germans. "The role of a leader," reads the manifesto, "is not to follow his troops, but to lead them by showing them the way. Here is what I ask you to undertake:"

Be among the first rank of those who struggle against poverty and demoralization, for the resumption of work and the return to normal life.

But do not believe that it is necessary to resist the occupying power; accept the fact of his victory and try rather to draw lessons therefrom so as to make of this the starting point for new social progress.

The war has led to the debacle of the parliamentary regime and of the capitalist plutocracy in the so-called democracies.

For the working classes and for socialism, this collapse of a decrepit world is, far from a disaster, a deliverance.

Despite all that we have experienced of defeats, sufferings, and disillusions, the way is open for the two causes that sum up the aspirations of the people: European peace and social justice.

Peace has not been able to develop from the free understanding of sovereign nations and rival imperialisms: it will be able to emerge from a Europe united by arms, wherein the economic frontiers have been leveled.

Social justice has not been able to develop from a system calling itself democratic but in which money powers and the professional politicians in fact predominate . . .

For years the double talk of the warmongers has concealed from you that [the Nazi] system, despite everything in it that strikes our mentality as alien, had lessened class differences much more efficaciously than the self-styled democracies, where capital continued to lay down the law.

Since then everyone has been able to see that the superior morale of the German army is due in large part to the greater social unity of the nation and to the resulting prestige of its authorities. In contrast, the plutodemocracies offer us the spectacle of authorities deserting their stations and the rich crossing the border by car without worrying about what happens to the masses.

By linking their fate to the victory of arms, the democratic governments have accepted in advance the verdict of the war. This verdict is clear. It condemns the systems where speeches take the place of actions.[4]

It seems quite obvious from his wartime journalistic pieces that the young Paul was, like his uncle, equally captivated by the Nazis' seeming revolutionary promise and shared entirely, at first, his uncle's faith in the authority and the vocation of his own leadership, and consequently his conviction that collaboration with the Germans was Belgium's only chance for national survival, and that the thrust of the Nazis' rise to power held nothing more, in stock, than the exhilarating prospect of a European reunification and the promise of a cataclysmic renewal of Western culture and the Western social fabric.

Language played an important role in this political conjuncture. As a bilingual country, Belgium's history had been marked by the oppression of the Flemish by the French-speaking minority. Identifying with their Flemish origins in spite of their assimilation into the cultural dominance of French, both Hendrik and Paul de Man tended to view the Germans as linguistic allies in the liberation of the Flemish from French superiority. This Germanic cultural alliance, however, while claiming the originality and worth of Flemish, was supposed to maintain the specificity of both the French and the Flemish within a diverse European culture.

My sense is that, in speaking for the Flemish, Hendrik's claims and his political focus as a leader seemed to offer his young nephew not only a renewed relation to the *mother tongue,* beyond the loss marked by the mother's suicide, but also, in a general way, a renewed *relation to the past,* which in Hendrik's theories and actions was constantly referred to as an inspiration for a critique—and a remaking—of the present. This question of the relation of the present to the past will become particularly relevant, of course, in trying to account for the different and more enigmatic form that Paul de Man's later relation to his past will necessarily assume: both in his silence, which I take to be (among other things) his consequent refusal of a discursive relation to the past that might have any shadow of resemblance to his past relation to the

[4]Hendrik de Man, "The Manifesto," *A Documentary Study of Hendrik de Man, Socialist Critic of Marxism,* ed. and trans. Peter Dodge (Princeton, N.J., 1979), pp. 326–327.

past, and in his later absolute rejection both of the politically conservative and of the politically radical notion of a return to origins.

During the war, however, Hendrik's radical analysis of history and his misguided understanding of the historical opportunity for a revolutionary return to origins seemed to guide Paul de Man's historical beliefs. "The main goal of all historical labor [is] to become a guide for the critical investigation of existing conditions," writes Paul in the newspaper *Het Vlaamsche Land.* "For what would be the use of keeping in touch with the past and of fathoming all its aspects if this knowledge does not teach us to pass judgment on what is happening around us *now?*[5] And in his review for *Le Soir* of the work of the French historian Daniel Halévy, who analyzed France's defeat by Nazi Germany in May 1940 by comparing it to two previous major disasters in French history, Paul de Man writes: "This [comparison] is not a vain historian's game. The only resource of a nation, when its institutions have been crushed, its land invaded, and when the problem of the choice between life and death presents itself, is to return upon its past. This in any case is the task of those who have the responsibility of giving directives and of searching for programs of action."[6]

This model of a leader who turns to the past so as to reassess and to rebuild the present implicitly takes its inspiration from Hendrik's sense of his historical endeavor. What the young Paul must have found compelling in his uncle's enterprise, what lures indeed both Paul and Hendrik in the German program, is the seductive Nazi ideology of *reconstruction* and *national salvation* (the need to save one's country from economic, social, and emotional bankruptcy): an ideology that might have seemed to hold the promise of making up for personal and political disasters and that appeared to be supported by the concrete historical example of Germany's effective economic reconstruction and national revival after its defeat and devastation in the First World War.

Thus it is that in December 1940, at a point when the Second World War seemed to many to have been definitively won by Germany, five months after the publication of his uncle's manifesto, and one month before the birth of his first son (who will also be named Hendrik), Paul de Man starts writing his art column for *Le Soir,* one of the two major

[5]Paul de Man, "Critiek en literatuurgeschiedenis" ["Criticism and Literary History"] (*Het Vlaamsche Land,* 7–8 June 1942), trans. Ortwin de Graef, *Wartime Journalism, 1939–1943,* ed. Hamacher, Hertz, and Keenan (Lincoln, Neb., 1988), p. 313.

[6]De Man, " 'Trois épreuves' par Daniel Halévy" (*Le Soir,* 14 Oct. 1941), *Wartime Journalism,* p. 153; my translation.

Belgian newspapers, which, at this point, are both controlled by the German occupation.

The Jewish Question

Of the 170 articles (literary, musical, and cultural reviews) he would contribute to *Le Soir* over the next two years, one stands out as truly compromising (beyond the general motif of admiration for German literature and culture and the occasional propounding of a cultural renaissance in light of this identification with the Germanic model culture): an article entitled "Jews in Contemporary Literature" ["Les Juifs dans la littérature actuelle"], published on March 4, 1941 in a special afternoon edition of *Le Soir* devoted to anti-Semitic propaganda, on a page entitled "The Jews and Us: The Cultural Aspects." The general subject obviously must have been assigned by the German propaganda controlling the newspaper. "All [Belgian] witnesses agree," writes Colinet, that Paul de Man fulfilled this assignment "reluctantly, fearing to lose his livelihood" ("P," 430).

"Vulgar anti-Semitism," writes de Man, "would willingly consider the postwar cultural phenomena (following the 1914–1918 war) as degenerated and decadent, because Jewified [*enjuivés*]. Literature has not escaped this lapidary judgment: it was enough to discover several Jewish writers under Latinized pseudonyms for the whole contemporary production to be judged as ominous and polluted."[7] But the article itself refutes this argument. Since the main contemporary writers— among whom de Man names "Gide, Kafka, Hemingway, Lawrence"— are not Jewish, Western literature has not, in fact, been penetrated by the foreign element of Jewish influence and its integrity, its impermeability to this influence, proves its vitality and health.

There seem to be two ways in which de Man's statements deviate from the straight anti-Semitic purpose of the newspaper's assignment: one is de Man's naming of Franz Kafka as one of the greatest—and non-Jewish—writers; the other is his taking issue with the so-called vulgar anti-Semitism's major thesis of Jewish world dominion, and, consequently, of the necessity of defending against such dominion by eliminating the Jewish threat. But even though it argues that there is no Jewish threat, the article does seem to carry over an anti-Semitic

[7]De Man, "Les Juifs dans la littérature actuelle" (*Le Soir*, 4 Mar. 1941), *Wartime Journalism,* p. 45; my translation.

tone in conceiving of the Jews, in opposition to an uncritical Aryan self-centeredness, as the foreign and contaminating Other, a conception that, although it takes care not to duplicate, is also not entirely in disagreement with, the Christian and the Nazi ideologies depicting Jews as the negative of truth.[8] The implication of the article, one might concede, is, much more benignly, that there is no need to defend against the Jews. But even though the only truth here claimed is that of literature (and of a literature problematically and paradoxically modeled on Kafka), still the basic underlying Christian premise of the inherent otherness of Jews to truth seems to be taken for granted as the unquestioned vestige of a Christian education, which is, presumably, unconsciously rehearsed by the new pressure, and the new channel, of the ideology of European revival and salvation. This is doubtless the most tainted piece of de Man's wartime writing.

In no other circumstance of his life did de Man propound—or consent to—anti-Semitism: not only did his intellectual and personal relationships, both during the war in Belgium, and, even more so, later in the United States, include quite crucial intimate friendships with Jews, but in 1942 or 1943, about a year after the journalistic publication of his compromising statement, he and his wife sheltered for several days in their apartment the Jewish pianist Esther Sluszny and her husband, who were then illegal citizens in hiding from the Nazis.[9] During this same period, de Man was meeting regularly with Georges Goriely, a member of the Belgian Resistance. According to Goriely's own testimony, he never for one minute feared denunciation of his underground activities by Paul de Man.[10]

---

[8]De Man thus writes: "One sees that the creation of a Jewish colony isolated from Europe will not entail any deplorable consequences for the literary life of the West." This statement has been read as condoning the Nazi Final Solution, that is, deportations of the Jews to extermination camps. But this is an anachronistic reading. Since the Nazi plans for the deportation of the Belgian Jews were put into operation only in late July 1942, and since rumors of extermination spread through the Jewish community only after this period (August 1942), it is unlikely that in March 1941, the date when "Les Juifs dans la littérature actuelle" was published, de Man's statement is in fact informed by the Nazi "solution" by extermination. It seems, rather, that what de Man's statement is alluding to is the political solution that had been debated since the beginning of the century in Jewish intellectual circles, that of a resettlement of Jews outside of Europe— in Palestine or in Madagascar (a colony the West would give to the Jews). There is no question here that de Man's summary argument—"to lose the Jews is to lose nothing"— is patently anti-Semitic (in compliance with the newspaper's coercive line), but not in the Nazis' murderous sense. Nothing would be lost for European literature, de Man argues, if the Jews were to leave for a resettlement in a Jewish colony outside of Europe.

[9]See "P," p. 436 n.12.

[10]I am indebted to Neil Hertz for confirmation of this testimony.

III

The Turning Point

When and how did Paul de Man, who—willingly or not—was writing as an ideologist, wake up to the seductive traps, to the deception and to the dangers, of Nazi ideology?

We have no explicit answers to this question, no explicit statement on de Man's part. It seems, however, that the sequence of de Man's wartime writings, read in juxtaposition with the chronology of historical events,[11] does enable us to recognize a turning point and a subtle change of focus and orientation, starting in the middle of 1942.

On June 1, 1942, the policy of the yellow star is for the first time implemented: Jews in Belgium and France are required by order of the German military command to wear a yellow Star of David on their outer clothing to mark their inferior racial identity as Jews. Six weeks later, on July 14, 1942 (the anniversary of the French Revolution), Paul de Man (then twenty-two years old) publishes for the first time in the pages of *Le Soir* a review of the French resistance journal *Messages* ("Continuité de la poésie française: À propos de la revue 'Messages' "). The review, which deals with contemporary trends of French poetry, claims the independence of literature with respect to political upheavals and defeats.[12]

A month later, in mid-August, rumors of extermination spread through the Jewish community in Belgium. About the same time, the Nazi *Propaganda Abteilung* tightens its censorship policy, requiring that newspaper articles be submitted for review before their publication.

Two weeks after this double turn of events, on September 1, 1942, the readers of *Le Soir* can read, under the signature of Paul de Man, a review entitled " 'The Massacre of the Innocents': A Poem by Hubert Dubois" [" 'Le Massacre des Innocents': poème de Hubert Dubois"].[13] The poem de Man chose to review, written by a Belgian author, is

---

[11]See the detailed chronology established by Hamacher, Hertz, and Keenan, kindly communicated to me by them last summer and now published in *Responses*, pp. xi–xxi.

[12]See de Man, "Continuité de la poésie française: À propos de la revue 'Messages' " (*Le Soir*, 14 July 1942), *Wartime Journalism*, pp. 250–251.

[13]See de Man, " 'Le Massacre des Innocents': poème de Hubert Dubois" (*Le Soir*, 1 Sept. 1942), *Wartime Journalism*, pp. 265–266.

a barely masked allegory of the Nazi extermination of the Jews. It underscores repeatedly the fact that the sacrilege of Herod's massacre of Jewish children (provoked by the prophecy of the advent of Christ) is taking place not in the past but (to use the poem's words) "in our time," in "our countries," and that the place of the original massacre, Rama, has extended itself today—this is the main thesis of the poem— to "the entire world of humans." The epigraph of the poem is drawn from Matthew 2, referring to a prophecy of the crucifixion and to the cry of Rachel bemoaning her children. The latent resistance connotation of the original French text is masked not merely by the Christian topos, but also by the reassuring symmetries of its rhymes and rhythms—by the conservative appearance of its traditional versification. I will attempt to point out its significant implicit political statements by quoting, in my necessarily awkward free and literal translation, some selected verses.

> Rama . . .
> Is no longer the Bethlehem of the Massacre . . .
> Rama, in our time, like an insubordinate people
> Overflowing its shore, has reached our countries.
> Rama is today the entire world of humans . . .
> Rachel has a thousand voices to claim her misery . . .
> Thus Rachel laments in each person today
> Her pain . . .
> And on the human Wailing Wall falls
> A rain of red lights like blood . . .[14]

De Man praises "the intellectual and moral superiority of this poem," and ventures to write, "One could easily call 'The Massacre of the Innocents' a meditation on the guilt which has led humanity to the awful state in which it is plunged at the present moment." The review also refers to a human history of "repeated crimes against the human person."[15]

The last of de Man's articles for *Le Soir* appears two months later, at the end of November 1942.

---

[14]Hubert Dubois, "Le Massacre des Innocents," *Messages* 11 (1942); my translation. I owe many thanks to Tom Keenan, who generously provided me with a copy of this text, as well as with a folder of copies of the *Le Soir* articles and with seven other folders of documents related to this case (including a copy of *Exercice du silence,* which I will be discussing later)—documents that have served as the informational basis for my reflection and without which this essay would not have been possible.

[15]De Man, " 'Le Massacre des Innocents,' " p. 265.

An Exercise of Silence

In December 1942 de Man helps to bring to light in Brussels, at l'Agence Dechenne, the German-controlled publishing house at which he works, a volume entitled *Exercice du silence,* whose publication in Paris in the poetic journal *Messages* (associated with the French intellectual resistance) has been censored by the Germans.

Thus 1942 marks a change in de Man's orientation, a change that, furthermore, *precedes* the turn of the fortunes of the war in the historical turning point that will take place only the following year, in February 1943, with the surrender of the German army in Stalingrad. Chronologically, this change of mind follows immediately, and thus seems to derive from, the tightening of Nazi censorship and the historical knowledge of the extermination of the Jews.

In March 1943, Paul de Man is fired from l'Agence Dechenne, three months after, and probably as a result of, his publication of the previously censored *Exercice du silence.*

This is the point at which de Man himself lapses into silence, a public silence that would last eleven years (until the reappearance of de Man's next literary essays in the French periodical *Critique* in the early fifties). Interestingly enough, the transgressive publication of *Exercice du silence* precedes de Man's own silence, a silence, therefore, perhaps not unrelated to the content of the publication of the French intellectual resistance he himself rescued from silence. What, then, is the nature of the silence that the publication claims to exercise?

The volume opens with a quotation from Georges Bernanos, which serves as its epigraph: "Keeping silent: what a strange word! It is the silence that keeps us." What, however, does it mean for the authors of this volume to keep silent in the very paradoxical performance of a discourse, of a writing? And what, in turn, does the silence here keep, or protect, if not the very action, and the very possibility, of resisting, of affirming—through contemporary poetry—that, as Pierre Seghers will put it, "France exists,"[16] exists, that is, autonomously with respect to its invaders, independent of its occupying forces? The editorial introduction, which recapitulates the title "Exercise of Silence," opens with yet another epigraph, from Pascal: "if those keep silent, the stones will speak." Somehow, therefore, *Exercice du silence*

---

[16]Pierre Seghers, "Signaux de Belgique," *Poetes prisonniers, Poésie 43, 14,* p. 95. At the bottom of the page, a footnote reads, "Brussels.—A palace revolution has evicted from the direction of certain editions Georges Lambrichs and Paul de Man, who defended the young French literature" (my translation).

is involved with a story that is not told in words but that the stones cry out. In its political protest through its poetical endeavor, the volume implies from the beginning that a certain way of keeping silent can make the stones speak—can intensify, in other words, a certain sort of testimony that, although unspoken, speaks for itself. I will later suggest that both de Man's silence and the testimony of his later work are informed by precisely such an exercise of silence.

But let me return to the sequence of significant events:

During his silent period and consequent to his being fired from l'Agence Dechenne, de Man devotes himself to the work of translation. (Could the work of translation—the rewriting of someone else's text, the acceptance of and attentive listening to another's language—itself be viewed as part of de Man's exercise of silence?) While his previous translations were from German and from Flemish into French, he for the first time now translates from English—and from American literature—into Flemish: *Moby-Dick* appears in Belgium in de Man's Flemish translation in 1945.

In the same year, during the collaboration trials following the war, the twenty-six-year-old de Man is asked to appear before a Belgian military tribunal and is released without charges of collaboration. Before this exonerating public sentence, de Man had been denounced, paradoxically and significantly, by both sides: in a pamphlet published by the resistance in 1943 for his writing for *Le Soir,* and by two collaborationist journals in 1943 for his publication of *Exercice du silence.*[17]

The Belgian authorities convict Paul's uncle, Hendrik, for having "knowingly and maliciously served the design of the enemy." Because of disagreements with Belgian socialists and his growing unwilling-ness to cooperate fully with the Germans, Hendrik de Man had left Belgium for France in 1941, and in 1944 obtained political asylum in Switzerland. He is sentenced in absentia to a twenty-year term of imprisonment, dedicates the rest of his life to writing books, and dies in a car accident (which may have been suicidal) in 1953.

Moby-Dick; or, The Whale

Paul de Man's 1945 publication of the American novel *Moby-Dick,* which he had probably been translating during the two preceding

[17]The Resistance pamphlet was *Galerie des traîtres;* the collaborationist journals were *Le Nouveau journal* and *Cassandre* (given in the chronology in *Responses,* xix).

Paul de Man denounced in *Galerie des traitres,* 1943 (age twenty three).

years, during the later (silent) phase of his experience of the war, prefigures, in more than one way, de Man's future. The new focus on a non-European, American novel precedes the American part of de Man's life, his first departure to America in 1947, and his definitive departure the following year to emigrate to the United States, where he will later marry a second time and become a student of comparative literature at Harvard University.

But *Moby-Dick,* which de Man produces at the conclusion of the Second World War, prefigures not merely de Man's future choice of America as a physical and cultural destination but the radical nature of the departure, which will create an absolute break with what pre-ceded, as he leaves behind everything connected to the Belgian past, including his own family, wife and children. In the same way, *Moby-Dick*'s protagonists, Captain Ahab and the narrator Ishmael, are indeed both marked, each in his own way, by a radical departure: Captain Ahab has left his wife and children to settle his account with the whale; Ishmael goes to sea, he tells us, when he is death-drawn and depressed, as a substitute for committing suicide. "This is my substitute for pistol and balls," he says. "With a philosophical flourish Cato throws himself upon the sword; I quietly take to the ship" (*M-D,* 6). Might both de Man's eleven-year-old silence and his radical departure be viewed as substitutes for suicide—suicide as the recognition that what has been done is absolutely irrevocable, which requires one in turn to do something irreversible about it? What appears to be an erasure of the past is in fact this quasi-suicidal, mute acknowledgment of a radical loss—or death—of truth, and therefore the acknowledgment of a radical loss—or death—of self: the realization that there can be no way back from what has happened, no possible recuperation. Already *Exercice du silence* had announced both literally and metaphorically the annihilation of the self, not only because the volume chose symbolically to open with a letter by Baudelaire announcing his own suicide ("I kill myself because I can no longer live, because the fatigue of falling asleep and the fatigue of waking up are both unbearable"),[18] but because the editorial introduction, entitled "Exercise of Silence," had included the following thoughts on the death of the self and its reduction to silence (thoughts that can uncannily be read as prophesying the silent violence of de Man's imminent departure):

> Nevertheless this adventure by which he [the self] had believed he was taking over, in turn has overtaken him. The possession of the world opens vacant on his death . . . [He] cannot come into the proximity of the emergence of a (finally) crucial reality unless he has renounced marking it by the seal of his belonging, and has carefully *burnt out the dictionaries of his memory* . . . At this point [he] recognizes that humbleness is his profession and that exile is henceforth his only condition.[19]

Like *Moby-Dick*'s narrator, de Man condemns himself to exile.[20] "Call me Ishmael" (*M-D*, 3) he too might have said in the "prosopopeia"[21] of the story that he had translated into Flemish but that, unlike *Moby-Dick*'s narrator, *he* will *not directly tell.*

Like Ishmael, however, de Man survives the fanaticism of the war

[18]"Lettre à Ancelle," *Exercice du silence* (Brussels, 1942), p. 6.

[19]*Exercice du silence*, pp. 3–5.

[20]In its strong sense, exile is not merely a departure but an act of self-expropriation and renunciation of one's origins. It is thus an abdication of one of the great resources of Nazi ideology, the recourse to the natural integrity and purity and to the organic unity of nation and of nationalism.

[21]This opening sentence of chapter 1 of *Moby-Dick* is a reference to Isaac's half-brother, Abraham's son by the bondservant Hagar, who was disinherited and thus, having to leave his father's land, condemned to exile (Gen. 21).

Prosopopeia, a figure of address (the way in which, for instance, the sentence "Call me Ishmael" is actively addressing an implicit listener or reader), will become one of de Man's favorite rhetorical figures, a key term in his theoretical vocabulary, and a key concept in his later writing about autobiography.

against the whales and the disaster of the shipwreck by uncannily and paradoxically—as Melville quite fantastically imagines it—*floating on a coffin:*

> It so chanced, that . . . the coffin life-buoy shot lengthwise from the sea, fell over, and floated by my side. Buoyed up by that coffin, for almost one whole day and night, I floated on a soft and dirge-like main . . . On the second day, a sail drew near, nearer, and picked me up at last. It was the devious-cruising Rachel, that in her retracing search after her missing children, only found another orphan. [M-D, 573]

De Man's future is foreshadowed, enigmatically and paradoxically, by *both* the destinies of Ahab and of Ishmael. He at the same time dies as Ahab and survives as Ishmael. He survives, that is, not as the same but as a radically transformed Other: what survives is not the memory of Ahab but the witnessing by Ishmael of the fact that Ahab's quasi-suicidal death provides no resolution to the struggle, because Ahab at the end becomes entangled with, and thus forever tied to, the very body of the stricken whale. " 'Oh, lonely death on lonely life,' "mutters Ahab in his last breath.

> "Oh, now I feel my topmost greatness lies in my topmost grief. Ho, ho! from all your furthest bounds, pour ye now in, ye bold billows of my whole foregone life, and top this one piled comber of my death! Towards thee I roll, thou all-destroying but unconquering whale; to the last I grapple with thee; from hell's heart I stab at thee . . . Sink all coffins and all hearses to one common pool! and since neither can be mine, let me then tow in pieces, while still chasing thee, though tied to thee, thou damned whale!" [M-D, 571–572]

Nazi ideology had seemed to offer a way out of political dead ends, a clear historical direction, a black-and-white solution, a cataclysmic resolution. But Ishmael remains not with a solution but with the irreducible ambiguity of the apocalyptic struggle. Ishmael's vision, or his vantage point, is thus different both from that of Ahab and from his own before the shipwreck and his own solitary survival.

" 'And I only am escaped alone to tell thee,' " reads, quoting from Job,[22] Melville's conclusion of *Moby-Dick,* opening the epilogue of

[22]In these words from Job 1:16, a witness and the sole survivor of a catastrophe comes to inform Job about the loss of everything he once owned or had, including his wife and children. Borrowing these very words, Ishmael, in turn, as the sole survivor and the only witness to the shipwreck, is "escaped alone," and his testimony (the text of *Moby-Dick*) will be marked by this radical "aloneness" of his position as a witness. "No one bears witness for the witness," writes Paul Celan. And yet, the witness is "escaped alone to tell thee," to tell, in other words, what he alone can henceforth tell, to testify, precisely, for the muteness of a corpse sunk in the ocean. With what language, with what silence, will Ishmael be able to speak for, speak *from within,* the very *dumbness* of that corpse, and yet, to also say the enigma of his own survival in a coffin

Ishmael's narrative. In the same way, de Man, like Ahab wrestling and forever tied up with the whale, survives, like Ishmael, in order to henceforth *position* both his silence and his later discourse precisely in the very core of Ishmael's doubleness of vision, in his inside knowledge of the compellingly seductive and radically delusional quality of the event, and in his later vision of the entanglement and the complicity, of the bankruptcy of all conventional historical divisions and the blurring of all boundaries. It is no longer possible to distinguish between heroes and knaves, regeneration and destruction, deliverance and entanglement, speeches and acts, history and faith, idealistic faith and (self-)deception, justice and totalitarianism, utmost barbarism and utmost civilized refinement, freedom of will and radical enslavement to historical manipulations and ideological coercions. Indeed, in his afterlife as Ishmael, in his later writings and his teaching, de Man, I would suggest, does nothing other than testify to the complexity and ambiguity of history as Holocaust. Like Ishmael rejoining life by floating on a coffin, like Ahab struggling and forever tied up with the whale, de Man will bear witness, in his later writings, to the Leviathan of a historical complexity with which his testimony will remain forever wrestling, in an ongoing testimonial struggle to which, the writings testify, there is no end and from which, they tell us, there is no possible escape.

IV

Theory and Testimony: The Later Writing

Why, then, did de Man not choose, like Ishmael, to *tell his story* if—as I am here suggesting—his afterlife was dedicated to bearing witness to its lesson?

Because the story is not simply over, known or given, in a totalizing overview of what happened in the past; and because the act of bearing witness can itself be—as de Man has learned from his war experience—an illusory endeavor. The young Paul de Man who was writing for *Le Soir* believed himself to be a *witness* to the history of his time, of which the journalistic writings were meant to be the testimonial records, as their very titles indicate: "Testimonies on the War in

---

covered with inscriptions, which thus keeps him afloat not merely on the figure of the grave but on the life-giving figure of a *writing?* "And I only am escaped alone to tell thee."

Paul de Man at Bard College, 1951 (age thirty one).

France" ["Témoignages sur la guerre en France"] (March 25, 1941); "French Literature before the Events" ["La Littérature française devant les événements"] (January 20, 1942); "Narratives and Testimonies" ["Récit et témoignages"] (February 3, 1942); "Biographies and History" ["Biographies et histoire"] (February 17, 1942); "Testimonies on Our Time" ["Témoignages de notre temps"] (March 10, 1942); and so on. However, I would suggest that once de Man realized the utter fallacy and aberration of his "war testimonies," the act of bearing witness could no longer be repeated as a simple narrative act but had to turn upon its own possibility of error to indicate—and warn us against—its own susceptibility to blindness.

In his only explicit statement about his past—a letter to the Harvard Society of Fellows written in 1955—de Man explained that he stopped writing for *Le Soir* "when Nazi thought-control did no longer allow freedom of statement."[23] But what de Man in fact discovered in the later phase of the Second World War, and what he bears witness to in his mature work, is not the simple factual tightening of Nazi censorship in 1942, but the way in which his former journalistic witnessing

[23]De Man, letter to Renato Poggioli, director of the Harvard Society of Fellows, Jan. 26, 1955, in *Responses*, p. 476.

had all along been inadvertently in some way predetermined by the unrecognized coerciveness of the Nazi rhetoric of promises. Retrospectively, de Man discovered the inescapable, pervasive way in which ideological coercion is surreptitiously built into language, into the very discourse one is inadvertently employing and the very writing of which one believes oneself to be the author.

"I cannot tell," writes Ishmael, "why this was exactly; yet, now that I recall all the circumstances, I think I can see a little into the springs and motives which being cunningly presented to me under various disguises, induced me to set about performing the part I did, besides cajoling me into the delusion that it was a choice resulting from my own unbiased freewill and discriminating judgment" (*M-D,* 7). In the same way, de Man discovers that his wartime witnessing of history and the part that *he* performed—his political convictions, his nationalistic faith, his belief in a new Europe, and his very journalistic dedication— were in turn "thought-controlled" and thus preempted as a testimony by the very grammar of their language.

The later writing, therefore, cannot simply "tell the story of the war," since it has to tell how the war story it had once told was historically voided of meaning, how witnessing does not provide narrative knowledge, since one cannot be sure, in one's position as a witness, either if one is in reality perceiving what one believes oneself to be perceiving or if one is in effect speaking in (if one has not already lost) one's own voice. The later testimony, in other words, is not that of (the belated narrative of) the returning speaking witness but rather that, precisely, of the failed witness, of the witness, that is, who failed to be and who has returned mute. "I must repeat," writes, from a different position, Primo Levi:

> we, the survivors, are not the true witnesses. This is an uncomfortable notion of which I have become conscious little by little, reading the memoirs of others and reading mine at a distance of years . . . Those who . . . have not returned to tell about it or have returned mute, . . . they are . . . the submerged, the complete witnesses, the ones whose deposition would have a general significance. [*DS,* 83–84]

Incorporating the silence of the witness who has returned mute into his very writing, de Man's entire work and his later theories bear implicit witness to the Holocaust, not as its (impossible and failed) narrator (a narrator-journalist whom the war had dispossessed of his own voice) but as a witness to the very blindness of his own, and others', witness, a firsthand witness to the Holocaust's historical disintegration of the witness.

Such second-degree testimony is complex and can no longer be direct. Because it seeks above all to preserve the distance necessary for the witnessing (the inner distance of the radical departure), it requires not the involved proximity of memory (that of the submersion of the witness) but the *distancing* of this submersion through the reflectiveness of *theory*. For it is, I would suggest, precisely de Man's *theories* that inscribe the testimony of the muted witness and that address the lesson of historical events, not (as some would have it) as a cover-up or a dissimulation of the past, but as an ongoing, active *transformation of the very act of bearing witness*. Here again, de Man could borrow Primo Levi's words:

> An apology is in order. This very book is drenched in memory; what's more, a distant memory. Thus it draws from a suspect source and must be protected against itself. So here then: it contains more considerations than memories, lingers more willingly on the state of affairs such as it is now than on the retroactive chronicle. [*DS*, 34–35]

History as Holocaust is mutely omnipresent in the theoretical endeavor of de Man's mature work. The war's disastrous historical and political effects are what is implicitly at stake in the text's insistent focus on, and tracking of, an ever-lurking blindness it underscores as the primary human (and historical) condition. De Man's entire writing effort is a silent trace of the reality of an event whose very historicity, borne out by the author's own catastrophic experience, has occurred precisely as the event of the preclusion—the event of the impossibility—of its own witnessing; an event that could thus name the very namelessness, the very magnitude, the very materiality of what de Man will constantly refer to as the ever-threatening *impossibility of reading*.

> The naïve historical question from which we started out—should the *Profession de foi* be called a theistic text?—must remain unanswerable. The text both is and is not the theistic document it is assumed to be. It is not the simple negation of the faith it seems to proclaim, since it ends up by accounting in a manner that cannot be refuted for the necessary occurrence of this faith. But it also denounces it as aberrant. A text such as the *Profession de foi* can literally be called "unreadable" in that it leads to a set of assertions that radically exclude each other. Nor are these assertions mere neutral constations; they are exhortative performatives that require the passage from mere enunciation to action. They compel us to choose while destroying the foundation of any choice. They tell the allegory of a judicial decision that can be neither

judicious nor just . . . One sees from this that the impossibility of reading should not be taken too lightly.[24]

The Referential Debt, or the Purloined Ribbon

In his important essay on Rousseau's *Confessions,* strategically placed at the conclusion of *Allegories of Reading* as de Man's last statement and ambiguously entitled "Excuses (*Confessions*)," de Man addresses posthumously, I would suggest (or in anticipation), the question so persistently asked today both by his critics and by his admirers, of why he has not satisfied the former's sense of justice and/ or cleared the latter's conscience, by giving both the satisfaction—or the reparation—of a public confession or a public declaration of remorse that would have at least proven his regret, his present repentance of past errors.

"Excuses (*Confessions*)" was entitled in its first version "The Purloined Ribbon," in an allusion to (and perhaps a critical rewriting of) Jacques Lacan's "Seminar on 'The Purloined Letter.' "[25] The essay discusses an episode from Rousseau's *Confessions,* in which Rousseau narrates a scene of youthful guilt in which he stole a ribbon, and then—to clear himself—gratuitously accused the servant Marion for having stolen it, an accusation that resulted in the firing of the maid. I would suggest that de Man's discussion of "the purloined ribbon," and of Rousseau's avowal of his "primal scene" of guilt, which de Man treats as a "paradigmatic event, the core of [Rousseau's] autobiographical narrative" (*AR,* 278–79), as well as the episode itself of the purloined ribbon and of Rousseau's gratuitous denunciation of the maid, can be read as an implicit evocation of the absent (purloined) referent of de Man's own past; the purloined referential letter of his wartime journalistic writings and, specifically, the truly compromising journalistic statement he now recalls, perhaps, as his gratuitous "denunciation" of the Jews.

Of course, de Man did not, properly speaking, "denounce" the Jews. But his statement on the Jews was published in a context, and spoken

[24]De Man, *Allegories of Reading: Figural Language in Rousseau, Nietzsche, Rilke, and Proust* (New Haven, Conn., 1979), p. 245; hereafter abbreviated *AR.*

[25]See Jacques Lacan, "Seminar on 'The Purloined Letter,' " trans. Jeffrey Mehlman, in *The Purloined Poe: Lacan, Derrida and Psychoanalytic Reading,* ed. John P. Muller and William J. Richardson (Baltimore, 1988), pp. 28–54. De Man, of course, must have read the original French version of this essay in Lacan's *Ecrits* (Paris, 1966).

in a historical situation, that, *de factum,* made it into a denunciation. Similarly (though on a lesser and more trivial scale), Rousseau's intention, in uttering the name of Marion, was not to *accuse* her but to *clear* himself. But in both cases, the verbal act (of naming, and of pointing to, the Other), turns out to have disastrous consequences unpredictable by either of its authors. The resonance between Rousseau's text and de Man's past thus lies not so much in a one-to-one resemblance between Rousseau's act and de Man's act, but in the structural resemblance of a primal scene of guilt that links an act of speaking with the unpredictable and devastating consequences of this act. Rousseau's confession must have retrospectively captured de Man's attention not simply in reference to de Man's own history but, specifically, in reference to *the turning point* in that history: de Man's eventual historical discovery of his own unexpected and unsuspected involvement with—and complicity in—a historical false accusation amounting to an actual "Massacre of the Innocents." Through its reflection on the consequences of the purloined ribbon and of Rousseau's speech act of accusation, "Excuses (*Confessions*)" thus implicitly outlines a meditation on the purloined letter of the journalistic collaborationist writing.

Behind de Man's text, there is, in addition to Rousseau, a whole network of associated texts that are elliptically—and yet consistently—present, that create in turn a whole network of unarticulated textual and historical associations. One of these, as I have suggested, is Lacan's "Seminar on 'The Purloined Letter,' " insofar as it is replicated by de Man's initial title for the piece, "The Purloined Ribbon." But it is Lacan's French title that is significant: the French name under which Lacan has recapitulated and rendered notorious Poe's text (according to Baudelaire's translation)—"La Lettre volée" ["The Stolen Letter"]—might have been oddly evocative, for de Man, of the pejorative political name by which the Belgian newspaper in which he wrote during the war, *Le Soir,* came to be known once it had been seized and taken over by the Nazis—a pejorative name that was meant to designate the usurpation of the paper from its rightful, independent Belgian owners in its period of forced collaboration with the Germans: *Le Soir volé* [*The Stolen Evening*].

Lacan's uncanny question with respect to *La Lettre volée*—"To whom does a letter belong?"[26]—could in fact be reiterated as a political question with respect to *Le Soir volé:* to whom does a newspaper

[26]Lacan, "Seminar on 'The Purloined Letter,' " p. 41.

belong? And how, conversely, does one paradoxically become the *owner* of a political false accusation whose historical significance one does not entirely own, but which was nonetheless historically put into effect by the very context in which one was writing, the context of the stolen, or the purloined, newspaper?

"Political and autobiographical texts," writes de Man, "have in common that they share a referential reading-moment explicitly built in within the spectrum of their significations, no matter how deluded this moment may be in its mode as well as in its thematic content: the deadly 'horn of the bull' referred to by Michel Leiris in a text that is indeed as political as it is autobiographical" (*AR,* 278). De Man's first footnote, at this point, refers us to Leiris' autobiographical work, *L'Age d'homme,*[27] and comments simply, "The essay [by Leiris] dates from 1945, immediately after the war" (*AR,* 278 n.1). Leiris's is, with Lacan's, the second major text elliptically present throughout de Man's text; if Lacan's text deals with the tracking of secrets (purloined letters), Leiris's text is a contemporary model of the genre of autobiography that, like Rousseau's, designates itself as a "confession." Now, what does Leiris mean by the "horn of the bull," a figure that de Man borrows both to designate and to implicitly *date* the "referential reading-moment" he has in mind as what "political and autobiographical texts have in common"—their common reference to a moment of historical reality—"no matter how deluded this moment may be" in its reading by others and/or in its reading by itself, in its own self-presentation and self-perception?

Leiris compares the act of writing to the ritual drama of bullfighting. Both take place on the " 'terrain of truth' which is the bullfighting term for the arena . . . Just as the matador . . . gives the measure of his value when he finds himself face to face and alone with the bull . . . so . . . man discovers himself confronting a reality" (*M,* 37).

The bull's horn comes to represent, in Leiris's allegory of (autobiographical) writing, the material effects of referential reality, and specifically three aspects of these effects:

1. the inescapable materiality of one's past;[28]

[27]See Michel Leiris, *L'Age d'homme: précédé de "De la littérature considérée comme une tauromachie"* (Paris, 1946); trans. Richard Howard, under the title *Manhood: A Journey from Childhood into the Fierce Order of Virility* (New York, 1963); hereafter abbreviated *M.*

[28]"To use materials of which I was not the master and which I had to take as I found them (since my life was what it was and I could not alter, by so much as a comma, my past, a primary *datum* representing for me a fate as unchallengeable as for the *torero* the beast that runs into the ring)" (*M,* 160).

2. the irreducible reality of the confrontation, through the writing, with a real danger deriving from a real event;[29]
3. the political and ethical effects of *writing* as itself *an act,* an act that provokes change and that thus itself has material consequences:

> To write a book that is an act—such is, broadly, the goal that seemed to be the one I must pursue. [*M,* 155]

Thus spoke Leiris in 1939, on the threshold of the war. This was doubtless also the intention of de Man as journalist: to *intervene* historically and politically: writing for the newspaper was meant to be an *act.* "Thus to complicate a fact certainly is: to act," writes de Man forty years later in "Excuses *(Confessions)*" (*AR,* 281). The converse, however, is also true: the facts complicate and subvert the act. When Leiris recapitulates his autobiographical text after the war (1945), the *fact* of the *interruption* of the war is inscribed (very like a bull's horn) in the very core of his autobiography as, indeed, a *complication,* a *disruption,* of his previous notion of the *act.*

> This was the preface I was writing . . . on the eve of the "phony war." I am reading it today in Le Havre, a city . . . to which I am bound by so many old ties (my friends . . . ; Sartre, who taught here and with whom I became associated in 1941 when most of the writers remaining in occupied France united against the Nazi oppression). Le Havre is now largely destroyed, as I can see from my balcony, which overlooks the harbor from a sufficient height and distance to give a true picture of the terrible *tabula rasa* the bombs made in the center of the city. [*M,* 152]

The historical perspective embodied in the image of the devastated city, a perspective out of which Leiris inscribes the splitting—the internal interruption and division—of his initial autobiographical project, is very like the perspective out of which de Man writes his "Excuses *(Confessions)*": the perspective of a memory contemplating (and reflecting on) the materiality of a *tabula rasa in the very center.*

---

[29]"Is not what occurs in the domain of style valueless," writes Leiris, "if it remains 'aesthetic,' anodyne, insignificant, if there is nothing in the fact of writing . . . that is equivalent . . . to the bull's keen horn, which alone—by reason of the physical danger it represents—affords the *torero's* art a human reality . . . ?" (*M,* 152). At a distance of six years, after the interruption of the Second World War, Leiris returns to this question by framing his early thought with an ironical and critical (historical and political) perspective, since the reality of the endangering event—the horn of the bull that penetrates and wounds the writing—is no longer that of the (imaginary or theatrical) bullfighting, but that of the magnitude both of the struggle and of the destruction of the Second World War.

The tabula rasa is, however, not the simple erasure of an event but its actual inscription. In much the same way as Leiris's autobiography is, de Man's "Excuses (*Confessions*)" is materially transpierced by the bull's horn of the war experience. Indeed, the irony and the *self-distance* with which, after the war, Leiris nevertheless returns to—both to subvert and to insist on—the initial question of the writing as an act, is in turn mutely spoken, or adhered to, by de Man. "At this point," says Leiris, "I am far from utterly immediate and dismaying events such as the destruction of a great part of Le Havre, so different today from the city I knew":

> I am far, indeed, from that authentic horn of the war of which I see, in the ruined houses, only the least sinister effects . . . Perhaps I should be less obsessed by my desire to make literature into an *act*, a drama by which I insist on incurring, positively, a risk . . . There would nonetheless remain that essential "engagement" one has the right to demand of the writer, the engagement . . . to make his words . . . always tell the truth. And on the intellectual or emotional level, he must *contribute evidence* to the trial of our present system of values. [*M*, 162; my emphasis]

To return to de Man's discussion of Rousseau's *Confessions:* in what way, then, is the "horn of the bull"—the referential deadly impact of the past and of the war, of danger confronted and of writing as an act with material consequences—present in de Man's text, and what, precisely, is the kind of *evidence* that de Man's text is involved with—and contributes—through Rousseau's *Confessions?*

I have suggested that the purloined ribbon might stand for the purloined letter of de Man's journalistic past (*Le Ruban volé, La Lettre volée, Le Soir volé*), and that the gratuitous denunciation of Marion might be resonant with the way in which de Man's 1941 journalistic text ("Les Juifs dans la littérature actuelle") might be read, by others and by the author retrospectively, as evidence of his gratuitous accusation of the Jews, and thus as evidence against him or as evidence about the nature of his past. The contemporary question of (Rousseau's actual and de Man's virtual) confession and of the referentiality of the purloined ribbon engages, thus, both the question of the factual effects of the original act of journalistic wartime writing and that of the contemporary difficulties and complexities resulting from using these texts retrospectively as evidence in an attempt to understand the past. "The distinction," writes de Man, "between the confession stated in the mode of revealed truth and the confession stated in the mode of excuse is that the evidence for the former is referential (the ribbon), whereas the evidence for the latter can only be verbal. Rousseau can convey his 'inner feeling' to us only if we take, as we say, his *word* for it, whereas the evidence for the theft is, at least in theory, literally available" (*AR*, 280).

The literal availability of the purloined journalistic *evidence*, however, is significant at present less for its historically dated semantic content (which so many of today's investigators, like the police in "The Purloined Letter," have set out to uncover and expose) than for the uncanny logic of the indestructible materiality of these outdated journalistic texts and by the predicament of their symbolic circulation.[30]

What, then, does de Man have to say about the literal availability of his journalistic texts and, in particular, about the bull's horn of his published slander of the Jews, implicitly evoked by Rousseau's reference to his gratuitous slander of Marion? "For one thing," writes de Man, "to excuse the crime of theft [could one read, the incriminating writing for *Le Soir volé?*] does not suffice to excuse the worse crime of slander which, as both common sense and Rousseau tell us, is much harder to accept" (*AR*, 284–285).

Rousseau invokes the way in which he was operating under the deception that his discourse was merely a fiction and, as such, was removed from the real world. As for what constitutes the fiction, he points to the absence of connection between his utterance and his intention (his lack of any real hostility toward Marion) as well as to the absence of connection between his utterance and its result (the real damage caused to Marion), discontinuities that both derive, he says, from the constitutional deviousness of language and its inherent freedom with respect to its referent, its inherent, built-in mechanism of fiction-making, which he has wrongly equated with unreality and with ineffectuality.

In a similar and yet inverse way, de Man's belief in the referential truth or the testimonial purpose of his journalistic pieces is shown by history and by his later writings to have been unwittingly involved with an ideologically productive linguistic *fiction*. In the same way, Leiris describes his prewar avowed realism (his writing with the resolution "to reject all fable, to admit as materials only actual facts")

---

[30]Ironically enough, de Man seems to describe the contemporary scene of the belated finding of the journalistic texts and the hectic energies of their exchanges and appropriations when he writes: "Once it is removed from its legitimate owner, the ribbon, being in itself devoid of meaning and function, can circulate symbolically as a pure signifier and become the articulating hinge in a chain of exchanges and possessions. As the ribbon changes hands it traces a circuit leading to the exposure of [the] hidden" (*AR*, 283).

as what the war will have belatedly revealed to him as only "a *falla-cious compromise* between real facts and the pure products of the imagination" (*M,* 156; my emphasis).

That history subverts its witnessing and turns out to be linguisti-cally involved with fiction does not prevent the fiction, however, from functioning historically and from having deadly factual and material consequences. Rousseau's speech act of gratuitous denunciation, his attempt at purloining the referential ribbon by only verbally accusing Marion, results in the actual firing of the servant. The purloined jour-nalistic letter of de Man's gratuitous (perhaps intendedly fictitious, perhaps unwilling) accusation of the Jews is amplified and followed by the Nazis' discourse of the Final Solution and by the actual extermi-nation of the Jews. The speech act of purloining the referential ribbon by a fictitious verbal accusation turns out to have unpredictable real effects and an awesome historical consequence and sequence in the imminent politics of the "yellow star" and in what might be called the deadly materiality of the yellow ribbon.

In underscoring the linguistic nature of Rousseau's predicament and in seeming to invoke, along with Rousseau, "the radical irresponsi-bility of fiction" (*AR,* 293), de Man does not, as some read him erron-eously, claim to *disown* responsibility, but rather shows, precisely, how the very irresponsibility of fiction turns out to be, in the most serious sense, historically (and referentially) responsible. Rousseau himself indicts his own apparent pleaded innocence in a reflection that, in recapitulating, de Man implicitly turns on himself: " 'the ab-sence of a purposefully harmful intent does not suffice to make a lie innocent; one must also be assured that the error one inflicts upon one's interlocutor can in no conceivable way harm him or anyone else' " (*AR,* 292).

If through the war de Man discovers both the fiction of what he took to be political reality (the change and the renewal promised by the Nazis) and the political reality of what he took to be fiction (writing about literature), what de Man henceforth calls language is not simply language as it is commonly understood to be: an alleged isolated verbal entity framed by a bracketing of history and politics. "Lan-guage" for de Man is, in that sense, almost a red herring, taken as an isolated, static term. Far from being either a foreclosed or a foreclosing concept, "language" should be understood dynamically and differen-tially, only in its interaction with the term "history." Language is, in matter, what resists; it is, in history, what differentiates it from itself, what designates the fact that history is never present to itself and cannot be guided; the fact that, as de Man puts it, "history is not human,"[31] that any attempt at a human guidance of history invariably turns out to be either deceptive or illusory. History is, at the same time, what designates the fact that language is, in turn, not present to itself. History, therefore, is not, as it is commonly understood to be, a mode of continuity that defines itself in opposition to the mode of fiction, but a mode of interruption in which the unpredictability and uncontrollability of fiction, acting itself out into reality, "becomes the disruption of the narrative's referential illusion" (*AR*, 292), in much the same way as the historical reality of the war has in effect been the historical disruption of the pseudoreferential narrative of the journalistic witnessing of history. Paradoxically enough, history is, on the one hand, a mode of interruption of consciousness' awareness, and perception, of reality, and on the other hand, a mode of unexpected continuity (the uncanny indestructible materiality) of signifiers and of their circulation, the material, purloined way in which linguistic utterances have real effects (make history), without any relation to their meaning, their intention, or their content.

The Impossible Confession

How can one belatedly *confess* to such a history without engaging, once again, in a deluded and deluding (pseudowitnessing, pseudocontinuity, pseudocognition, of yet another) referential narrative? And what would be the inescapable performative production of the linguistic utterance of such confession? "What I did not realize," writes Leiris after the war about the referential illusion, the pseudorealism of his autobiographical narrative from before the war, "was . . . that every confession contains a desire to be absolved" (*M*, 154).

But how can one *absolve* the mystified historical collaboration with the Nazis? If the act of the journalistic collaborationist writing was, in a sense, a lie, would not the linguistic act of the confession—in recapitulating language as a straightforward referential witness, and in claiming to relieve or "overcome guilt . . . in the name of truth" (*AR*, 279)—simply amplify and magnify the lie?

[31]De Man, *The Resistance to Theory,* Theory and History of Literature, vol. 33 (Minneapolis, 1986), p. 92; hereafter abbreviated *RT*. De Man elaborates, "History is not human, because it pertains strictly to the order of language . . . You can apprehend . . . but after a certain point you can't comprehend what you apprehend . . . The 'inhuman,' however, is not some kind of mystery, or some kind of secret; the inhuman is: linguistic structures, . . . linguistic events that occur, possibilities which are inherent in language—independently of any intent or any drive or any wish or any desire we might have" (*RT*, 92, 95, 96.)

The question takes us to the *Fourth Rêverie* and its implicit shift from reported guilt to the guilt of reporting, since here the lie is no longer connected with some former misdeed but specifically with the act of writing the *Confessions* and, by extension, with all writing. [*AR*, 290]

In pointing out the lie inherent in any confession, as well as the demand for absolution that every confession necessarily implies,[32] de Man's discussion of Rousseau at once enumerates and radically rejects the whole series of excuses that have been, in fact, historically used by the Nazis.

Should de Man say that he simply *followed* what was dictated by someone else, someone who ranked higher and who had more authority? Should he say that he was young, that Nazism, as well as the political faith of his uncle (after the loss of both mother and brother), was *the first thing that came across his way,* and that his journalistic statement about the Jews, like Rousseau's chance utterance of the name of Marion, was a mere unconscious "slip, a segment of the discourse of the other" (*AR*, 288), and adhere, thus, to Rousseau's excuse and explanation? " 'Viciousness was never further from me than at this cruel moment, and when I accused the hapless girl,' " writes Rousseau, " 'it is bizarre but it is true that my friendship for her was the cause of my accusation. She was present to my mind, I excused myself on the first thing that offered itself. I accused her of having done what I wanted to do and of having given me the ribbon because it was my intention to give it to her' " (*AR*, 284, 288). De Man, however, like Rousseau himself, does not find this effort to absolve successful, and he points out the discrepancy in the very logic of the excusing argument: "But the use of a vocabulary of contingency . . . within an argument of causality is arresting and disruptive" (*AR*, 288).

Should he say, then, in the manner of Rousseau, that he was *caught in a machine* "that seduce[d] him into dangerously close contact" (*AR*, 298), a machine of language whose functioning turned out to be beyond his power and control? Rousseau writes: " 'It is certain that neither my judgment, nor my will dictated my reply, but that it was

---

[32]About two months after the completion of the present text and its submission to *Critical Inquiry*, I had the privilege of hearing at Yale (on November 16, 1988) a lecture by Ortwin de Graef (the original discoverer of the early journalistic texts) on de Man's "Excuses (*Confessions*)," a lecture whose remarkably subtle and complex analysis of de Man's text came uncannily close to my focus here on the link between confession and absolution, which makes confession an impossible solution for de Man. Since Ortwin de Graef and myself had no knowledge of each other's work, I think the intersections between some of our conclusions on this point bear uncanny witness to the accuracy of the paths we have both chosen in de Man's text.

the automatic result [*l'effet machinal*] of my embarrassment' " (*AR,* 294). But de Man articulates a critical position with respect to the machine's capacity to serve as an excuse:

> The machinelike quality of the text . . . is more remarkable still when, as in the Marion episode, the disproportion between the crime that is to be confessed and the crime performed by the lie adds a delirious element to the situation. By saying that the excuse is not only a fiction but also a machine one adds to the connotation of referential detachment, . . . that of the implacable repetition of a preordained pattern . . . There can be no use of language which is not . . . mechanical, no matter how deeply this aspect may be concealed by aesthetic . . . delusions.
>
> The machine not only generates, but also suppresses, and not always in an innocent or balanced way . . . The addition of examples leads to the subversion of the cognitive affirmation of innocence which the examples were supposed to illustrate. At the end of the text, Rousseau knows that he cannot be excused. [*AR,* 294]

Should de Man say, then, that he *did not know,* at the beginning of the war, all the historical implications of Nazism and, specifically, that he *did not know* about the extermination of the Jews, and invoke, in the archetypal way in which the Nazis have excused themselves in court, the legal or the psychoanalytic plea of innocence by virtue of unconsciousness or ignorance?

> Excuse occurs within an epistemological twilight zone between knowing and not-knowing; this is also why it has to be centered on the crime of lying and why Rousseau can excuse himself for everything provided he can be excused for lying. When this turns out not to have been the case, when his claim to have lived for the sake of truth . . . is being contested . . . , the closure of excuse . . . becomes a delusion. [*AR,* 286]

One by one, the essay rejects all the possibilities of excuse, the pleas of innocence that have historically been articulated by the Nazis. Neither does de Man accept the Christian excuse of the fact of suffering as itself an expiation of the crime or as a ground for absolution:

> The injury done to Marion is compensated for by the subsequent suffering inflicted on Rousseau by nameless avengers acting in her stead. The restoration of justice naturally follows the disclosure of meaning. Why then does the excuse fail and why does Rousseau have to return to an enigma that has been so well resolved? [*AR,* 287–288]

The essay shows how all these possibilities of excuse (of a confession asking for absolution) are *not at the disposal* of its author, who knows that no excuse, and no confession, can undo the violence of his initial wartime writing and of his journalistic speech act: "For the initial violence . . . can only be half erased, since . . . language . . . never ceases to partake of the very violence against which it is directed."[33]

"Excuses (*Confessions*)" thus rejects not only the historical excuses of the Nazis but any mode of possible apologetic discourse.[34]

> Excuses generate the very guilt they exonerate, though always in excess or by default . . . No excuse can ever hope to catch up with such a proliferation of guilt. On the other hand, any guilt . . . can always be dismissed as the gratuitous product of . . . a radical fiction: there can never be enough guilt around to match the text-machine's infinite power to excuse. [*AR*, 299]

The trouble with excuses (with confessions) is that they are all too *readable:* partaking of the continuity of conscious meaning and of the illusion of the restoration of coherence, what de Man calls "the readability of . . . apologetic discourse" (*AR*, 290), pretends to reduce historical scandals to mere sense and to eliminate the unassimilable shock of history, by leaving "the [very] assumption of intelligibility . . . unquestioned" (*AR*, 300).[35] Confessions (or excuses) thus allow one, through the illusion of understanding they provide, to forgive and to forget. But de Man precisely faces, in the history that cannot be confessed, what is both unforgivable and unforgettable.

> The interest of Rousseau's text is that . . . the confession fails to close off a discourse which feels compelled to modulate from the confessional into the apologetic mode.

[33]De Man, *The Rhetoric of Romanticism* (New York, 1984), pp. 118–119; hereafter abbreviated *RR*.

[34]It is here that de Man definitely parts ways with his uncle Hendrik, who did engage in an apologetic discourse and who, in general, was keen on writing his autobiography in the guise of what (perhaps in reference to Rousseau) he himself liked to refer to as "confessions." Thus, in his foreword to *The Remaking of a Mind*, Hendrik de Man writes, in relation to the First World War: "As soon as evidence ceases to be personal, not much reliance can be place on its accuracy. And subjective accuracy is all I claim for these *confessions*. I will make them documentarily autobiographical" (*The Remaking of a Mind: A Soldier's Thoughts on War and Reconstruction* [New York, 1919], p. ix).

In "The Age of Doom," published in its German and French versions in 1945, immediately after the Second World War, Hendrik de Man again refers to his autobiographical reflections as "a confession" when he writes, with the sort of pathos that Paul de Man will at once avoid and precisely deconstruct in "Excuses (*Confessions*)": "We are witnessing 'the end of history,' . . . I should not hesitate to call this end a catastrophe . . . the catastrophic outcome in the ordinary sense of the word—apocalyptic possibilities not being excluded—seems far more probable to me than the opposite . . . After this *confession*, I feel more at ease to say that I should consider this book to have missed its purpose with anybody who would feel discouraged . . . by its conclusions" (Hendrik de Man, "The Age of Doom," *A Documentary Study of Hendrik de Man*, pp. 344–346; my emphasis).

[35]"The scandal of random denunciation of Marion . . . could have been explained away by the cognitive logic of understanding. The cognition would have been the excuse, but this convergence is precisely what is no longer conceivable" (*AR*, 298–299).

> Neither does the performance of the excuse allow for a closing off of the apologetic text ... some ten years later, in the *Fourth Rêverie,* [Rousseau] tells the entire story all over again ... Clearly, the apology has not succeeded in becalming his own guilt to the point where he would be allowed to forget it. [*AR*, 282]

In deconstructing, in his rigorous commitment to the truth of history, the conceptual system of all apologetic discourses and their very claim to restore an ethical balance—to be "epistemologically as well as ethically grounded and therefore available as meaning, in the mode of understanding" (*AR*, 287)—de Man keeps reiterating, and demands that we keep facing, the historical *impossibility of reading* (or the Holocaust) as an unredeemable scandal of injustice and of injury.

In the testimony of a work that performs actively an exercise of silence not as simple silence but as the absolute refusal of any trivializing or legitimizing discourse (of apology, of narrative, or of psychologizing explanation of recent history), de Man articulates, thus, neither—as some have argued—an empirical (or psychological) hidden confession nor—as others have suggested—an empirical (or psychological) refusal to confess, but the incapacity of apologetic discourse to account for history as Holocaust, the ethical impossibility of *a confession that, historically and philosophically, cannot take place.* This complex articulation of the impossibility of confession embodies, paradoxically enough, not a denial of the author's guilt but, on the contrary, the most radical and irrevocable assumption of historical responsibility.

> Cast in the tone of a pietistic self-examination, [the text] sounds severe and rigorous enough in its self-accusation to give weight to the exoneration it pronounces upon its author—until Rousseau takes it all back in the penultimate paragraph which decrees him to be "inexcusable." [*AR,* 290]

> At the end of the text, Rousseau knows that he cannot be excused. [*AR,* 294]

In trying to force the secret out of the journalistic evidence of the wartime newspapers (or of today's press), in trying to force de Man's biography to a *confession* he told us could not be historically articulated, we naively believe that we can simply overcome (explain away) his silence, and in this way forget our own.

We thus forget what de Man has taught us through the figure of Wordsworth—about history as "a defacement of the mind" and about autobiography as muting or as "muteness"—in a reading lesson that might describe not merely the historical experience of his own autobiography but our own posthumous reading relation to him, our own incapacity of facing our own history both in the mutedness of his defaced biography and in the silent testimony of his writing:

> It would be naive to believe that we could ever face Wordsworth [or de Man] . . . outright. But it would be more naive still to think we can take shelter from what he knew by means of the very evasions which this knowledge renders impossible. [*RR,* 92]

> A certain misuse of language is denounced in the strongest of terms: "Words are too awful an instrument for good and evil to be trifled with . . ."
>
> Wordsworth says of evil language, which is in fact all language including his own language of restoration, that it works "unremittingly and *noiselessly*" . . . To the extent that, in writing, we are dependent on this language we all are . . . deaf and mute—not silent, which implies the possible manifestation of sound at our own will, but silent as a picture, that is to say eternally deprived of voice and condemned to muteness. [*RR,* 79, 80]

> Autobiography veils a defacement of the mind of which it is itself the cause. [*RR,* 81]

V

The Task of the Translator

If history does not allow for a confession as a mode of either explanation or reparation, if confession can no longer serve as a viable language of historical accountability, how can one nevertheless attest to the "defacement of the mind" the Holocaust has been? There remains, suggests de Man, a positive necessity of accounting, a positive historical endeavor that Walter Benjamin, profoundly and suggestively, has named "The Task of the Translator." And if it is, indeed, in his last lecture (published posthumously) that de Man addresses Benjamin's essay on "The Task of the Translator," it is, I would suggest, because translation, as opposed to confession, itself becomes a metaphor for the historical necessity of bearing witness and because the "task"—which can be read as de Man's testament—describes at once de Man's endeavor in his later writings and his radically revised position as belated witness to the events of World War II. While the conclusion of the Second World War coincides with de Man's silence and with his translation of *Moby-Dick* (1945), the conclusion of his later career of writing and of teaching coincides with his last statement on "The Task of the Translator" and on the silence that at once inhabits, and threatens to disrupt, this task. Thus, in Benjamin's example, which de Man reemphasizes, Hölderlin has literally and historically gone mad after finishing his superb translation of Sophocles. It is as though the translator, by the very power of his rendering the silence that inhabits Sophocles' tragedies, were himself exploded and aspired by that very silence.

> In the process of translation, as Benjamin understands it—which has little to do with the empirical act of translating, as all of us practice it on a daily basis—there is an inherent and particularly threatening danger. The emblem of that danger is Hölderlin's translations of Sophocles:
>
> ". . . Hölderlin's translations in particular [says Benjamin] are subject to the enormous danger inherent in all translations: the gates of a language thus expanded and modified may slam shut and *enclose the translator with silence.* Hölderlin's translations from Sophocles were his last work, in them meaning plunges from abyss to abyss until it threatens to become *lost* in the bottomless depths of language." [*RT,* 84; my emphasis]

It is not a coincidence, indeed, that de Man ends his career in a reflection not merely on translation and on silence but specifically on Walter Benjamin.

Benjamin is mentioned for the first time by de Man in "The Rhetoric of Temporality," where the reference to his theory of allegory, which de Man espouses in his revision of the conventional conception both of temporality and of literary history, will later be acknowledged by de Man not as a simple influence or reference but as the inscription of a major change in his own work, a turning point in his own critical thought. In his 1983 foreword to the revised second edition of *Blindness and Insight,* a few months before the delivery of his last lecture on "The Task of the Translator," de Man writes:

> With the deliberate emphasis on rhetorical terminology, ["The Rhetoric of Temporality"] augurs what seemed to me to be a change, not only in terminology and in tone but in substance. This terminology [borrowed from Benjamin] is still uncomfortably intertwined with the thematic vocabulary of consciousness and of temporality that was current at the time, but it signals a turn that, at least for me, has proven to be productive.[36]

[36]De Man, "Foreword to Revised, Second Edition," *Blindness and Insight: Essays in the Rhetoric of Contemporary Criticism,* 2d ed., rev., Theory and History of Literature, vol. 7 (Minneapolis, 1983), p. xii.

Benjamin thus stands for *a change* de Man has undergone, and the choice of Benjamin for de Man's last lecture signifies that de Man's testament, his legacy, consists in nothing other than the imperative, and implications, of this change. I would suggest that this change, which has found its first explicit formulation in the conceptual shift marked by "The Rhetoric of Temporality" (1971) and which "The Task of the Translator" will in turn discuss at the conclusion of de Man's life (1983) is the same process of change that began in 1942 during the war, with de Man's own silence, at the turning point of the interruption of his journalistic interventions and of his transgressive publication of *Exercice du silence,* followed by his translation of *Moby-Dick.*

"The Task of the Translator" has thus not only critical and theoretical, but also biographical and autobiographical, implications. And it is not by chance that these final autobiographical considerations about a change happen to take place in conjunction with the name of Benjamin, the German-Jewish critic who died as a superfluous, ironic, and accidental casualty of the Second World War. As Hitler rises to power, Benjamin, boycotted as a Jew and an undesirable writer, emigrates from Germany to France, yet continues to publish in periodicals in German. After France's declaration of war on Germany, he declines an opportunity to leave for the United States and is imprisoned for three months in a camp in Nevers. In 1940, the year in which de Man starts writing for *Le Soir,* Benjamin joins a group of refugees who attempt to escape from France by crossing the Spanish Pyrenees. Responding to an unfounded verbal threat of being turned over to the Gestapo, Benjamin commits suicide during the night; the other fugitives will escape to safety without being intercepted.

My conjecture is that not only Benjamin's philosophy but also his biography—and his death—have left a powerful impression on de Man and on his work. Benjamin's suicide might have resonated with the suicides that framed de Man's own life. Benjamin's aborted departure might have evoked de Man's own radical departure and his violent annihilation—or erasure—of his Belgian self. If the question remains open of whether de Man, like Ishmael, departed as a substitute for committing suicide, Benjamin commits suicide when he is in the process of departure and when he believes (mistakenly) this process to be disrupted.[37]

[37]Previous to his definitive departure following the war, de Man in fact experienced, very much like Benjamin, an aborted departure during the war. After the surrender of the Belgian army to Germany on May 28, 1940, de Man and his wife fled (along with many other Belgians) to Bagneres de Luchon in the French Pyrenees, where they spent the summer months waiting, unsuccessfully, for permission to cross to Spain, before their reluctant return to Brussels in August. Thus, in the very year (1940) and the very

Walter Benjamin, 1892–1940.

De Man's life would thus seem to be the opposite of Benjamin's. De Man escaped while Benjamin failed to escape. De Man survived the war while Benjamin drowned in it. De Man left for the United States, whereas Benjamin postponed and failed to reach this destination. Benjamin was Jewish; de Man published a time-piece against the Jews.

And yet, the opposition is too symmetrical to not also suggest a

---

geographical region (French Pyrenees) in which Benjamin took his own life, de Man in turn found himself entrapped, with no possibility of escape and with the war closing in on him.

subtle doubling between the two life stories and between the two experiences of being totally engulfed and cognitively overwhelmed by the war. Although politically positioned on two different sides, although de Man collaborates while Benjamin is persecuted as a Jew, both Benjamin and de Man experience the events of the Second World War essentially as a mistake, as an impossibility of reading (or of witnessing), as a historical misreading that leads both men to a misguided action. The one dies as a consequence of his misreading of the war whereas the other survives in spite of it and constructs his later life as a relentless struggle with the powers of historical deception, including his own former historical misreading.

No wonder, then, if through his own translation of "The Task of the Translator" de Man implicitly has recognized in Benjamin a double and a brother (a brother who can be related to, once more, only belatedly, as a *dead brother*), since Benjamin's biography is an ironic mirror image of de Man's autobiography, and since the mutedness of both life stories, the inarticulate articulation and the articulated inarticulation of both biographies, translates something that is historically and crucially significant beyond both individuals, something essential (and inarticulable) about the history of the Second World War.

Although unmentioned, Benjamin's suicide is referentially inscribed within de Man's survival as well as within "The Task of the Translator" (both de Man's and Benjamin's), in much the same way as Shelley's death is referentially inscribed, in de Man's interpretation, within the manuscript of his unfinished poem, paradoxically entitled *The Triumph of Life,* a poem whose writing process was historically and materially interrupted by the author's accidental drowning. At a point when de Man himself is terminally ill and when his own work is about to be interrupted by his imminent death, de Man offers the following reflections on Shelley's drowning, which, I would suggest, could equally describe the inscription and the presence of Benjamin's historic death—and of the dead bodies of the Holocaust—in his own text on "The Task of the Translator":

> [The] defaced body is present in the margin of the last manuscript page and has become an inseparable part of the poem. At this point, figuration and cognition are actually interrupted by an *event which shapes the text but which is not present in its represented or articulated meaning.* It may seem a freak of chance to have a text thus molded by an actual occurrence, yet the reading of *The Triumph of Life* establishes that this mutilated textual model exposes the wound of a fracture that lies hidden in all texts . . .

> In Shelley's absence, the task of . . . reinscribing the disfiguration now devolves entirely on the reader. The final test of reading, in *The Triumph of Life*, depends on *how one reads the textuality of this event, how one disposes of Shelley's body* . . .
>
> For what we have done with the dead Shelley, and with all the other dead bodies . . . is simply to bury them, to bury them in their own texts made into epitaphs and monumental graves . . . They have been transformed into historical and aesthetic objects. [*RR*, 120–21; my emphasis]

De Man refuses to *dispose* of Benjamin's body, to make of Benjamin (or, for that matter, his own work) a "historical and aesthetic object"; he refuses, that is, to treat history as a totalized, settled, understood, and closed account, to engage in a semblance of historical reading of the Holocaust that would be, in fact, a speech act of disposing of the scandal of the bodies.

The task of the translator, on the contrary—in opposition both to confessional, apologetic discourse and to traditional historical cognition—is to read the textuality of the original event *without disposing of the body,* without reducing the original event to a false transparency of sense. De Man insists, thus, on the fact that the German word for "task" also means a "giving up," a defeat or failure; and that Benjamin's text is not merely about the task or the endeavor but, correlatively and essentially, about the failure, the defeat, of the translator:

> One of the reasons why he takes the translator rather than the poet is that the translator, per definition, fails. The translator can never do what the original text did. Any translation is always second in relation to the original, and the translator as such is lost from the very beginning. He is per definition underpaid, he is per definition overworked, he is per definition the one history will not really retain as an equal . . . If the text is called "Die Aufgabe des Übersetzers," we have to read this title more or less as a tautology: *Aufgabe,* task, can also mean the one who has to give up . . . he doesn't continue in the race anymore. It is in that sense also the defeat, the giving up, of the translator. The translator has to give up in relation to the task of refinding what was there in the original.
>
> The question then becomes why this failure with regard to an original text . . . is for Benjamin exemplary. [*RT,* 80]

I would suggest that what the translator has to give up is the temptation to translate history by making sense of it, that is, by using an apologetic or apocalyptic discourse. What the translator fails to do is to erase the body, to erase the murder of the original:

> All these activities ... relate to what in the original belongs to language, and not to meaning as an extralinguistic correlate ... They disarticulate, they undo the original, they reveal that the original was always already disarticulated. They reveal that their failure, which seems to be due to the fact that they are secondary in relation to the original, reveals an essential failure, an essential disarticulation which was already there in the original. They kill the original, by discovering that the original was already dead. [*RT,* 84]

De Man shows in specific and striking detail how the official English and French translations of Benjamin (by Harry Zohn and Maurice de Gandillac, respectively) both misrepresent, at crucial points, what Benjamin is saying and thus again *kill the original,* and testify unwittingly to its murder:

> Even the translators, who certainly are close to the text, ... don't seem to have the slightest idea of what Benjamin is saying; so much so that when Benjamin says certain things rather simply in one way—for example he says that something is *not*—the translators, who at least know German well enough to know the difference between something *is* and something *is not,* don't see it! ... This is remarkable, because the two translators ... are very good translators. [*RT,* 79]

> [Benjamin's] assertion is so striking, so shocking in a way, ... goes so much against common sense, that an intelligent, learned, and careful translator *cannot see it, cannot see what Benjamin says.* [*RT,* 81; my emphasis]

> The translations confirm, brilliantly, ... that it is impossible to translate. [*RT,* 74]

The failure of the translator, including that of Benjamin's translators, is thus exemplary in that it is a *failure to see,* a failure to witness history in its original occurrence. The original is killed because there is no possible witnessing of the original event; and this impossibility of witnessing is, paradoxically, inherent in the very position of the translator, whose task is nonetheless to try to render—to bear witness to—the original.

De Man thus formulates not just his autobiographical, but, more important, his *philosophical* encounter with Benjamin's blindness and insight, with Benjamin's historical experience, and with his historic definition of the task of the translator. Benjamin articulates, precisely, *the position out of which de Man speaks* in his later writings, the position out of which de Man *translates* the Second World War as a historic incapacity of witnessing an original occurrence, a belated testimonial position he has occupied since 1942, since the period of his silence following his recognition of the failure, or the error, of his wartime journalistic witnessing. De Man encounters Benjamin precisely at this point of philosophical silence, this point of the historical disruption of his discourse out of which he joins, in turn, Benjamin's historical and philosophical relentless wrestling with the disfiguring Leviathan of history.

In this ongoing struggle, the need to testify to history as Holocaust repeatedly comes up against the impossibility of witnessing the original event; and yet, in the acknowledgment—in the historical translation—of this impossibility, *there is a witness*. It is thus that, in "The Task of the Translator," through Benjamin's articulation of a radical inarticulateness of contemporary history, de Man historically bears witness.

This witness, unlike a confession, is not personal; it is not directed, in the exhibitionistic way a theatrical (confessional) performance would be, toward an audience: " 'No poem,' " Benjamin has written, " 'is intended for the reader, no picture for the beholder, no symphony for the listener' " (*RT,* 78). History, like the original, is written in a foreign language, a language that the reader who relies on a translation cannot understand. A history that is "not human," cannot, furthermore, be totally translated, or intended for, or owned by, any subject.

> Things happen in the world [insists de Man] which cannot be accounted for in terms of the human conception of language. And . . . the relation [to] language is always involved when they have [happened] . . . To account for them historically, to account for them in any sense, a certain initial discrepancy in language has to be examined . . . —it cannot be avoided. [*RT,* 101]

Translation is thus necessarily a *critical* activity, a mode of *deconstruction,* that is, the undoing of an illusory historical perception or understanding by bearing witness to what the "perception" or the "understanding" precisely fails to see or fails to witness. After the Holocaust, this critical subversion of the witness has become unavoidable: deconstruction is a necessary way of examining events. "A certain kind of critical examination . . . *has* to take place, it has to take place not out of some perversity, not out of some hubris of critical thought . . . , it has to take place because it addresses the question of what actually happens" (*RT,* 101).

The way in which the translator can bear witness to *what actually happens* in the original is, however, paradoxically, not by imitation but only by a new creation, a creation that, although it insures the literal survival of the original, is itself only the testimony of an afterlife:

> [Translation] is associated with another word that Benjamin constantly uses, the word *überleben,* to live beyond your own death in a sense. The translation belongs not to the life of the original, the original is already dead, but the translation belongs to the afterlife of the original, thus assuming and confirming the death of the original. [*RT,* 85]

Here again, translation, insofar as it is deconstructive, insofar as it incorporates a passage through death that takes the original off center, is opposed precisely to confession, which attempts a synthesis by taking itself (taking the self) as center, thus denying in its very mode that the center, the original, is dead. De Man himself bears witness, or translates, like Ishmael, from both the philosophical and the auto-biographical position of an afterlife and of a radical exile. "Unlike a work of literature," writes Benjamin, "translation does not find itself in the center of the language forest but on the outside facing the wooded ridge; it calls into it without entering."[38] "What translation does," echoes de Man, "is that it implies—in bringing to light what Benjamin calls 'die Wehen des eigenen'—the suffering of what one thinks of as one's own—the suffering of the original language" (*RT,* 84). This suffering, however, does not consist in the pathos of an individual but in the structural historical movement of the decanoni-zation and the disintegration of the original:

> This movement of the original is a wandering, an *errance,* a kind of permanent exile if you wish, but it is not really an exile, for there is no homeland . . .
> Now it is this motion, this errancy of language which never reaches the mark, which is always displaced in relation to what it meant to reach, . . . this illusion of a life that is only an afterlife, that Benjamin calls history. [*RT,* 92]

Autobiography itself thus turns out to be, paradoxically, an *impersonal witness* to a history of which it cannot talk but to which it nonetheless bears witness in a theory of translation, which is, at the same time, its new historical creation.

This new articulation that constitutes historical translation does not afford, however, a totalizing view of history (or of the original historical occurrence) as a whole but is, on the contrary, a constant fragmentation of such a view, a continuous disarticulation of any illusion of historical closure or historical totalization. Benjamin thus writes in Zohn's translation:

[38]Walter Benjamin, "The Task of the Translator: An Introduction to the Translation of Baudelaire's *Tableaux Parisiens,*" *Illuminations,* ed. Hannah Arendt, trans. Harry Zohn (New York, 1969), p. 76.

"A translation, instead of resembling the meaning of the original, must . . . incorporate the original's mode of signification, thus making both the original and the translation recognizable as fragments of a greater language, just as fragments are part of a vessel." [*RT,* 91]

But de Man corrects the English translation:

"Just as fragments are part of a vessel" is a synecdoche; "just as fragments," says Benjamin, "are the *broken* parts of a vessel"; as such he is not saying that the fragments constitute a totality, he says the fragments are fragments, and that they remain essentially fragmentary . . . The translation is the fragment of a fragment, is breaking the fragment— so the vessel keeps breaking, constantly—and never reconstitutes it; there was no vessel in the first place, or we have no knowledge of this vessel, or no awareness of it, no access to it. [*RT,* 91]

Like the shipwrecked vessel in *Moby-Dick,* historical translation keeps breaking into fragments against the whale. History, however, is neither the historical pathos of remembering a state from before the fragmentation nor the subjective, individual pathos of this fragmentation, but its objective structural determination, the structural necessity—and occurrence—of a change that is neither simply objective nor simply subjective, but that changes (or displaces) the very nature of the opposition between subject and object.

It is not this pathos of remembrance, or this pathetic mixture of hope and catastrophe and apocalypse . . . It is not the pathos of a history . . . between the disappearance of the gods and the possible return of the gods. It is not this kind of sacrificial, dialectical, and elegiac gesture, by means of which one looks back on the past as a period that is lost. [*RT,* 86]

Translation thus itself becomes a metaphor for history, not only in that it demands the rigor of a history devoid of pathos, but in that it opens up the question of *how to continue when the past, precisely, is not allowed any continuance.* Translation is the metaphor of a new relation to the past, a relation that cannot resemble, furthermore, any past relation to the past but that consists, essentially, in the historical performance of a radical discontinuity:

Finally, translation is like history, and that will be the most difficult thing to understand . . . it is like history to the extent that history is not to be understood by analogy with any kind of natural process. We are not supposed to think of history as ripening, as organic growth, or even as a dialectic . . . We are to think of history rather in the reverse way: we are to understand natural changes from the perspective of history, rather than understand history from the perspective of natural changes.

162

If we want to understand what ripening is, we should understand it from the perspective of historical change. [*RT,* 83]

The perspective of historical change is not simply what is *stated* by the translation but what is, in effect, *accomplished* by it. The translation is thus not quite a cognition but, rather, a performance of historical change to which it testifies in the very process of achieving it, of putting the change into effect: "The process of translation, if we can call it a process, is one of change and of motion" (*RT,* 85). The testimony is itself a form of action, a mode not merely of accounting for, but of going through, a change: as opposed to a confession, the meaning of the testimony is not completely known, even by its author, before and after its production, outside of the very process of its articulation, of its actual writing. Historical change cannot fully come into cognition but testifies to its own process of occurring.

The Occurrence

In explaining how, in Benjamin, translation *happens,* de Man comments:

> There is not in Benjamin, at this point, a statement about history as occurrence, as that which occurs . . . [But] I think that what is implied, that what occurs, for example, is—translation is an occurrence. At the moment when translation really takes place, for example Hölderlin's translation of Sophocles, which undid Sophocles, undid Hölderlin, and revealed a great deal—that's an occurrence. That's an event, that is a historical event. As such, an occurrence can be textual,, . . . but it is an occurrence, in the sense that it is not . . . the end of an error, but the recognition of the true nature of that error. [Benjamin] has described Hölderlin in his constant falling, and he says, "*Aber es gibt ein Halten.*" Which one tends to read as saying, "but there is a stop to this" . . . [However,] you can read it to mean, "*Aber es gibt ein Halten,*" in which you hold on . . . obstinately, to this notion of *errance,* . . . you stay with it, in a sense. Then something occurs in the very act of your persisting in this . . . you don't give in to everything that would go in the other direction. At that moment, translation occurs. In Hölderlin, translation *occurs* . . . When Luther translated . . . the Bible . . . something happened . . . there are, in the history of texts, texts which are occurrences. [*RT,* 104]

The present essay has been trying to suggest how de Man's work— in the very terms of its own statement about Benjamin—*makes translation happen.* What does the "happening" consist of? What does it mean for a translation to occur? It means that the original, or history, has been given not a voice that redeems it from its muteness and says it properly, but *the power to address us* in its very silence.

In compelling us to try to grasp, through the complexity of the relation between silence and speech, life and writing, language and reality, the nonsimplicity of reference in the shadow of the trauma of contemporary history; in compelling us to radically rethink the very notions of autobiography and history as the inescapable, nonfictional, nonpathetic, and nontrivial real texture of both literature and literary criticism, de Man's testimony in his later writings invokes the Holocaust as the very figure of a silence, of a historical forgetting, which our very efforts at remembering—through the unwitting use of ready-made cultural discourses—only reenact and keep repeating, but which a certain silent mode of testimony can *translate,* and thus make us remember, "not," however, as "the end of an error, but [as] the recognition of the true nature of that error." Paradoxically enough, de Man's work does not cancel out forgetfulness, but it gives our own historical forgetting *the power to address us,* to remind us that we have forgotten, once again, the horror, and the threat, and the murder, and the radical impossibility of witnessing, of the original.

If it is true that, as de Man points out, there are in history translations that made such a *difference* that they have had themselves the impact of historical events—if "an occurrence can be textual" and if "there are, in the history of texts, texts which are occurrences"—I would suggest that, in the history of texts as well as in that of events, the silent testimony of de Man's work in his later writings, and the translation it makes happen, is precisely one such textual and historical *occurrence.*

S I X

The Betrayal of the Witness:
Camus' **The Fall**

SHOSHANA FELMAN

If, in the wake of Nazism, *The Plague* (1947) inaugurates the Age of Testimony as the age of the imperative of bearing witness to the trauma and the implications of survival, *The Fall,* appearing nine years later (1956), rewrites the problematic of an Age of Testimony in a different manner, since its dilemma and its drama do not so much *bear witness to survival* as they obscurely struggle through the question: *how does one survive the witnessing?*

I

The Missed Encounter

Some years ago, the narrator was the chance witness of a suicide: a woman he had just passed by suddenly jumped off the bridge into the Seine. Stunned, the narrator froze for a brief moment, then continued his itinerary: this involuntary witnessing was not part of his life. But the scene has kept haunting him and, in its very absence, has brought about a radical disorientation and a gradual disintegration of everything that, in his life before it, had seemed safe, familiar, given.

> That particular night in November . . . I was returning to . . . my home by way of the Pont Royal. It was an hour past midnight . . . On the bridge I passed behind a figure leaning over the railing and seeming to stare at the river. On closer view, I made out a slim young woman dressed in black . . . I had already gone some fifty yards when I heard the sound—which, despite the distance, seemed dreadfully loud in the midnight silence—of a body striking the water. I stopped short, but without turning around. Almost at once I heard a cry, repeated several times, which was going downstream; then it suddenly ceased. The

Camus by Cartier-Bresson

silence that followed, as the night suddenly stood still, seemed interminable. I wanted to run and yet didn't stir. I was trembling, I believe from
cold or shock. I told myself that I had to be quick and I felt an irresistible
weakness steal over me. I have forgotten what I thought then. "Too late,
too far . . ." or something of the sort. I was still listening as I stood
motionless. Then, slowly under the rain, I went away. I informed no
one.

But here we are, here's my house . . . That woman? Oh, I don't know.
Really I don't know. The next day, and the days following, I didn't read
the papers. [pp. 69–70][1]

[1]Camus, *The Fall,* trans. Justin O'Brien, New York: Vintage Books, 1956. Page numbers will refer to this edition. References to the original French will be to Camus, *La
Chute,* Paris: Gallimard, 1956 ("Folio": 1978). The abbreviations "*F*" and "*P*" will be used
to differentiate *The Fall* (F) from *The Plague* (P).

The scene, which the narrator introduces—not before the middle of the narrative—as "my essential discovery," "the adventure I found at the center of my memory" and "which I cannot any more put off relating, despite my digressions" (69, *tm*), describes at once the absolute transience and the absolute indelibility of a moment of a missed encounter with reality, an encounter whose elusiveness cannot be owned and yet whose impact can no longer be erased, in taking hold of the entire movement of the narrator's life which will henceforth unwittingly, compulsively strive toward an impossible completion of the missed experience. In the half-lit transience of the scene itself, there is an enigmatic sense of doom, but there is also something warmly intimate about the "slim young woman dressed in black." "The back of her neck, cool and damp between her dark hair and coat collar, stirred me. But I went on after a moment's hesitation" (70). In continuing his own itinerary, the narrator does not recognize the sense of doom—the condemnation emanating from the figure—and does not acknowledge, on the other hand, that they are both alive. "I had already gone some fifty yards." What are fifty yards, fifty human steps? The narrator puts a real distance between himself and the young woman, as though she will always be there. But the unexpected sound of a body suddenly striking the water intercepts at once the distance and "the midnight silence," and its "dreadful loudness" breaks into the silence of his own life. "I stopped short, but without turning around." The reverberation of a cry behind him goes downstream and in turn drowns in silence. In his paralysis, the narrator is unable not merely to *do* something about the drowning, but to experience and to truly *know* what is occurring: what is occurring outside him and in himself as well. "I had forgotten what I thought then. Too late, too far, or something of the sort. I was still listening as I stood motionless. Then, slowly under the rain, I went away. I informed no one." It is not only the others that the reluctant witness does not inform. Essentially—the narrative will let us know—he fails precisely to inform himself.

A Transformed Scene of Witnessing

At first sight, the subject of *The Fall* seems altogether different from that of *The Plague*. And yet, in much the same way as *The Plague*, *The Fall* in turn revolves around a scene of witnessing. And *The Fall* in turn seems to be alluding, though far less explicitly than did *The Plague*, to European history:

> Still let us take care not to condemn [our Parisian fellow citizens] . . .
> for all Europe is in the same boat. I sometimes think about what future
> historians will say of us. [6]

Whatever the relation of *The Fall* to European history might be, however, the scene of witnessing that it embodies differs radically from
the historical scene of witnessing narrated by *The Plague.*

I propose now to sketch out a reading of *The Fall* that would indeed
consider it as, fundamentally and crucially, a *transformation* of *The
Plague,* a narrative of critical rethinking of the stakes of witnessing in
history and a recapitulation, at a distance of nine years, of the relation
between testimony and contemporary history, in a retrospective commentary on his own highly successful novelistic wartime writing, by
a Camus whose transformation and whose difference from himself
and from his own successful image has not yet begun, I would suggest,
to be appreciated.

In reflecting on his role as a key witness of historical events, Dr.
Rieux insisted in *The Plague:* "The narrator's business is only to say:
this is what happened, when he knows that it actually did happen, that
it affected the life of a whole populace, and that there are thousands of
eyewitnesses who can appraise in their hearts the truth of what he
writes":

> In any case the narrator . . . would have little claim to competence for
> a task like this, had not chance put him in the way of gathering much
> information, and had he not been, by the force of things, closely involved
> in all that he proposes to narrate. *This is his justification for playing the
> part of the historian.* Naturally, a historian, even an amateur, always
> has data, personal or at second hand. The present narrator has three
> kinds of data: first, what he saw himself; secondly, the accounts of other
> eyewitnesses; and lastly, documents that subsequently fell into his
> hands. [*P,* 6][2]

In *The Plague,* the scene of witnessing is thus the scene of the historical recording—and of the historical documenting—of an event. In
The Fall, the scene of witnessing is, paradoxically enough, the scene
of the non-recording and of the non-documenting of an event: "I
informed no one. The next day, and the days following, I didn't read
the papers" (*F,* 70–71). In *The Plague,* the event is witnessed insofar as
it is fully and directly *experienced.* In *The Fall,* the event is witnessed
insofar as it is *not experienced,* insofar as it is literally *missed.* The
suicide in effect is *not seen* and the falling in itself is not perceived:
what is perceived is the woman before the fall, and the sound of her

---

[2]Camus, *The Plague,* trans. Stuart Gilbert, op. cit. Page numbers refer to this edition.

body striking the water after the fall; there is a seeing which takes place before the occurrence and a hearing which takes place after it, but too late. *The Fall* bears witness, paradoxically enough, to the *missing* of the fall.

While the narrator of *The Plague* thus naturally feels, from his key position as "a faithful witness" (270, *tm*) that, "decidedly, it was up to him to speak for all" (281), the narrator of *The Fall,* though formerly, in his profession as defense attorney, spokesman for the victims and an eloquent champion of "noble causes" (16), does not speak to anyone about his witness of the suicide but is rather, paradoxically, reduced to silence by his very role as witness. "I informed no one."

> I must admit that I ceased to walk along the Paris quays. When I would ride along them in a car or bus, *a sort of silence would descend on me.* [42]

Rieux can "speak for all" because he understands—and shares in— the explosion of the cry which he is witnessing:

> Gradually he found himself drawn into the seething, clamorous mass and *understanding more and more the cry* that went up from it, *a cry that, for some part at least, was his.* [278]

Jean-Baptiste Clamence (as the narrator of *The Fall* chooses to call himself) *does not* understand, and *does not* share in, the reverberation of the cry which *he* is witnessing, but which—in contrast to Rieux— he believes precisely not to be of his concern because *not his own.*

Met with silence and reduced to silence, the unacknowledged cry emitted by the other's voice is thus perceived as the voice of no one, coming from nowhere. But this *nowhere* from which the other's voice has at the same time reached and failed to reach his ears will hence- forth lie in wait for the narrator *everywhere,* as the obsession of a vocal echo and in the delirious form of visual and accoustic hallucinations.

> I had gone up on the Pont des Arts . . . I . . . was about to light a cigarette when, at that very moment, a laugh burst out behind me. Taken by surprise, I suddenly wheeled around; *there was no one there* . . . I turned back toward the island and, again, heard the laughter behind me, a little farther off as if it were going downstream. I stood there motionless. The sound of the laughter was decreasing, but I could still hear it distinctly behind me, *come from nowhere* unless from the water. [38–39]

The Disintegration of the Witness

Having missed his chance encounter with the real, having failed to witness both the suicide and the other's cry, the narrator paradoxically will turn into an obsessive witness of an outside world totally confused with his own delusions. This disintegration of the witness, this breakdown of his ethical and psychological integrity and consequently, this radical collapse of his reliability, of his authority as witness, is, of course, a very different story from the story of *The Plague*. And yet, in the midst of its affirmation of the integrity of its own witness and of its relief at a possible return to the normal, *The Plague* contained already a shrill note of dissonance, a puzzling and explosive residue of madness, in the figure of a sniper unexpectedly emerging at its very ending:

> "Sorry, Doctor," a policeman said, "but I can't let you through. There's a crazy fellow with a gun, shooting at everybody." [281]

> "It's Cottard!" Grand's voice was shrill with excitement. "He's gone mad!" [284]

Why is Cottard shooting at everybody? The text alludes to the reasons for his mental breakdown in a previous conversation where Cottard discusses with Tarrou the forthcoming, and already visible, ending of the plague:

> "Granted!" Cottard rejoined. "But what do you mean by a return to normal life?"
> Tarrou smiled. "New films at picture-houses." But Cottard didn't smile. Was it supposed, he asked, that the plague wouldn't have changed anything and the life of the town would go on as before, exactly as if nothing happened? Tarrou thought that the plague would have changed things and not changed them; naturally, our fellow citizens' strongest desire was, and would be, to behave as if nothing had changed and for that reason nothing would be changed, in a sense. But—to look at it from another angle—one can't forget everything. [259]

Thus, in the midst of "the vast joy of liberation" (276), the explosive madness of the sniper ending the triumphant novel by his shooting at the celebrating crowds is itself in some ways a residual testimony to the Plague, a concurrent testimony to the testimony of Rieux which, in the very madness of its shooting through the crowds, bears witness both against and through the crowd's denial of the plague in its jubilant obliviousness:

> These ecstatic couples, locked together . . . proclaimed in the midst of the tumult of rejoicing, with the proud egoism and injustice of happy people, that the plague was over, the reign of terror ended. Calmly they denied, in the teeth of evidence, that we had ever known a crazy world in which men were killed off like flies, or that precise savagery, that

calculated frenzy of the plague ... In short, they denied that we had ever been that hag-ridden populace a part of which was daily fed into a furnace and went up in oily fumes ... [276–277]

I would suggest that the delirium of the witness in *The Fall* picks up precisely on the vision of the sniper in *The Plague.* The madness of the sniper communicates both with the madness of the woman jumping and with that of the narrator of *The Fall,* in breaking through the layers of apparent resolution of the former novel and in shooting through the "calm" of those who "deny in the teeth of evidence that we had ever known a crazy world."

Thus, the story of the *ending* of the Plague becomes the story of the *non-cessation* of the Fall.

The Disintegration of the Narrative

Because what has been witnessed cannot be made whole and integrated into an authoritative telling, *The Fall* has lost at once the narrative consistency of *The Plague* and the claim of the former novel to historical monumentality. What is witnessed, here as in *The Plague,* is the Other's death. But the scene of witnessing has lost the amplifying resonance of its communality, the guarantee of a community of witnessing. It is no longer a collective, but a solitary scene. It does not carry the historical weight, the self-evident significance of a group limit-experience, but embodies, rather, the *in-significance,* the ineffectuality of a missed encounter with reality and of a non-encounter between two solitudes. Unlike *The Plague,* whose testimony celebrated and recorded the significance of the dead, *The Fall* bears witness to the failure of the Other's death to claim significance. And yet, this very insignificance *claims the narrative,* since it decenters and defocalizes the significance of all the rest.

In line with this decentering, this defocalization of signification, and in this modified perspective of what constitutes historical perspective, *The Fall,* I would suggest, in opposition to *The Plague,* explores the roots of the disasters of contemporary history not in the evil of the enemies (some external bacillus of Plague) but, less predictably, in the betrayal of the friends. "Have you ever," writes Camus, "suddenly needed sympathy, help, friendship?"

> Yes, of course. For my part, I have learned to be content with sympathy ... It comes cheap, after catastrophes. Friendship is less simple ... Don't think for a minute that your friends will telephone you every

171

evening, as they ought to, to find out if this doesn't happen to be the evening when you are deciding to commit suicide . . . As for those who by definition are supposed to love us—I mean parents and *allies*[3] (what a curious expression!)—those are another matter. They find the right word, all right, and it hits the bull's eye; they telephone as if shooting a rifle . . .

What? What evening? I'll get to it, be patient with me. In a certain way I *am* sticking to my subject with that story about friends and allies [D'une certaine manière d'ailleurs, je suis dans mon sujet, avec cette histoire d'amis et d'alliés (*36*)]. [31–32, *tm*]

II

The Betrayal of the Allies

How does "cette histoire d'amis et d'alliés"—this "story" or this "history" of the betrayal of the "allies"—tie in with what appears to be the central temporal event and the main subject of *The Fall*, the suicide scene and the elusiveness of the suicide scene? ("What? What evening? I'll get to it, be patient with me.") Let me, in Camus' own footsteps, now take this detour of the "allies" as a way of getting at some deeper, less immediately apparent levels of the meaning and of the significance of the suicide scene.

*

"The most convincing keys to the shock of *La Chute* were autobiographical," writes Camus' biographer Herbert Lottmann.[4] Camus' most influential ally in the French and European intellectual scene had been Jean-Paul Sartre, who, in 1943, had acknowledged publicly Camus' preeminence as a modern writer and thinker in a noted article he had published in *Les Cahiers du sud* on Camus' first novel, *L'Etranger* (*B*, 262). In the years that followed the ending of the Second World War, Camus and Sartre shared each other's literary sympathies, frequented the same circles and were thought to belong to the same intellectual

---

[3]The word is mistranslated in the official English version as "connections," thus missing altogether the political connotations of the French word *alliés*, connotations underscored by the following expression, "what a curious expression" (*quelle expression!*, Folio, 35). The crucial importance of the concept of the "allies" in this text will be gradually clarified in what follows.

[4]Herbert Lottmann, *Albert Camus: A Biography*, New York: Doubleday, 1979, p. 591. Hereafter designated by the abbreviation "*B*," followed by page number.

group. But the 1951 publication of Camus' philosophical essay *L'Homme revolté (Man in Revolt)* was to bring about, dramatically, in 1952, four years before the publication of *The Fall,* a momentous break between Camus and Sartre, when a negative review of Camus' essay—taking Camus altogether by surprise—was published in Sartre's periodical *Les Temps modernes* (May 1952), giving rise in turn to an angered exchange between Camus and Sartre published in a later issue of the same periodical (August 1952), an exchange consisting in a virulent articulation of Camus' and Sartre's mutual criticisms and consummating a political and personal rupture both of their friendship and of their intellectual alliance. The complaint of the narrator of *The Fall* concerning the betrayal of the friends can thus refer to what Camus could not but feel as a betrayal on the part of Sartre. And indeed, Sartre himself, as well as other readers of the novel, took *The Fall* at its autobiographical *face value* and interpreted the enigmatic forms of Camus' narration as the barely disguised figures of a personal *confession.*

And yet, Camus himself insisted on the fact that the form of confession which ostentatiously structures his novel is itself deceptive and misleading, since it is primarily a rhetorical device which—in the expert mouth of the narrator—is precisely *used,* exploited, with the skills of an attorney. At the very least, the confession is not simple, since its desire to confess is directed by a calculation. In the blurb initialed by the author on the cover of the book, Camus thus wrote:

> The man who speaks in *The Fall* delivers himself of a calculated confession. Exiled in Amsterdam in a city of canals and cold light, where he plays the hermit and the prophet, this former attorney waits for willing listeners . . . Thus he hastens to try himself but he does so so as to better judge others.
>
> Where does the confession begin, where the accusation? Is the man who speaks in this book putting himself on trial, or his era? Is he a particular case, or the man of the day? A sole truth, in any case, in this studied play of mirrors: pain, and what it promises. [Quoted in *B,* 593]

To his friend the actress Maria Casarès, Camus repeated that the book was not a confession, but "the spirit of the times, and even the confused spirit of the times" (*B,* 593).

The Controversy about History

"The confused spirit of the times" implied, of course, a diagnosis of contemporary history. And in fact, the clash between Camus and

Sartre revolved around their differing diagnoses of—and their differing approach to—history. With the 1951 publication of *L'Homme révolté,* Camus emerged as an outspoken critic of dogmatic Marxism and, in particular, of the political labor camps of Soviet totalitarianism, which he analyzes in his book as an exemplary historical degeneration—through ideological exacerbation and fetishization—of the constitutively human revolutionary impulse and of what originated as legitimate political revolt. Sartre, on the other hand, was a firm political and philosophical apologist for Stalinism: in Sartre's primary preoccupation with history as a process of dialectical *totalization,* and in his constant search for a perspective of coherent explanations of historical processes viewed in their entirety, Stalin's rule appeared to him to yield, precisely, a totalizing legibility of Russian history; it justified itself in making clear the ultimate *intelligibility* of Soviet society after the Russian Revolution.

Camus, however, was wary of totalizations. In the perspective sketched out in *L'Homme révolté,* the totalitarian impulse of a historicism that believes it can account for everything is shown to be as harmful and as deluded as the totalitarian impulse of the ideology that seems to be its opposite, that of idealist anti-historicism. Camus *puts side by side* the blindness and the contradictions of historicism and the blindness and the contradictions of antihistoricism. "He who believes *nothing but history* is walking toward terror," warns Camus; but at the same time, "he who believes *nothing of history* is authorizing terror" (*TM,* 323).[5] Because of their totalitarianism and of their similar purism, both attitudes, Camus claims, are in fact historically inefficacious. "There are two sorts of impotence," he argues, "the impotence of Good and the impotence of Evil." Although on different ends of the moral scale, both are historically disabling, for both are tied up with specific—although different—forms of *denial of the real.* "To deny history is to deny, in fact, the real," but "neither more nor less," insists Camus, than the denial of the real which historicism dramatizes in its ideological fetishization of history itself: "one takes a distance from the real by wanting to consider history as a totality sufficient unto itself" (*TM,* 323). It is only at the price of this denial of the real that history can be considered as a self-contained whole with no referential residue and whose every aspect is entirely subsumed by its own transparent intelligibility.

Under the signature of Francis Jeanson, the negative review of

---

[5] Camus, "Lettre au directeur des *Temps modernes,*" *Les Temps modernes,* August 1952. This issue of *Les Temps modernes* is designated here by the abbreviation "*TM,*" followed by page number. Quotations from this issue are in my translation.

Camus' book in *Les Temps modernes* in effect responded to Camus' critique in the implicitly *collective* name of the whole group of intellectuals (Existentialists, Marxists and Communists) that had crystallized around Sartre. Jeanson, and by implication Sartre's group, accused Camus' critique of consisting in a negative antihistoricism, and of thus amounting to a nihilistic advocacy of abstentianism.

> Is Camus' hope [Jeanson protested] really to halt the movement of the world by refusing every endeavor in the world? He blames the Stalinists (but also existentialism) for being totally captive of history; but they are not more so than he is, they are only captive in another way.[6]

When Camus in turn responded to Jeanson by saying he had never said, in fact, "that existentialism was (like Stalinism) a prisoner of history," but rather, that "for the moment, existentialism was in turn subjugated to historicism and thus subject to its contradictions" (*TM*, 324), Sartre felt compelled to respond in person to take issue on Camus' authority on history, in terms even harsher and more bluntly personal than the ones deployed in Jeanson's critique.

A Reply to Albert Camus

Indeed, Sartre acknowledged, Camus once *did* speak with authority on history, but *no more:* at the present day Camus was nothing other than a man, precisely, of the past. In his "Reply to Albert Camus," Sartre thus writes:

> You have been for us . . . the admirable conjunction of a person, an action and a work. That was in 1945; one discovered Camus, the Resistant, as one discovered Camus, the author of *L'Etranger.* And when one put together the editor of the clandestine [journal] *Combat* with this Meursault . . . that our society condemned to death, when one knew, especially, that you were and have not ceased being both the one and the other, this apparent contradiction made us progress in our knowledge of ourselves and of the world, you were not far from being exemplary. *In you were summed up the conflicts of our time, and you surmounted them by your eagerness to live them.* You were a person, the most complex and the richest . . .
>
> You introduced a new note of morality into our literature . . .
> How we loved you then. [*TM*, 345–346; emphasis mine]
>
> The equilibrium that you thus realized could produce itself [, however,] only once, for one moment, in one man: you were lucky that the

[6]Francis Jeanson, "Albert Camus ou l'âme révoltée," *TM*, May 1952.

175

common fight against the Germans symbolized in your eyes and in our own the union of all men against inhuman fatalities. In choosing injustice, the German, of his own accord, had cast himself among the blind forces of Nature and you could, in *The Plague,* assign his role to the bacteria . . .

[But once the war was over,] suddenly the Germans did not count any more . . . We had believed that there was only one way of resisting, and we discovered that there were two ways of envisaging Resistance . . .

It is possible to think that the circumstances, even the most painful, of your life, have elected you to *bear precisely witness* to the fact that *personal salvation* [le salut personnel] *was accessible to all . . .*

[But] your personality, which was real and alive as long as the event was nourishing it, has become now an illusory mirage: In 1944 it was the future, in 1952 it is the past . . . You had to change if you wanted to remain yourself and you were afraid of changing. [*TM,* 350–351]

It is interesting that, in the middle of his quarrel with Camus and in the very act of blaming him for having failed to change, Sartre experiences nostalgia for the Camus of 1945, the heroic editorialist of the Resistance journal and as such, the exemplary postwar *key witness* whose very painful circumstances (Sartre alludes here to Camus' tuberculosis) have become a living testimony to the fact that a cure— or, as Sartre puts it, "personal salvation"—is "accessible to all." These are indeed the very terms of Camus' assumption of his role as witness in *The Plague.* Far from experiencing, however, a nostalgia for his own successful past and for his witnessing authority, the author of *The Fall* precisely *deconstructs* the very ideology of salvation and the very witnessing authority which, governing *The Plague,* gave it its momentum as an exemplary *therapeutic* testimony.

*

The Fall, indeed, looks back at history in a different manner. Was *The Plague, The Fall* seems now to ask, essentially a *rescue operation,*[7]

[7]It is doubtless no coincidence if *The Plague,* in its heroic effort toward—and perception of—the war struggle as primarily a rescue operation, was conceived and published in its first version (the Resistance publication in 1942) in Le Chambon-sur Lignon, the French farming village which effectively conspired to resist the Vichy government and succeeded in sheltering five thousand Jews from the Nazi deportations. "In Le Chambon," says Pierre Sauvage, author of the 1988 French film which documents and dramatizes Le Chambon's wartime "conspiracy of goodness," "the situation was easier than it was in parts of Poland and Germany. [Generally] those who hid Jews lived in fear of their neighbors. Sometimes their own children turned them into the Gestapo. In Le Chambon there was none of that fear, since everyone was doing the same thing."

as it once had seemed to be? Was the trauma of the inhumanity of the occurrence a *disease*—a simple stroke of history—from which we can now simply be *cured?*

Let us think back, for a moment, to the suicide scene. The event, *The Fall* seems to suggest, was never really about *salvation* but about the lost chance of encounter with the *possibility of rescue.* It is not simply that salvation has not, as yet, taken place. Rather, with the chance of rescue missed through a missed historical encounter with the real, the event seems to consist in the *missing* of salvation and, henceforth, in its radical historical and philosophical impossibility. Sartre acknowledges that he liked Camus when Camus was a communal witness of salvation, of a cure accessible to all. Sartre dislikes Camus when Camus seems to become a witness of incurability and of perdition. What, however, if Camus' "election"—as Sartre puts it— to the testimonial task or, to put it more objectively, what if the contemporary trauma of the testimonial crisis which compelled Camus to write, far from having ended in the resolution of *The Plague,* had only then in fact begun? "I realized definitively," says the narrator of *The Fall,* "that I was not cured, that I was still cornered and that I had to make shift with it" (109).

What, indeed, if it is Sartre, rather than Camus who, since the war, has in some ways *failed to change,* Sartre who, in advocating Stalinism and prophetic Marxism, is caught precisely in the movement of the jubilance which marks the ending of *The Plague,* still celebrating the historical advent of cure, salvation and redemption, still looking for a new beginning that will altogether do away with the contamination of disease, a new beginning that, indeed, would totally erase, forget, deny the Plague?

> For it cannot be said [comments the narrator of *The Fall*] that there is no more pity; no, good Lord, we never stop talking of it. On dead innocence the judges swarm, the judges of all races, those of Christ and those of the Antichrist . . . Do you know what has become of one of the houses in this city that sheltered Descartes? A lunatic asylum. Yes, general delirium . . . it's a real madhouse. Prophets and would be healers multiply everywhere; they hasten to get there with a good law or a flawless organization before the world is deserted. [116–118, *tm*]

While Sartre thinks Camus has failed as witness since he has ceased to be the witness of a cure, Camus thinks it is Sartre who is failing as

---

On Le Chambon's rescue of Jews, see also Philip Hallie, *Lest Innocent Blood Be Shed,* New York, Harper & Row: 1979.

a witness, since he neglects to witness and to take into account the labor camps in Soviet Russia, and fails to recognize through them the non-cessation of the Plague. While Sartre sees Camus as a *man of the past* who fails to recognize the progress made by history and thus essentially *fails to march toward the future,* Camus sees Sartre as a man who, in the name not of the real future but of the prophetic gesture—and projection—of an ideology, fails to *recognize the present* and thus *denies,* specifically, *the implications of the past* and the ineradicability of these implications from any possible future construction.

Sartre, however, replies succinctly to Camus' critique, and seeks to undercut it by reclaiming the priority of history as *action* and of politics as *practice* over contemplation of the past.

> Involved in history, like you, I do not see it in your manner. I do not doubt that history indeed shows this absurd and horrifying face to all those who look at it from Hell: *but those who look at it from Hell have nothing more in common with those who are involved in making it.* [*TM,* 351; emphasis mine]

What does it mean, I will now ask, to *look at history from Hell?* What is the relation (or the difference in topography) between history and hell? What is the relation between "looking" and "making"? How does Camus' position differ radically from Sartre's, both on the nature and significance of the relation between "looking at history" and "making history", and on the nature and significance of what "looking at history from Hell" specifically implies? How is *The Fall* tied up with, and in what way does *The Fall* attempt to answer, all those questions?

III

"Methodical Deafness"

In his response to Jeason's critique, publicly addressed to Sartre on the pages of *Les Temps modernes,* Camus explains why he has felt compelled to answer. Referring to the negative review of his *L'Homme revolté* in the article signed by Jeanson but that Sartre's publication in effect implicitly approved and sanctioned as an authorized dismissal of Camus' analysis and of his proposed critique, Camus writes:

> If your article had only been frivolous and if its tone had only been hostile, I would have kept silent. But for reasons of intellectual comfort, its author has pretended *not to understand* what he was reading and

not to see *what face of our history* I had been trying to retrace [son auteur a fait mine de se tromper sur ce qu'il lisait et de ne pas voir celui des visages de notre histoire que j'ai essayé de retracer] . . . Consequently, silence was no longer possible for me. (*TM,* 333; emphasis mine)

Camus' central reproach to Jeanson's critique addresses therefore not the substance of the disagreement, *not* Jeanson's choice to adhere to communism while Camus is critical of what he takes to be the ideological fetishization of this doctrine, but rather, Jeanson's misreading and thus misrepresentation of Camus' text in his pretension *not to understand*—and *not to see*—what face of history Camus is trying to retrace. At the core of Jeanson's misreading, Camus' analysis locates and underscores a project of avoidance, an attempt to *look away* both from Camus text and from the specificity of that particular historical face. Camus writes:

Asserting that the sky is blue, if you make me say that I judge the sky to be black, I have no other choice but to cast myself a madman or to declare my interlocutor a deaf man. Fortunately, this does not affect the reality of the color of the sky or, in this case, of the argument discussed. This is why I have now to examine your collaborator's reasons, in order to determine either *my madness* or *his deafness.*

Rather than a deaf man, he seems to me, in truth, someone who insistently *will not hear.* [*TM,* 322]

Thus, Camus proceeds to analyze, and to respond to, what he feels as a wall of deafness in Jeanson, a deafness whose opaqueness and whose impermeability seem to him too systematic and "too methodical" [cette trop méthodique surdité, *TM,* 327] not to be willful, not to be, in other words, symptomatic of a crucial method of denial. What is it, therefore, in his writing, that has triggered such a vehement denial? It is not simply his critique of Stalinism, although this appears to be the core of the debate. In an understated and allusive manner, Camus attempts to point to the locus of the deafness, by recapitulating not simply his argument but the specific question that Jeanson, and by implication Sartre, refuse to hear. Camus concedes—and Sartre would agree, of course—that Soviet communism's rise to power was the most important revolution of the twentieth century: Sartre's apologies for Stalin are based precisely on the rationale of Stalin's need to strengthen this radically unprecedented socialist regime. But this is where Camus insists on the necessity of paying careful historical attention:

If one holds that *authoritarian socialism* is the principal revolutionary experience of our era, it is difficult not to pronounce upon the terror it entails, today precisely, and, for instance, to remain within the bounds of reality, it is difficult not to pronounce upon *the fact of a concentration-camp universe* [le fait concentrationnaire]. [*TM,* 328]

Authoritarian Socialism and Its Double

Since "le fait concentrationnaire"—the "fact of a concentration-camp universe"—is posited not simply as a fact but as a concept, a new concept forged by our era and whose capacity for generalization as a concept exceeds the specific fact of concentration camps in Stalin's Russia, the corollary concept of "authoritarian socialism" is given the potential to allude not merely to the Communist authoritarianism of the rule of Stalin but also, to the pseudo-socialist authoritarianism of the rule of Hitler, to Nazi Germany and to the revolutionary claims of national socialism. But it is precisely this similarity of pattern in the recurrent structure of a concentration-camp universe, this recurrent intellectual seduction of the ideology of a new order and the consequent apocalyptic rationalization of its oppressive measures, to which Jeanson and Sartre insist on remaining deaf, in Sartre's specified refusal "to look at history from hell" and in Jeanson's pretention "not to see what face of our history" Camus was "trying to retrace."

Indeed, the divagations of the narrator of *The Fall* are a "confession" only insofar as they betray the blind spot—and the *unacknowledged meeting ground*—of all twentieth-century apocalyptic and redemptive ideologies, in their common confusion of salvation and "definitive" (final) "solutions." In denouncing the delusion of salvation of the ending of *The Plague, The Fall* portrays, by the same token, a parodic picture of the contradictions of an entire generation of entrapped European intellectuals, unwittingly still struggling with the Second World War and, in the grips of history as Plague but hoping to erase it by a new beginning, falling for the rationalizations both of Marxism and of fascism. "You see in me, *très cher,*" says the narrator of *The Fall,* mimicking the discourse of the European intellectual in its intellectualizations and its rationalizations of one authoritarian socialism or of the other,

> an enlightened advocate of slavery.
> Without slavery, as a matter of fact, there is *no definitive solution.*
> [*F,* 131–132]

> There are always reasons for murdering a man. That's why crime always finds lawyers, and innocence only rarely. [*F,* 112]

Testimony and Alliance

If, however, in giving voice to the contradictions of an entire generation as well as to his own and to his own former delusions, the narrator
of *The Fall* chooses to name himself, ironically, Jean-Baptiste (John
the Baptist), it is by reference to the voice of that other witness who
was, precisely, "crying in the desert." Facing the deafness of the
collaborators of *Les Temps modernes*—supposedly the group of his
friends and of his historical allies—to his analysis and to his testimony
in *L'Homme révolté*, Camus now realizes that the real witness is a
dissident by definition, doomed by his very function to remain alone.
"Death is solitary," says elliptically the narrator of *The Fall*, "whereas
slavery is collective . . . All together at last, but on our knees and
heads bowed" (*F,* 136).

The betrayal of the friends and of the allies, which the narrator of
The Fall—let us recall—has underscored as somehow linked to his
main subject, can thus refer to Camus' experience of Sartre's betrayal
and to the dissolution—over what might be called the *querelle des
Temps modernes*—of their personal and political alliance.

> May heaven protect us, *cher Monsieur,* from being set on a pedestal by
> our friends! As for those who by definition are supposed to love us—
> I mean parents and allies (what a curious expression!)—those are
> another matter. They find the right word, all right, and it hits the bull's
> eye; they telephone as if shooting a rifle . . .
> What? What evening? I'll get to it, be patient with me. In a certain
> way I *am* sticking to my subject, with that story about friends and allies
> [D'une certaine manière, je *suis* dans mon sujet, avec cette histoire
> d'amis et d'alliés]. [*F,* 32, tm]

Since, however, in Camus' perspective, Sartre's betrayal is not
just personal but intellectual and ethical, the reference in *The Fall*
to the betrayal of the allies carries connotations that go far beyond
the story of Camus' autobiography, far beyond the story of the
dissolution of this one particular alliance. For what is here at stake,
I would suggest, and what is more profoundly linked to the main
subject, is a *transvaluation of the very concept of alliance*—and a
disintegration of the very notion of the ally—through the particular
relation of both concepts to the contemporary testimonial crisis.

Camus now realizes that the very moral core that gave its momentum to *The Plague*—the establishment of a community of witnessing—was itself in some ways a distortion, a historical delusion.
Inasmuch as the authentic feeling of community helped in fact to fight

against the Plague, the *fight* against the Plague was itself already a distraction from what history as Plague was really like. The Plague is such that, by its very nature, it cannot be testified to by any *alliance.* Camus now understands that, in the face of history as Plague, the witness, like the victim, has no ally. "No one bears witness for the witness," Celan's verse knows. And in the context of *The Fall,* it is ironically significant that this knowledge borne by Celan's verse is precisely uttered and articulated by one who was himself a Nazi labor camp survivor, one who was himself, in other words, by chance *saved* from the Plague, but who nonetheless, through a belated and delayed effect of history, finished his life not as a *saved* but as a *drowned,*[8] in choosing in his turn, after years of bearing witness through his poetry, to commit suicide and in jumping in his turn—like the woman in *The Fall*—from a bridge into the Seine.[9]

Who is the saved, therefore, and who has drowned? Can the saved be separated from the drowned? What is the significance of the body's fall and of the sound and the impact of its striking the water? What is the meaning of the death, and what is the significance of the survival, of the witness in *The Fall?* What is the significance of speech? What is the significance of silence? And what, henceforth, is the significance of deafness? What, in other words, is there to hear?

> If your article had only been frivolous and if its tone had only been hostile, I would have kept silent . . . But for reasons of intellectual comfort, its author has pretended not to understand what he was reading and not to see what face of our history I had been trying to retrace . . . Consequently, *silence was no longer possible for me.* [*TM,* 222]

> If one holds that authoritarian socialism is the principal revolutionary experience of our era, it is difficult not to pronounce upon the terror it entails, today precisely, and, for instance, to remain within the bounds of reality, it is difficult not to pronounce upon the fact of a concentration-camp universe. [*TM,* 328]

> Your article seems to say yes to a doctrine and to *shroud with silence* the politics it entails [*faire silence* à la politique qu'elle entraîne]. [*TM,* 331]

[8]I am borrowing, of course, the power and the resonance of these suggestive terms from Primo Levi's *The Drowned and the Saved,* translated from the Italian from Raymond Rosenthal, New York: Summit Books, 1988.

[9]There is a terrible irony in the fact that Primo Levi also later, like Celan, took his own life by jumping to his death. Behind the cry of the woman drowning, it is possible to hear the lonesome cry, now silenced, of all these former witnesses and historical belated suicides of concentration camp survivors: Celan, Levi, Améry, Borowski, Kosinski . . .

What is at stake in the debate between Camus and Sartre—a debate whose thrust can be viewed as generic, in a way, to all historical debates and all polemics about history—is thus less the substance of the issues, the political correctness of one doctrine as opposed to the political correctness of another doctrine—than the significance of silence insofar as it defines in and of itself an act, a political behavior that is both a symptom of, and a crucial factor in, historical developments. While Sartre claims that, unlike Camus who "looks at history from hell," he is in the business not of "looking" but of "*making* history," Camus reproaches Sartre that he is literally "*making silence*" ("dire oui à une doctrine et *faire silence* à la politique qu'elle entraîne"), that in not avowing—in not making a pronouncement upon—Soviet concentration camps, he is literally shrouding the reality of concentration camps in silence.

The Making(s) of a Silence

Shrouding with silence is, however, what the narrator of *The Fall* precisely does during and after the suicide scene.

> I had already gone some fifty yards when I heard the sound—which, despite the distance, seemed *dreadfully loud* in the *midnight silence*— of a body striking the water. I stopped short, but without turning around. Almost at once I heard a cry, repeated several times, which was going downstream; then it suddenly ceased. *The silence that followed, as the night stood still, seemed interminable . . .* I informed no one. [*F,* 69–70]

> I must admit that I ceased to walk along the Paris quays. When I would ride along them in a car or bus, *a sort of silence would descend on me.* [*F,* 42]

Silence here is not a simple absence of an act of speech, but a positive avoidance—and erasure—of one's hearing, the positive *assertion* of a deafness, in the refusal not merely to know but to acknowledge—and henceforth respond or *answer to*—what is being heard or witnessed. In this defeat of the presence of the witness to reality, silence is the active *voiding of the hearing,* the voiding of the act of witnessing of a reality whose transmission to awareness is obstructed and whose content is insistently denied as known—insistently asserted (reasserted) as *not known*—because essentially remaining *unacknowledged.*

That woman? *I don't know.* Really *I don't know.* The next day, and the days following, I didn't read the papers. [*F,* 71]

Rethinking the debate with Sartre, *The Fall,* indeed, rethinks the ways in which the "*making*" of a history is tied up with the makings of a *silence* (faire silence) intent upon *not knowing* and *not looking* ("not looking at history from hell"). The relation between silence and not knowing, and the question of what knowing and not knowing mean in practice and in theory—in the practice and the theory of history— is what the debate between Camus and Sartre and the drama of *The Fall* are, in fact, profoundly all about. The narrator of *The Fall* reflects, indeed, at once upon how history is made by, and rewritten through, the silence of the censor, and how massacres historically repeat themselves—from the ancient Jesus to the closer horrors of the contemporary aberrations—through history's replaying of its subtle vascillation between knowing and not knowing:

> There are always reasons for murdering a man . . . That's why crime always finds lawyers, and innocence only rarely . . .
>
> *He knew* that he was not altogether innocent. If he did not bear the weight of the crime he was accused of, he had committed others—even though he *didn't know* which ones. Did he really *not know* them? He was at the source, after all, he must have heard of a certain Massacre of the Innocents. The children of Judea massacred while his parents were taking him to a safe place—why did they die if not because of him? Those blood-spattered soldiers, those infants cut in two filled him with horror . . . I am sure he could not forget them. And as for that sadness that can be felt in his every act, wasn't it the incurable melancholy of a man who heard night after night the voice of Rachel weeping for her children and refusing all comfort? . . .
>
> *Knowing what he knew,* familiar with everything about man—ah, who would have believed that crime consists less in making others die than in not dying oneself!—he found it too hard for him to hold on and continue . . .
>
> He was not upheld, he complained, and as a last straw, *he was censored.* Yes, it was the third evangelist I believe, who first *suppressed his complaint.* "*Why has thou forsaken me?*"—it was a *seditious cry,* wasn't it? Well then, the scissors! Mind you, if Luke had suppressed nothing, the matter . . . would not have assumed such importance. Thus the censor cries aloud what he proscribes. The world's order likewise is ambiguous.
>
> Nonetheless, the censored one was unable to carry on. And I know, *cher,* whereof I speak . . . In certain cases carrying on . . . is superhuman. And he was not superhuman, you can take my word for it. He cried aloud his agony . . .

The unfortunate thing is that he left us . . . to carry on . . . *knowing in turn what he knew,* but incapable of doing what he did and of dying like him . . .

Peter, you know, the coward, Peter denied him. "*I know not the man . . . I know not what thou sayest* . . . etc." [*F,* 112–114; *tm,* emphasis mine]

Modes of Knowing and Not Knowing

Thus, *The Fall* reflects upon how "knowing" and "not knowing" are translated into *actions,* and what they in effect mean in the practice and the theory of history.

Jesus, in Camus' atheological perspective, is himself not a man-God but an archetypal *human witness,* witness to human suffering and pain in general and in particular, witness to history as outrage, as the outrage of the Massacre of the Innocents.[10] The extent of the massacre is such, however, that the *witness* cannot not be in his turn *tainted,* implicated in the guilt of its occurrence by his very witnessing of it, by his very *knowledge* of the massacre—and of his own survival. "Knowing what he knew" . . . "*He* knew he was not altogether innocent." And it is *because he knows,* and because his knowledge must be hushed (denied as knowledge and asserted—through an active silence—as non-knowledge), that he in effect must die, and that his voice, his testimony, and his outcry, must be censored. Paradoxically, the allegorical figure of Christ appears in the arena of *The Fall* not as a saviour, but as a witness to the fact, and as a bearer of the knowledge of the fact, that human history precludes any salvation. Since the witness is a dissident by definition, since the witness can, by definition, have no ally, Christ in turn is betrayed by his own allies, and his testimony, met by deafness and repressed by silence, is ironically denied by his own apostles. Christ's canonization and his transformation into God henceforth insures the deafness to his testimony and the impermeability to his "seditious cry."

Amplified and recapitulated in the silence of the Censor—in his canonical textual deletion of the outcry of the dying Jesus—the initial silence of the witness of *The Fall* and the reassertion of his deafness— his "not knowing"—likewise consists in censorship, in a *suppression of the cry:* a muffling—in the witnesses's own ears and, as a result, in

[10]Of course, the history of Jesus cannot not encompass here—in its resonances of the massacre of the children of Judea—the atrocities, as well, of the Second World War.

the awareness of the world—of the outcry of the drowning woman. It is a similar suppression that is enacted by the systematic deafness of *Les Temps modernes* and by Sartre's reasserted silence on Stalin's oppressions, a similar censorship both of the victims' cry and of Camus' own outcry as a witness, in the concerted muffling of his dissident voice, crying in the desert against Soviet concentration camps. In this *double suppression of the cry* of *both* the victim and the witness, what is particularly grave and particularly rich in implications in the vision of *The Fall* is that Sartre, or *the fellow intellectual,* has betrayed the testimonial task, *betrayed, precisely, as a fellow witness,* since he chose not to acknowledge Russian concentration camps and not to look at history from hell.

IV

The Concentric Circles of Hell

In contrast to Sartre's refusal, the whole thrust of *The Fall* is to reclaim, precisely, the relation between history and hell.

> For we are [says Jean-Baptiste Clamence] at the heart of things here. Have you noticed that Amsterdam's concentric canals resemble the circles of *hell?* . . . When one comes from the outside, as one gradually goes through those circles, life—and hence its crimes—becomes denser, darker. Here, we are in the last circle. The circle of the . . . Ah, you know that? By heaven, you become harder to classify. But you understand then why I can say that the center is here, although we stand at the tip of the continent. [*F,* 14–15]

The fact that both Camus and Sartre use "hell" as a metaphor for a historical reality is itself, I would suggest, charged with historical significance. Whatever "hell" might be, it designates in both Camus' and Sartre's usage something within history that neither one of them can speak about directly, something that they can refer to but *not name* and that can therefore only be alluded to by indirection. In this respect, it is significant that the narrator of *The Fall* is interrupted by his listener, or else interrupts himself, when he is about to name "the last circle" of hell. The last circle of hell remains unnamed.

What, however, does "hell" mean, at once in Sartre's metaphoric designation of his own refusal "to look at history from hell" and in Camus' ironic recapitulation of the metaphor of hell in the concentric circles introduced at the beginning of *The Fall?* I would suggest that the word *concentric,* in Camus' perspective and in the vision of *The Fall,* resonates with implications that extend beyond the mere description of the shape of the canals of Amsterdam. In addition to its geometrical or geographical significance, (as well as to the literary, allegorical allusion to the circularity of hell in Dante), "concentric" in effect is pregnant with another meaning which derives its resonance from the debate with Sartre, and, referring quite specifically to the political context and to the history evoked by the debate, connotes Camus' allusion to—and insistence on—the historically indubitable *fait concentrationnaire,* the fact of a concentration-camp universe. Camus' is thus not merely a *concentric* but a *concentrationary* hell, the very one whose ghost is now returning in Stalin's Russia, but that Sartre chooses not to look at, not to acknowledge both as a political reality and as a necessary vantage point for any vision of, and view on, history.

The whole performance of the narrative repeats in turn, in *The Fall,* the shape of its concentric circles: the movement of the plot has a pronounced, repetitive, *concentric* thrust, as though searching for a silent center that remains, however, absent from the circles and *excentric* to their *concentration.* Indeed, the circling of *The Fall* revolves around an effort at—but also, paradoxically, an impossibility of—getting at the center. What then might the center be?

In some ways, it is the suicide scene which could be thought of as the center of the narrative, a sort of primal scene around which the narrative's concentric movement keeps precisely turning and returning. When a description of the suicide scene emerges for the first time half-way through the novel—that is, at its typographical and spatial center—it is indeed referred to by the voice of the narrator as "my essential discovery," "the adventure that I found at the *center* of my memory" (*F,* 69, *tm*). Significantly, though, the suicide scene here functions as a center only insofar as the narrator's discourse, made of digressions, continually tries to *turn away from it,* at the same time that, compulsively, it keeps returning to it. The central status of the suicide scene is thus established, paradoxically, both through the effort to recover it and through the effort to avoid it and to turn away from it.

There is, however, yet another silent center which is inscribed outright at the beginning of the book, a center, it is true, which the reader is most likely to bypass and which appears to be itself disorientingly peripheral ("you understand then why I say that the center is here, although we stand at the tip of the continent," 15), but which is nonetheless alluded to as somehow crucial and as *literally central* in the geography of Amsterdam and in the space of its concentric circles. It is presented, quite significantly, at the opening of the novel, as a topography which the narrator and his listener will precisely *go around.* This center of avoidance and yet also of encounter, appears when the narrator, who has just met his listener in a bar in Amsterdam, offers to show his guest the way back to his hotel:

> *Your way back?* [Votre chemin?] . . . Well . . . the easiest thing would be for me to accompany you as far as the harbor. Thence, by *going around the Jewish quarter* [en contournant le quartier juif] you'll find those fine avenues with their parade of streetcars full of flowers . . . Your hotel is one of them. [*F,* 10]

The Jewish Quarter

The "Jewish quarter" is thus mentioned at the outset of *The Fall,* as though *in passing,* with the subtle but, I would suggest, with the full charge of the historical implications of the movement of *by-passing*—of turning away from, and of going round—something that is nonetheless the center. The geographical or topographical guidance the narrator offers could itself be emblematic, I would venture to propose, of a larger search and of an allegorical/historical attempt to get one's bearings: to find in history one's way—the right way; to find in history a way back home. We might choose, *The Fall* seems to suggest, to bypass certain quarters of our history or not to look at history from hell. And yet, the way back home passes through that one place—that one hell—we want most of anything to avoid: the Jewish quarter.

> *Your way back?* . . . Well . . . the easiest thing would be for me to accompany you as far as the harbor. Thence, by *going around the Jewish quarter* you'll find those fine avenues with their parade of streetcars full of flowers . . . Your hotel is one of them . . .
> *I live in the Jewish quarter* [Moi, j'habite le quartier juif] or *what was called so* until our Hitlerian brethren made room. What a cleanup! Seventy-five thousand Jews deported or assassinated; that's real vacuum cleaning. I admire that diligence, that methodical patience. When one has no character one *has* to apply a method. Here it did wonders incontrovertibly, and I am living on the site of one of the greatest crimes in history [J'habite sur les lieux d'un des plus grands crimes de l'histoire] [10–11]

It is therefore not the Soviet concentration camps but the Jewish ones that, like the innermost circle of hell, are implicitly at the center of the novel: a center that remains, as such, unspeakable. The Jewish quarter "or what was called so" is itself a name that is no longer valid, a displaced, anachronistic designation that names—improperly—only an absence and a silence. Unlike the silence with which Sartre has surrounded Soviet concentration camps by not talking about them, by not avowing them, the silence of the Jewish concentration camps can no longer be dispelled by an avowal. The last circle of hell is inhabited by those who are no longer there, those who, from within the very center of the circle, have precisely been obliterated. The Jewish quarter—or the ultimate concentric circle—is inhabited by silence, a silence we can no longer dispel, denounce, deplore or simply understand. "When one comes from the outside, as one gradually goes through those circles, life—and hence its crimes—becomes denser, darker" (14).

What is the connection, the question now arises, between this denser, darker, and unnamable center of silence in the midst of Amsterdam's concentric circles and the other silent center of the plot's concentric movement—the scene of the woman's drowning? What is the relation between the conspicuously marginal narrative divagation on the Jewish quarter at the opening of the novel and the inconspicuously pivotal episode of the suicide? I would suggest that the opening remark, in creating a significantly audible subtext of the very silence of extermination, is meant to cue the reader to the fact that the real subject of the novel (of the testimony) is, precisely, this subtext: what does it mean to inhabit the (exterminated) Jewish quarter of Amsterdam (of Europe)? What does it mean to *inhabit history* as crime, as the space of the annihilation of the Other?

The Silence of the Western Allies

Framed by such a question, the suicide episode—in its insistent evocation of the bystander's silence and of the narrator's failure to become a responsive witness—can be interpreted as an allegory of the deafness and the muteness of the world facing the extermination of the Jews. Despite the shock that swept the world when the Nazi death camps were first liberated in 1945, information about the extermination had been communicated to the Allies since at least 1941. The Polish underground had played a key role in the transmission of the news about the Nazi gas chambers to the West, but its information—like the testimony, later, of some rare escapees of concentration camps—had been met with "disbelief" and accused of "exaggeration."

The Nazi genocide occurred by virtue of the fact that *all sides of the war* maintained a terrible but *universally shared secret:* "the fact of a concentration-camp universe." Walter Laqueur sums up the situation:

> From this time up to the end of the war the number of victims given in the official declarations of the Allied Governments was consistently too low. Even after it had been accepted in London and Washington that the information about the mass slaughter was correct, the British and US governments showed much concern that it should not be given too much publicity . . . 1942 was a critical year in the course of the war, strategists and bureaucrats were not to be deflected in the pursuit of victory by considerations not directly connected with the war effort . . . The Office of War Information in the US and the Ministry of Information in Britain were inclined to soft pedal publicity about the mass murder in 1942–43 for a variety of reasons: because the public would never believe it, because it would stir up anti-semitism in the West, because it would not be unpopular in some European countries, because it would have a devastating effect on the morale of the European resistance, etc.[11]

Thus, Camus' allegory in *The Fall,* unlike that of *The Plague,* addresses, in what turned history into a Holocaust, not the magnitude of the event but, on the contrary, the tendency to its minimization that allowed it to occur through systematic deafness, silence and suppression of information: "That woman? I don't know. Really I don't know. The next day and the days following, I didn't read the papers." Camus' allusion to the betrayal of the "allies" would thus have, in addition to the reference to Sartre's betrayal as a friend, as an allied intellectual and as a fellow witness, this further connotation and further historical allusion to the Western Allies—and to their failure to become responsive and effective witnesses vis-à-vis the Nazi genocide. The "plague" is such that it cannot be testified to by any alliance.

A Legacy of Silence

The concept of alliance has thus undergone a philosophical and moral bankruptcy, even though its practice has achieved political and military victory. In the very act of striving to defeat the executioners, the Allies failed to be true allies either of the witnesses or of the victims, suppressing in effect at once the victim's and the witness' cry. To borrow Sartre's terms once again, the Allies in their turn refuse

[11]Walter Laqueur, *The Terrible Secret-Suppression of the Truth about Hitler's "Final Solution,"* New York, Penguin Books: 1980, pp. 201–204.

to look at history from hell. And as in Sartre's case, the Allies' rationale is, likewise, the necessity of *making history:* "Strategists and bureaucrats were not to be deflected in the pursuit of victory by considerations not directly connected with the war effort . . . Too much publicity about the mass slaughter was . . . thought to be detrimental to the war effort."[12] Like Sartre, the Allies are involved in *making history* by *not looking* at it, and in particular, by *overlooking hell.* Hell—not simply as the space of genocide but as the space of a compulsive overlooking, the terrifying space of looking and not seeing—hell as the silent center of a concerted oversight is thus the cultural legacy of World War II.

It is doubtless no coincidence if, even in his militant dismantling of the ideology of anti-Semitism in the magnanimous, momentous book he publishes immediately after the war, Sartre still unwittingly continues to maintain the Allies' silence and to look away from hell: *Reflexions sur la question juive,* published in 1946, launches a war on anti-Semites and defends the Jews against their venom, but neglects to mention, even in one word, the Holocaust. The "Jewish quarter" thus unwittingly remains the silent or unspoken center of the "Jewish question," not merely in Sartre's discourse, but in the general postwar intellectual production of the West, in the protracted postwar silence on the Holocaust of both the European and the American intellectuals.[13]

[12]Laqueur, *Ibid.*

[13]Camus, indeed, is one of the rare writers who at least *inscribe* the silence. See *The Plague,* p. 226: "There were other camps of much the same kind in the town, but the narrator, for lack of first-hand information and in deference to veracity, has nothing to add about them."

As for the silence of American intellectuals, see Robert Westbrook's remarkable essay "The Responsibility of People: Dwight Macdonald and the Holocaust," in Sanford Pinsker and Jack Fischel, eds., *America and the Holocaust (Holocaust Studies Annual,* Vol. I, Greenwood, Fla.: Penkeville, 1984), pp. 35–36:

On the basis of retrospective accounts . . . one would expect to find an outpouring of critical reflection by American intellectuals on the implications of the Holocaust . . . Moreover, one would expect such reflection to be a particularly prominent feature of the work of that community that has come to be known as "the New York intellectuals" . . . a group of intellectuals, most of them Jewish, who had by the late forties begun to move to the forefront of American cultural life . . .

[But] the response of the New York intellectuals to the Holocaust was, with a few notable exceptions, slow to come, and, when it did come, it was "limited and oblique." During the war and immediate postwar years, *Partisan Review,* which had been accurately described as "the very voice and soul of the New York intelligentsia," was virtually silent about the destruction of the Jews. The other principal journal of these intellectuals in the 1940s, *Commentary,* did provide its readers with valuable documents and accounts of the Holocaust . . .

The Fall is then a book not merely about silence, but about the ways in which one silence masks another, the ways in which one concentrationary universe outlines another. The suicide scene becomes a figure for historical occasions in which silence reasserts itself, a metaphor for history as the assertion and the reassertion—as the displacement and *the repetition*—of a silence.

V

Accomplices

The narrator witnessing the suicide scene without response, in much the same way as the Marxist intellectuals accepting Stalin's labor camps and the Western Allies witnessing the genocide with a conspiracy of silence, become, in fact, historical participants, *accomplices* in the execution of the Other.

Unlike *The Plague, The Fall* revisits thus contemporary history as a story not of resistance but of complicity.

Nonetheless, although the shadow of Nazi terror hung over everything published in this magazine in its early years, few of its contributors ventured beyond a description of the horrors of the "war against the Jews" toward a direct effort to understand the meaning and implications of this war. Ten years after the end of World War II, *Commentary* reviewer, Solomon Bloom, commented on this continuing silence, noting that "the facts are incontrovertible, yet it is easier to believe that these things have happened than that they *could* have happened. The senses cry truth, but the mind hesitates, for it can see only through understanding." Not until the explosive controversy over Hannah Arendt's *Eichmann in Jerusalem* in 1963 would many New York intellectuals directly and openly confront this problem of understanding."

Cf. Irving Howe's profound retrospective explanation of this situation in *Margin of Hope,* New York: Harcourt Brace Jovanovich, 1982, pp. 248–250:

"People don't react to great cataclysms with clear thought and eloquent emotions: they blink and stumble, they retreat to old opinions, they turn away with fear . . . To be human meant to be unequipped to grapple with the Holocaust. We had no precedent in thought or experience . . . We had no metaphors that could release the work of the imagination. All efforts to understand what happened in Europe required as their premise a wrenching away from received categories of thought—but that cannot happen overnight, it isn't easy to check in your modest quantity of mental stock . . .

The beginning of moral wisdom was to acknowledge one's intellectual bewilderment, to acknowledge we were witnessing a sharp break in the line of history. And that readiness could not come easily: our minds had been formed in the pre-Holocaust era and, strong or weak, they were the only minds we had . . . The Holocaust had extended the nature and meaning of Western history, we therefore had to reconsider man's nature, possibilities, and limits within that history."

You don't understand what I mean? . . . I've lost the lucidity to which my friends used to enjoy paying respect. I say "my friends," moreover, as a convention. I have no more friends; I have nothing but accomplices. To make up for this, their number has increased; they are the whole human race. And within the human race, you first of all. [73]

What kind of narrative event can be told only from accomplice to accomplice? What kind of story is it, whose legibility becomes transmissible only within a network of complicity? If narrative in general can be defined, according to Maurice Blanchot, as "the tension of a secret around which it is elaborated, and which declares itself without thereby being elucidated, announcing only its own movement,"[14] *The Fall,* unlike *The Plague* (whose narrative consists in making testimony *public*), perceives the historical uniqueness of the Holocaust as what turns history itself (and no longer a mere individual story) into the narrative of such a secret. But if the contemporary witness has become, by definition, no longer the Socratic spokesman for the truth but on the contrary, *the bearer of the silence [Geheimnissträger]*, the *secret sharer* in a muted execution; if the very making of contemporary history is bound with the narrative movement of secrecy, then witnessing itself needs to be redefined, rethought: it no longer is the unproblematical phenomenon—the transparent mediation between seeing and telling, private experience and public testimony—that grounds *The Plague* and grants it its self-evident historical authority.

This modified perspective, in *The Fall,* on what it means to witness (or what constitutes the energy of the perception of a historical event), radically displaces, moreover, the very concept of what history is, in relation to narration. This displacement, from now on, renders impossible the very style of an account like *The Plague.* And *The Fall,* indeed, reflects on this historical narrative impossibility.

A Primal Scene

In narrating how the Fall is missed, is not experienced, and in thus dramatizing allegorically "the sharp break in the line of history,"[15] *The*

[14]*Après-Coup,* Paris: Minuit, 1983, p. 96; my translation. In general, translation from French is mine unless otherwise stated.

[15]Cf. again Irving Howe, *Margin of Hope,* op. cit., pp. 248–250: "All efforts to understand what happened in Europe required as their premise a wrenching away from received categories of thought—but that cannot happen overnight . . . The beginning of moral wisdom was to acknowledge one's intellectual bewilderment, to acknowledge we were witnessing a sharp break in the line of history. And that readiness could not come easily."

Fall narrates the way in which the still conventional ethical and political categories of *The Plague* fail to contain the Holocaust; the way in which the very eloquence of the Plague, the very legibility of Rieux's "unqualified testimony," which affords him and the reader a direct, unmediated access to events, fails precisely to account for the specificity of a disaster that consisted in a radical failure of witnessing, an event to which the witness had no access, since its very catastrophic and unprecedented nature as event was to *make the witness absent:* absent to the very presence of the event; present in, but not to, what was taking place. "I was absent," says the narrator of *The Fall,* "when I took up the most space" (88).

The Holocaust in Western history functions, thus, in much the same way as a *primal scene* functions in psychoanalysis. It is a witnessing that cannot be made present to itself, present to consciousness.

> Yet I must admit that I ceased to walk along the Paris quais. When I would ride along them in a car or bus, a sort of silence would descend on me ... But I would cross the Seine, *nothing would happen,* and I would breathe again. [42]

Whereas the narrator of *The Plague* solemnly announces, "*this is what happened,*" the narrator of *The Fall* is struggling to articulate what is behind the urgency of the assertion, "*nothing happened,*" but the question is then: What? What Happened? *The event is not a given.* In the same way, to come to grips with the historical experience of the Holocaust is to realize our inability to simply say: "This is what happened." As Dwight Macdonald put it in 1945:

> Something has happened to the Germans—to some of them, at least; something has happened to Europe—to some of it, at least. What is it?[16]

The Empty Rectangle

Something happened. What is it? The very struggle of the narrative to articulate this question which insistently resists thematization, is in turn dramatized in *The Fall* through the story of the stolen painting. "Notice," says the narrator at the very opening of the novel," ... that

---

[16]"The Responsibility of Peoples", in *Politics* 2, July 1945, pp. 203–204. See also Robert B. Westbrook, "The Responsibility of Peoples: Dwight Macdonald and the Holocaust," in Sanford Pinsker and Jack Fischel, eds., *America and the Holocaust* (*Holocaust Studies Annual I,* Greenwood, Fla.: Penkeville, 1984).

empty rectangle marking the place where a picture has been taken down" (5). The narrator thus seems to introduce his listener (and the reader) not to a picture, but to the absence of a picture. In much the same way that he will, in a minute, talk about the fact that he inhabits the vacated, emptied Jewish quarter of Amsterdam, he points to the emptied space of a visual representation that is missing.[17]

> Indeed, there *was* a picture there, and a particularly interesting one, a real masterpiece. Well, I was present when the master of the house received it and when he gave it up. [5]

The painting, incidentally, was entitled *Les Juges intègres* (*The Just Judges*). We will later learn that it had been stolen, and the narrator, at the end, confesses to his complicity in the theft:

> I always hope, in fact, that my interlocutor will be a policeman and that he will arrest me for the theft of "The Last Judges." For the rest— am I right?—no one can arrest me. But for that theft, it falls within the provisions of the law and I have arranged everything so as to make myself an accomplice; I am harboring that painting and showing it to whoever wants to see it. [145]

Obviously, the historical complicity at stake in the narrative is differ- ent from the one to which the speaker is confessing: of a graver nature, it is less tangible to legal definitions than this question of the possession of the painting. I would venture to suggest, however, that the allegory of the stolen painting, in representing, on the one hand, the usurped position of all those who, on the subject of the Holocaust, still claim to speak from a position of a moral rightness ("Juges intègres"), and in embodying within the painting, on the other hand, art's claim to thematize a possible integrity of human justice and of human judgement—this allegory of the stolen painting could refer, among its other meanings, to the very novel of *The Plague*, whose effort was to testify from the perspective of the honest witness, and whose narrative could still hope to transmit a clear *picture* of events, a visual, coherent, legible representation of the Holocaust. But *The Fall* suggests that no one can legitimately claim the ownership or the possession of such a picture: we can only contemplate its trace, acknowledge that we are living, in its absence, on its *site:* "the site of one of the greatest crimes in history." In retrospect, *The Plague,* perhaps, has fallen victim in its turn to the complicity, or the compla-

---

[17]The marking of vacancies, of empty space, is part of the novel's use of "negative landscapes": "Isn't it the most beautiful negative landscape? Just see on the left that pile of ashes they call a dune here ... Is it not universal obliteration, everlasting nothingness made visible?" (72)

cency, of its own unquestioned faith in the untainted innocence of its own justice,[18] in the *integrity* (wholeness and truthfulness) of its own testimony, in the uncompromised position, that is, of its narrator/ witness as a "juge intègre."

Guilty of Innocence

But the Holocaust has not left innocence—the witness' innocence—intact. On the site of "one of the greatest crimes in history," innocence can only mean lack of awareness of one's participation in the crime. From the perspective of *The Fall*, one can only be, thus, paradoxically enough, *guilty* of one's very *innocence.* The irony is totally disanchored: there is no longer any place of innocence from which to testify.

> We cannot assert the innocence of anyone, whereas we can state with certainty the guilt of all. Every man testifies to the crimes of all the others—that is my faith and my hope. [110]

> In philosophy as in politics, I am for any theory that refuses to grant man innocence, and for any practice that treats him as guilty. [131–132]

If innocence is an illusion, guilt is not a *state* opposed to innocence, it is a *process* of coming to awareness: a process of *awakening* which, as a process, is not theory but, as Camus here puts it, an actual *practice:* a practice, or a process, of a constantly renewed wrenching apart.

The Lawyer's Stance

No wonder, then, if the narrator of *The Fall* no longer testifies from the uncompromised position of the doctor, of the healer who rubs shoulders with the Plague and with its victims and yet miraculously somehow stays himself clear of the contamination. In demystifying

---

[18]Cf. *The Fall,* 81: "From that point of view, we are all like that little Frenchman at Buchenwald who insisted on registering a complaint with the clerk, himself a prisoner, who was recording his arrival. A complaint? The clerk and his comrades laughed: "Useless, old man. You don't lodge a complaint here." "But you see, sir," said the little Frenchman, "my case is exceptional. I am innocent." Could the little Frenchman possibly also designate Rieux?

the illusory untaintedness of the healer's testimonial stance, *The Fall* significantly chooses to bear witness from the infinitely more ambiguous position of a *lawyer.* And it is doubtless no coincidence that the lawyer, by mistake, is referred to as a doctor.

> Here is our gin at last . . . Yes, the ape [the Dutch host] opened his mouth to call me doctor. In these countries everyone is a doctor . . .
> I am not a doctor. If you want to know, I was a lawyer. [8]

Unlike the narrative of the physician, whose testimony is "the record of what had to be done" (*The Plague,* 287), the lawyer's story is the history of what failed to be done. Unlike the doctor, whose "profession put him in touch" with the raging plague and who was thus "well placed for giving a true account of all he saw and heard" (*P,* 280), the lawyer does not speak by virtue of his presence to events but by virtue, on the contrary, of his skill to mediate events through language, and thus to manipulate their plausibility. Unlike the doctor, who has "deliberately taken the victims' side" (*P,* 280), the lawyer only *represents* the victim. *The Fall,* indeed, enacts the Holocaust as a radical *failure of representation,* in both senses of the word: failure of representation in the sense of *making present* the event; failure of representation in the sense of truly *speaking for* the victim, whose voicelessness no voice can represent. This does not, of course, prevent the lawyer from "talking through his hat" (130–131).

> I had a specialty: noble cases . . . It was enough for me to sniff the slightest scent of victim on a defendant for me to swing into action. And what action! A real tornado! My heart was on my sleeve. You would have thought that justice slept with me every night.

"I was sure," continues the narrator of *The Fall*—and the alerted reader cannot but recall *The Plague*—"you would have admired the rightness of my tone, the appropriateness of my emotion, the persuasion and warmth, the restrained indignation of my speeches before the courts . . . :"

> I was buoyed up by . . . the satisfaction of being on the right side of the bar . . .
> But after all, I was on the right side; that was enough to satisfy my conscience . . .
> I ran no risk of joining the criminal camp . . . [17–19]

A lawyer can, however, by definition, plead the case of either side, *switch sides.* It is this very certainty of being "on the right side of the bar," this *total separation between crime and testimony* in which *The*

Plague was grounded and which was guaranteed by the profession of the healer, which the profession of the lawyer serves to put in question in *The Fall,* and of which the narrator can no longer recover the assurance after his unwitting, silent witness of the suicide. In the interval that separates the publication of *The Fall* (1956) from that of *The Plague* (1942, 1947), contemporary history seems to inscribe itself, by deferred action, as the breakdown of received political and ethical divisions through the possibility (of which the lawyer is a figure) of legal switch between opposed sides of the bar, as well as between various stances and positions in the courtroom. Perhaps the essence of the Holocaust was to enact this historical reversibility of conventionally opposite juridical and cultural roles, this unprecedented *permutation* between victims, executioners, accomplices, bystanders.

In any case, Camus perceives the "sharp break in the line of history" as this effective permutation of roles, which renders testimony all the more necessary even as it undercuts the self-assured integrity of any witness. "As an artist," Camus was asked in an interview published in the fifties, "have you chosen the role of the witness?" And he answered:

> One would have to be quite pretentious to do that . . .
>
> The tyrannies of today have become a great deal more perfected; they admit neither of silence nor of neutrality. One has to pronounce upon them . . .
>
> But this does not mean choosing the comfortable role of the witness . . . And don't forget, moreover, that *today the judges, the accused and the witnesses are permuted.*[19]

VI

The Witness's Fall

The narrative moment of "the fall," as the crucial turning point of the story, can be read, in that way, as an allegory of the Second World War as a turning point in history. But the question could be asked: at the moment when the narrator/witness sees the woman fall into her death by drowning, *whose fall is being told?* Is the fall narrated the fall missed, the literally missed fall of the *drowned,* or is it rather, at the same time, the fall, precisely, of the *saved?* Does the title designate, in other words, the woman's fall or the narrator's own fall? What the

---

[19]*Actuelles,* vol. II, 1948–1953 (Paris: Gallimard/Ideés), pp. 172–173.

novel in fact dramatizes is the way in which, when the woman is precisely *not seen* falling off the bridge, at the moment when her fall is being *missed,* when the body strikes the water—and when history strikes—with no seeing and no hearing, with the failure of the passer-by—of the historical bystander—to be a witness, the scene of history is symbolically and radically transformed. Physically and metaphorically, the bridge no longer is a bridge: a safe passage from one bank of the Seine to the other. A bridge, from now on, can always lead nowhere, end in a dead end, or fall apart, lead to an abyss, not only for the woman but for her witness, whose own life also loses its continuity, its sense, its ground and its balance:

I, too,—says the narrator—am drifting. [97]

I lose the thread of what I am saying. [73]

You are wrong, *cher,* the boat is going at top speed. But the Zuider Zee is a dead sea, or almost. With its flat shores, lost in the fog, *there's no saying where it begins or ends.* So we are steaming along without any landmark. [97]

Unlike *The Plague,* where there is still a bridge to the other end of History as Plague, *The Fall* narrates the Holocaust as the history of the *collapse of bridges*—from one gaze to another, from one death to another, from one life to another. "History," writes Camus in his famous essay *Neither Victims Nor Executioners,* "is in the hands of blind and deaf forces, which will heed neither cries of warning, nor advice, nor entreaties":

The years we have gone through have killed something in us. And that something is simply the old confidence man had in himself, which led him to believe that he could always elicit human reactions from another man if he spoke to him in the language of a common humanity . . .
Mankind's long dialogue has just come to an end . . . The result is that . . . a vast conspiracy of silence has spread all about us, a conspiracy accepted by those who are frightened and who rationalize their fears in order to hide them from themselves.[20]

The question for contemporary testimonial narrative is, then, how can it *bridge,* speak over, the collapse of bridges, and yet, narrate at the same time the process and event of the collapse?

[20]Camus, *Neither Victims Nor Executioners,* World Without War Publications: 1972, p. 20.

Camus by Izis.

Response-Ability

In bearing witness to the witness's inability to witness—to the narrating subject's inability to cross the bridge towards the Other's death or life—*The Fall* inscribes the Holocaust as the impossible historical narrative of an event without a witness, an event eliminating its own witness. Narrative has thus become the very writing of the

200

impossibility of writing history. "Narrative," Maurice Blanchot writes elliptically, "from before Auschwitz" [récit d'avant Auschwitz]:

> At whatever date it might have been written, each narrative henceforth will be from before Auschwitz.[21]

I would suggest, now, that the cryptic forms of modern narrative and modern art always—whether consciously or not—partake of that historical impossibility of writing a historical narration of the Holocaust, by bearing testimony, through their very cryptic form, to the *radical historical crisis in witnessing* the Holocaust has opened up.

This is why contemporary narrative—the narrative of that which, in the Holocaust, cannot be witnessed—has by necessity inaugurated a contemporary Age of Testimony, and why the *age of testimony* has also turned out to be, paradoxically enough, the somewhat unique *age of historical prooflessness:* the age of the professional denial, by "revisionist" historians, of the very *evidence* of the historical existence of the Holocaust. "I have analyzed thousands of documents," declares for instance Robert Faurisson. "I have tirelessly pursued specialists and historians with my questions. I have tried in vain to find a single former deportee capable of proving to me that he had really seen, with his own eyes, a gas chamber."[22]

"Suppose," retorts the philosopher François Lyotard, "that an earthquake destroys not only lives, buildings, and objects but also instruments used to measure earthquakes . . .":

> The scholar says he knows nothing about it; . . . Mutatis mutandis, the silence that the crime of Auschwitz imposes on the historian is a sign for the common person. Signs are not referents to which are attached significations validatable under the cognitive regimen; they

---

[21]Maurice Blanchot, *Après-Coup*, Paris, Minuit: 1983. In his essay "Blanchot at *Combat:* Of Literature and Terror", in *Legacies of Anti-Semitism in France* (Minneapolis: University of Minnesota Press, 1983), pp. 6–22, Jeffrey Mehlman insists on the pro-rightist, pro-terrorist, pro-fascist sympathies of Blanchot in his political essays in *Combat* in the 1930's, and suggests that, as of 1942, Blanchot's stance as a literary theorist and the particular characterizations of his view of literature in fact evolve from an abdication of his political views and from "Blanchot's own liquidation of an anti-Semitic past" (p. 16). Although I do not subscribe to Mehlman's analysis, which I find exaggerated and distorting, the possibility of its correctness would not undercut, for me, Blanchot's authority as one of the preeminent literary theorists of our time, since the crucial insight of contemporary literature—insofar as it reflects on contemporary history—seems to me to be in any case inherently tied up (as in *The Fall*) with this second-stage perception of the self-subversive story of a radical—and inescapable—*complicity.*

[22]Robert Faurisson, in *Le Monde,* Jan. 16, 1979. Cited in Pierre Vidal-Naquet, "A Paper Eichmann," translated by Maris Jolas, in *Democracy,* vol. 1, no. 2, 1981, p. 81.

indicate that something that should be able to be put into phrases cannot be phrased in the accepted idioms . . .

With Auschwitz, something new has happened in history, which is a sign and not a fact . . . *Phrases are in abeyance of their becoming event.* But the historian must then break with the monopoly over history granted to the cognitive regimen of phrases, and he must venture forth by lending his ear to *what is not presentable under the rules of knowledge.* Auschwitz is the most real of realities in this respect. Its name marks the confines wherein historical knowledge sees its competence impunged.[23]

What Camus does in *The Fall* is to make, precisely, of the *silence* both of the historian and of history a *sign,* by placing the impossibility of history (of witnessing) as itself a *figure* in a larger literary, dialogic (testimonial) context, and by deflecting, thus, the inherent muteness of the narrative *outside,* toward the present/future referentiality of the Other, of the reader.

Mon cher compatriote! Search your memory and perhaps you will find some similar story that you'll tell me later on. [65]

But of course you are not a policeman; that would be too easy. What? . . . In Paris you practice the noble profession of lawyer! I sensed that we were of the same species. Are we not all alike, constantly talking and to no one, forever up against the same questions . . . ? Then please tell me what happened to you one night on the quays of the Seine and how you managed never to risk your life. You yourself utter the words that for years have never ceased echoing through my nights, and that I shall at last say through my mouth: "O young woman, throw yourself into the water again so that I may a second time have the chance of saving both of us!" A second time, eh, what a risky suggestion! Just suppose, *cher maître,* that we should be taken literally? We'd have to go through with it. Brr . . . ! The water's so cold! But let's not worry. It's too late now. It will always be too late. Fortunately! [147]

"It's too late now": it's history. In the Holocaust, the Other—as a witness—did not answer. But in deflecting the position of the Other toward ourselves; in deflecting the *too lateness* and the *answerlessness,* the impossibility of narrating history as Holocaust, toward the future of our own reality; in urging us not just to listen to, but to articulate the very inarticulateness of the narrative, to *be* the story and to repeat its unrepeatability; in performatively passing on to us

---

[23]François Lyotard, "The Différend," in *Diacritics,* Vol. 14, no. 13, Fall 1984, last page.

a dialogical historical responsibility, including the responsibility for history as silence and for the rather noisy silence of the revisionist historian, Camus succeeds in giving to the very silence of a generation—and to very voicelessness of history—the power of a *call:*[24] the possibility, the chance, of our *response-ability*.

[24]"From the evening that I was called—for I was really called—I had to answer or at least to seek an answer" (84). Cf. p. 108: "Then I realized, calmly as you resign yourself to an idea the truth of which you have long known, that that cry which had sounded over the Seine behind me years before had never ceased, carried by the river to the waters of the Channel, to travel throughout the world, across the limitless expanse of the ocean, and that it had waited for me there until the day I had encountered it."

SEVEN
The Return of the Voice:
Claude Lanzmann's Shoah

SHOSHANA FELMAN

I

History and Witness, or the Story of an Oath

"If someone else could have written my stories," writes Elie Wiesel, "I would not have written them. I have written them in order to testify. My role is the role of the witness . . . Not to tell, or to tell another story, is . . . to commit perjury."[1]

To bear witness is to take responsibility for truth: to speak, implicitly, from within the legal pledge and the juridical imperative of the witness's oath.[2] To testify—before a court of law or before the court of history and of the future; to testify, likewise, before an audience of readers or spectators—is more than simply to report a fact or an event or to relate what has been lived, recorded and remembered. Memory is conjured here essentially in order to *address* another, to impress upon a listener, to *appeal* to a community. To testify is always, metaphorically, to take the witness stand, or to take the position of the witness insofar as the narrative account of the witness is at once engaged in an appeal and bound by an oath. To testify is thus not merely to narrate but to commit oneself, and to commit the narrative, to others: to *take responsibility*—in speech—for history or for the truth of an occurrence, for something which, by definition, goes beyond the personal, in having general (nonpersonal) validity and consequences.

But if the essence of the testimony is impersonal (to enable a

---

[1] "The Loneliness of God," published in the journal *Dvar Hashavu'a* (magazine of the newspaper *Davar*), Tel-Aviv, 1984. My translation from the Hebrew.

[2] "To tell the truth, the whole truth, and nothing but the truth"; an oath, however, which is always, by its very nature, susceptible to perjury.

decision by a judge or jury—metaphorical or literal—about the true nature of the facts of an occurrence; to enable an objective reconstruction of what history was like, irrespective of the witness), why is it that the witness's speech is so uniquely, literally irreplaceable? "If someone else could have written my stories, I would not have written them." What does it mean that the testimony cannot be simply reported, or narrated by another in its role as testimony? What does it mean that a story—or a history—cannot be told by someone else?

It is this question, I would suggest, that guides the groundbreaking work of Claude Lanzmann in his film *Shoah* (1985), and constitutes at once the profound subject and the shocking power of originality of the film.

A Vision of Reality

Shoah is a film made exclusively of testimonies: first-hand testimonies of participants in the historical experience of the Holocaust, interviewed and filmed by Lanzmann during the eleven years which preceded the production of the film (1974–1985). In effect, *Shoah* revives the Holocaust with such a power (a power that no previous film on the subject could attain) that it radically displaces and shakes up not only any common notion we might have entertained about it, but our very vision of reality as such, our very sense of what the world, culture, history and our life within it are all about.

But the film is not simply, nor is it primarily, a historical document on the Holocaust. That is why, in contrast to its cinematic predecessors on the subject, it refuses systematically to use any historical, archival footage. It conducts its interviews, and takes its pictures, in the present. Rather than a simple view about the past, the film offers a disorienting vision of the present, a compellingly profound and surprising insight into the complexity of the *relation between history and witnessing.*

It is a film about witnessing: about the witnessing of a catastrophe. What is testified to is limit-experiences whose overwhelming impact constantly puts to the test the limits of the witness and of witnessing, at the same time that it constantly unsettles and puts into question the very limits of reality.

Art as Witness

Second, *Shoah* is a film about the *relation between art and witnessing*, about film as a medium which *expands* the capacity for witnessing. To understand *Shoah*, we must explore the question: what are *we* as spectators made to witness? This expansion of what we in turn can witness is, however, due not simply to the reproduction of events, but to the power of the film as a work of art, to the subtlety of its philosophical and artistic structure and to the complexity of the creative process it engages. "The truth kills the possibility of fiction," said Lanzmann in a journalistic interview.[3] But the truth does not kill the possibility of art—on the contrary, it requires it for its transmission, for its realization in our consciousness as witnesses.

Finally, *Shoah* embodies the capacity of art not simply to witness, but to *take the witness stand*: the film takes responsibility for its times by enacting the significance of our era as an *age of testimony*, an age in which witnessing itself has undergone a major trauma. *Shoah* gives us to witness a *historical crisis of witnessing*, and shows us how, out of this crisis, witnessing becomes, in all the senses of the word, a *critical* activity.

On all these different levels, Claude Lanzmann persistently asks the same relentless question: what does it mean to be a witness? What does it mean to be a witness to the Holocaust? What does it mean to be a witness to the process of the film? What does testimony mean, if it is not simply (as we commonly perceive it) the observing, the recording, the remembering of an event, but an utterly unique and irreplaceable topographical *position* with respect to an occurrence? What does testimony mean, if it is the uniqueness of the *performance of a story* which is constituted by the fact that, like the oath, it cannot be carried out by anybody else?

The Western Law of Evidence

The uniqueness of the narrative performance of the testimony in effect proceeds from the witness's irreplaceable performance of the act of seeing—from the uniqueness of the witness's "seeing with his/her own eyes." "Mr. Vitold," says the Jewish Bund leader to the Polish Courrier Jan Karski, who reports it in his cinematic testimony thirty-five years later, in narrating how the Jewish leader urged him—and persuaded him—to become a crucial visual witness: "I know the Western world. You will be speaking to the English ... It will

---

[3]*The Record*, Oct. 25, 1985; an interview with Deborah Jerome ("Resurrecting Horror: The Man behind *Shoah*").

strengthen your report if you will be able to say: *'I saw it myself* " (p. 171).[4]

In the legal, philosophical and epistemological tradition of the Western world, witnessing is based on, and is formally defined by, first-hand seeing. "Eyewitness testimony" is what constitutes the most decisive law of evidence in courtrooms. "Lawyers have innumerable rules involving hearsay, the character of the defendant or of the witness, opinions given by the witness, and the like, which are in one way or another meant to improve the fact-finding process. But more crucial than any one of these—and possibly more crucial than all put together—is the evidence of eyewitness testimony."[5]

Film, on the other hand, is the art par excellence which, like the courtroom (although for different purposes), calls upon a *witnessing* by *seeing*. How does the film use its visual medium to reflect upon eyewitness testimony, both as the law of evidence of its own art and as the law of evidence of history?

Victims, Perpetrators, and Bystanders: About Seeing

Because the testimony is unique and irreplaceable, the film is an exploration of the *differences* between heterogeneous points of view, between testimonial stances which can neither be assimilated into, not subsumed by, one another. There is, first of all, the difference of perspective between three groups of witnesses, or three series of interviewees: the real characters of history who, in response to Lanzmann's inquiry, play their own role as the singularly real actors of the movie, fall into three basic categories[6]: those who witnessed the disaster as its *victims* (the surviving Jews); those who witnessed the disaster as its *perpetrators* (the ex-Nazis); those who witnessed the disaster as *bystanders* (the Poles). What is at stake in this division is not simply a diversity of points of view or of degrees of implication and emotional involvement, but the *incommensurability* of different topographical and cognitive positions, between which the discrep-

---

[4]*Shoah*, the complete text of the film by Claude Lanzmann, New York, Pantheon Books, 1985. Quotations from the text of the film will refer to this edition, and will be indicated henceforth only by page number (in the parenthesis following the citation).

[5]John Kaplan, Foreword to Elizabeth F. Loftus, *Eyewitness Testimony*, Cambridge, Mass.: Harvard University Press, 1979, p. vii.

[6]Categories which Lanzmann borrows from Hilberg's historical analysis, but which the film strikingly *embodies* and rethinks. Cf. Raul Hilberg, *The Destruction of the European Jews*, New York: Holmes and Meier, 1985.

ancy cannot be breached. More concretely, what the categories in the film give to see is *three different performances of the act of seeing.*

In effect, the victims, the bystanders and the perpetrators are here differentiated not so much by what they actually see (what they all see, although discontinuous, does in fact follow a logic of corroboration), as by what and how they *do not see,* by what and how they *fail to witness.* The Jews see, but they do not understand the purpose and the destination of what they see: overwhelmed by loss and by deception, they are blind to the significance of what they witness. Richard Glazar strikingly narrates a moment of perception coupled with incomprehension, an exemplary moment in which the Jews fail to read, or to decipher, the visual signs and the visible significance they nonetheless see with their own eyes:

> Then very slowly, the train turned off of the main track and rolled . . . through a wood. While he looked out—we'd been able to open a window—the old man in our compartment saw a boy . . . and he asked the boy in signs, "Where are we?" And the kid made a funny gesture. This: (draws a finger across his throat) . . .
> *And one of you questioned him?*
> Not in words, but in signs, we asked: "what's going on here?" And he made that gesture. Like this. We didn't really pay much attention to him. We couldn't figure out what he meant. [34]

The Poles, unlike the Jews, *do* see but, as bystanders, they do not quite *look,* they avoid looking directly, and thus they *overlook* at once their responsibility and their complicity as witnesses:

> You couldn't look there. You couldn't talk to a Jew. Even going by on the road, you couldn't look there.
> *Did they look anyway?*
> Yes, vans came and the Jews were moved farther off. You could see them, but on the sly. In sidelong glances. [97–98]

The Nazis, on the other hand, see to it that both the Jews and the extermination will remain unseen, invisible: the death camps are surrounded, for that purpose, with a screen of trees. Franz Suchomel, an ex-guard of Treblinka, testifies:

> Woven into the barbed wire were branches of pine trees . . . It was known as "camouflage" . . . So everything was screened. People couldn't see anything to the left or right. Nothing. You couldn't see through it. Impossible. [110]

It is not a coincidence that as this testimony is unfolding, it is hard for us as viewers of the film to see the witness, who is filmed secretly:

Polish peasants from Treblinka

as is the case for most of the ex-Nazis, Franz Suchomel agreed to answer Lanzmann's questions, but not to be filmed; he agreed, in other words, to give a testimony, but on the condition that, as witness, *he* should not be seen:

> *Mr. Suchomel, we're not discussing you, only Treblinka. You are a very important eyewitness, and you can explain what Treblinka was.*
> But don't use my name.
> *No, I promised . . .* [54]

In the blurry images of faces taken by a secret camera that has to shoot through a variety of walls and screens, the film makes us see concretely, by the compromise it unavoidably inflicts upon *our* act of seeing (which, of necessity, becomes materially an act of *seeing through*), how the Holocaust was an historical assault on seeing and how, even today, the perpetrators are still by and large invisible: "Everything was screened. You couldn't see anything to the left or right. You couldn't see through it".

Figuren

The essence of the Nazi scheme is to make itself—and to make the Jews—essentially invisible. To make the Jews invisible not merely by killing them, not merely by confining them to "camouflaged," invisible

209

death camps, but by reducing even the materiality of the dead bodies to smoke and ashes, and by reducing, furthermore, the radical opacity of the *sight* of the dead bodies, as well as the linguistic referentiality and literality of the *word* "corpse," to the transparency of a pure form and to the pure rhetorical metaphoricity of a mere *figure*: a disembodied verbal substitute which signifies abstractly the linguistic law of infinite exchangeability and substitutability. The dead bodies are thus verbally rendered invisible, and voided both of substance and specificity, by being treated, in the Nazi jargon, as *figuren*: that which, all at once, *cannot be seen* and can be *seen through.*

> The Germans even forbade us to use the words "corpse" or "victim." The dead were blocks of wood, shit. The Germans made us refer to the bodies as *figuren*, that is, as puppets, as dolls, or as *Schmattes*, which means "rags."[13]

But it is not only the dead bodies of the Jews which the Nazis, paradoxically, do not "see." It is also, in some striking cases, the living Jews transported to their death that remain invisible to the chief architects of their final transportation. Walter Stier, head of Reich Railways Department 33 of the Nazi party, chief traffic planner of the death trains ("special trains," in Nazi euphemism), testifies:

> *But you knew that the trains to Treblinka or Auschwitz were—*
> Of course we knew. I was the last district. Without me the trains couldn't reach their destination . . .
> *Did you know that Treblinka meant extermination?*
> Of course not . . . How could we know? I never went to Treblinka. [135]
>
> . . . .
> *You never saw a train?*
> No, never . . . I never left my desk. We worked day and night. [132]

In the same way, Mrs. Michelshon, wife of a Nazi schoolteacher in Chelmno, answers Lanmann's questions:

> *Did you see the gas vans?*
> No . . . Yes, from the outside. They shuttled back and forth. I never looked inside; I didn't see Jews in them. I only saw things from outside. [82]

The Occurrence as Unwitnessed

Thus, the diversity of the testimonial stances of the victims, the bystanders and the perpetrators have in common, paradoxically, the incommensurability of their different and particular positions of not seeing, the radical divergence of their topographical, emotional and epistemological positions not simply as witnesses, but as witnesses who *do not witness,* who let the Holocaust occur as an event essentially unwitnessed. Through the testimonies of its visual witnesses the film makes us *see* concretely—makes us *witness*—how the Holocaust occurs as the unprecedented, inconceivable historical advent of *an event without a witness,*[7] an event which historically consists in the scheme of the literal *erasure of its witnesses* but which, moreover, philosophically consists in an accidenting of perception, in a *splitting of eyewitnessing* as such; an event, thus, not empirically, but cognitively and perceptually without a witness both because it precludes seeing and because it precludes the possibility of a *community of seeing*: an event which radically annihilates the recourse (the appeal) to visual corroboration (to the commensurability between two different seeings) and thus dissolves the possibility of any *community of witnessing.*

Shoah enables us to see—and gives us insight into—the occurrence of the Holocaust as an absolute historical event whose literally *overwhelming evidence* makes it, paradoxically, into an *utterly proofless event*: the age of testimony is the age of prooflessness, the age of an event whose magnitude of reference is at once below and beyond proof.

The Multiplicity of Languages

The incommensurability between different testimonial stances, and the heterogeneous multiplicity of specific cognitive positions of seeing and not seeing, is amplified and duplicated in the film by the multiplicity of languages in which the testimonies are delivered (French, German, Sicilian, English, Hebrew, Yiddish, Polish), a multiplicity which necessarily encompasses some foreign tongues and which necessitates the presence of a professional translator as an intermediary between the witnesses and Lanzmann as their interviewer. The technique of dubbing is not used, and the character of the translator is deliberately not edited out of the film—on the contrary, she is quite often present on the screen, at the side of Lanzmann, as another one of the real actors of the film, because the process of translation is itself an integral part of the process of the film, partaking both of

[7]See Chapter 3, II, "An Event Without a Witness."

its scenario and of its own performance of *its* cinematic testimony. Through the multiplicity of foreign tongues and the prolonged *delay* incurred by the translation, the splitting of eyewitnessing which the historical event seems to consist of, the incapacity of seeing to translate itself spontaneously and simultaneously into a meaning, is recapitulated on the level of the viewers of the film. The film places us in the position of the witness who *sees* and *hears*, but *cannot understand* the significance of what is going on until the later intervention, the delayed processing and rendering of the significance of the visual/acoustic information by the translator, who also in some ways distorts and screens it, because (as is attested by those viewers who are native-speakers of the foreign tongues which the translator is translating, and as the film itself points out by some of Lanzmann's interventions and corrections), the translation is not always absolutely accurate.

The palpable foreignness of the film's tongues is emblematic of the radical foreignness of the experience of the Holocaust, not merely to us, but even to its own participants. Asked whether he has invited the participants to see the film, Lanzmann answered in the negative: "In what language would the participants have seen the film?" The original was a French print: "They don't speak French."[8] French, the native language of the filmmaker, the common denominator into which the testimonies (and the original subtitles) are translated and in which the film is thought out and gives, in turn, its own testimony happens (not by chance, I would suggest) not to be the language of any of the witnesses. It is a metaphor of the film that its language is a language of translation, and, as such, is doubly foreign: that the occurrence, on the one hand, happens in a language foreign to the language of the film, but also, that the significance of the occurrence can only be articulated in a language foreign to the language(s) of the occurrence.

The title of the film is, however, not in French and embodies thus, once more, a linguistic strangeness, an estrangement, whose significance is enigmatic and whose meaning cannot be immediately accessible even to the native audience of the original French print: *Shoah*, the Hebrew word which, with the definite article (here missing), designates "The Holocaust" but which, without the article, enigmatically and indefinitely means "catastrophe," here names the very foreignness of languages, the very namelessness of a catastrophe which cannot be possessed by any native tongue and which, within the language of

---

[8]Interview given by Lanzmann on the occasion of his visit to Yale University, and filmed at the Fortunoff Video Archive for Holocaust Testimonies at Yale (interviewers: Dr. Dori Laub and Laurel Vlock) on May 5 1986. Hereafter, citations from this videotape will be referred to by the abbreviation *Interview*.

translation, can only be named as the *untranslatable*: that which language cannot witness; that which cannot be articulated in *one* language; that which language, in its turn, cannot witness without *splitting*.

The Historian as a Witness

The task of the deciphering of signs and of the processing of intelligibility—what might be called *the task of the translator*[9]—is, however, carried out within the film not merely by the character of the professional interpreter, but also by two other real actors—the historian (Raul Hilberg) and the filmmaker (Claude Lanzmann)—who, like the witnesses, in turn *play themselves* and who, unlike the witnesses and like the translator, constitute *second-degree witnesses* (witnesses of witnesses, witnesses of the testimonies). Like the professional interpreter, although in very different ways, the filmmaker in the film and the historian on the screen are in turn catalysts—or agents—of the process of *reception*, agents whose reflective witnessing and whose testimonial stances aid our own reception and assist us both in the effort toward comprehension and in the unending struggle with the foreignness of signs, in processing not merely (as does the professional interpreter) the literal meaning of the testimonies, but also, (some perspectives on) their philosophical and historical significance.

The historian is, thus, in the film, neither the last word of knowledge nor the ultimate authority on history, but rather, one more topographical and cognitive position of *yet another witness*. The statement of the filmmaker—and the testimony of the film—are by no means *subsumed* by the statements (or the testimony) of the historian. Though the filmmaker does embrace the historical insights of Hilberg, which he obviously holds in utter respect and from which he gets both inspiration and instruction, the film also places in perspective—and puts in context—the discipline of history as such, in stumbling on (and giving us to see) the very limits of historiography. "*Shoah*," said Claude Lanzmann at Yale, "is certainly not a historical film . . . The purpose of *Shoah* is not to transmit knowledge, in spite of the fact that there is knowledge in the film . . . Hilberg's book *The Destruction of the European Jews* was really my Bible for many years . . . But in spite of this, *Shoah* is not a historical film, it is something else . . . To condense

---

[9]See Walter Benjamin, "The Task of the Translator," in *Illuminations*, trans. Harry Zohn, ed. Hannah Arendt (New York: Schocken Books, 1969), pp. 69–82.

in one word what the film is for me, I would say that the film is an *incarnation,* a *resurrection,* and that the whole process of the film is a philosophical one."[10] Hilberg is the spokesman for a unique and impressive knowledge on the Holocaust. Knowledge is shown by the film to be absolutely necessary in the ongoing struggle to resist the blinding impact of the event, to counteract the splitting of eyewitnessing. But knowledge is not, in and of itself, a sufficiently active and sufficiently effective act of seeing. The newness of the film's vision, on the other hand, consists precisely in the surprising insight it conveys into the radical ignorance in which we are unknowingly all plunged with respect to the actual historical occurrence. This ignorance is not simply dispelled by history—on the contrary, it *encompasses* history as such. The film shows how history is used for the purpose of a historical (ongoing)*process of forgetting* which, ironically enough, *includes* the gestures of historiography. Historiography is as much the product of the passion of forgetting as it is the product of the passion of remembering.

Walter Stier, former head of Reich railways and chief planner of the transports of the Jews to death camps, can thus testify:

> *What was Treblinka for you? . . . A destination?*
> Yes, that's all.
> *But not death.*
> No, no . . .
> *Extermination came to you as a big surprise?*
> Completely . . .
> *You had no idea.*
> Not the slightest. Like that camp—what was its name? It was in the Oppeln district . . . I've got it: Auschwitz.
> *Yes, Auschwitz was in the Oppeln district . . . Auschwitz to Krakow is forty miles.*
> That's not very far. And we knew nothing. Not a clue.
> *But you knew that the Nazis—that Hitler didn't like the Jews?*
> That we did. It was well known . . . But as to their extermination, that was news to us. I mean, even today people deny it. They say there couldn't have been so many Jews. Is it true? I don't know. That's what they say. [136–138]

To substantiate his own amnesia (of the name of Auschwitz) and his own claim of essentially *not knowing,* Stier implicitly refers here to the *claim of knowledge*—the historical authority—of "revisionist

---

[10]"An Evening with Claude Lanzmann," May 4 1986; first part of Lanzmann's visit to Yale, videotaped and copyrighted by Yale University. Transcript of the first videotape (hereafter referred to as *Evening*), p. 2.

historiographies," recent works published in a variety of countries by historians who prefer to argue that the *number* of the dead cannot be *proven* and that, since there is no scientific, scholarly hard evidence of the *exact extent* of the mass murder, the genocide is merely an invention, an exaggeration of the Jews and the Holocaust, in fact, never existed.[11] "But as to their extermination, that was news to us. I mean, even today, people deny it. They say there could not have been so many Jews. Is it true? I don't know. That's what they say." I am not the one who knows, but there are those who know who say that what I did not know did not exist. "Is it true? I don't know."

Dr. Franz Grassler, on the other hand (formerly Nazi commissioner of the Warsaw Ghetto), comes himself to mimic, in front of the camera, the very gesture of historiography as an alibi to *his* forgetting.

> *You don't remember those days?*
> Not much . . . It's a fact: we tend to forget, thank God, the bad times
> . . .
> *I'll help you to remember. In Warsaw you were Dr. Auerswald's deputy.*
> Yes . . .
> *Dr, Grassler, this is Czerniakow's diary. You're mentioned in it.*
> It's been printed. It exists?
> *He kept a diary that was recently published. He wrote on July 7, 1941*
> . . .
> July 7, 1941? That's the first time I've relearned a date. May I take notes? After all, it interests me too. So in July I was already there! [175–176]

In line with the denial of responsibility and memory, the very gesture of historiography comes to embody nothing other than the blankness of the page on which the "notes" are taken.

The next section of the film focuses on the historian Hilberg holding, and discussing, Czerniakow's diary. The cinematic editing that follows shifts back and forth, in a sort of shuttle movement, between the face of Grassler (which continues to articulate his own view of the ghetto) and the face of Hilberg (which continues to articulate the content of

[11]For instance, the Frenchman Robert Faurisson wrote: "I have analyzed thousands of documents. I have tirelessly pursued specialists and historians with my questions. I have tried in vain to find a single former deportee capable of proving to me that he had really seen, with his own eyes, a gas chamber" (*Le Monde, Jan. 16 1979*). We have "a selective view of history," comments Bill Moyers. "We live within a mythology of benign and benevolent experience . . . It is hard to believe that there exist about a hundred books all devoted to teach the idea that the Holocaust was a fiction, that it did not happen, that it had been made up by Jews for a lot of diverse reasons." Interview with Margot Strom, in *Facing History and Ourselves*, Fall 1986, pp. 6 and 7.

the diary and the perspective that the author of the diary—Czernia-kow—gives of the ghetto). The Nazi commissioner of the ghetto is thus confronted structurally, not so much with the counter-statement of the historian, but with the first-hand witness of the (now dead) author of the diary, the Jewish leader of the ghetto whom the ineluctability of the ghetto's destiny, led to end his leadership—and sign his diary—with suicide.

The main role of the historian is, thus, less to narrate history than to *reverse the suicide*, to take part in a cinematic vision which Lanzmann has defined as crucially an "incarnation" and a "resurrection." "I have taken a historian," Lanzmann enigmatically remarked, "so that he will incarnate a dead man, even though I had someone alive who had been a director of the ghetto."[12] The historian is there to embody, to give flesh and blood to, the dead author of the diary. Unlike the Christian resurrection, though, the vision of the film is to make Czerniakow *come alive precisely as a dead man.* His "resurrection" does not cancel out his death. The vision of the film is at once to make the dead writer come alive as a historian, and to make, in turn, history and the historian come alive in the uniqueness of the living voice of a dead man, and in the silence of his suicide.

The Filmmaker as a Witness

At the side of the historian, *Shoah* finally includes among its list of characters (its list of witnesses) the very figure of the filmmaker in the process of the making—or of the creation—of the film. Traveling between the living and the dead and moving to and fro between the different places and the different voices in the film, the filmmaker is continuously—though discretely—present in the margin of the screen, perhaps as the most silently articulate and as the most articulately silent witness. The creator of the film speaks and testifies, however, in his own voice, in his triple role as the *narrator* of the film (and the signatory—the first person—of the script), as the *interviewer* of the witnesses (the solicitor and the receiver of the testimonies), and as the *inquirer* (the artist as the subject of a quest concerning what the testimonies testify to; the figure of the witness as a questioner, and of the asker not merely as the factual investigator but as the bearer of the film's philosophical address and inquiry).

[12]Statement made in a private conversation in Paris, Jan. 18, 1987: *"J'ai pris un historian pour qu'il incarne un mort, alors que j'avais un vivant qui était directeur du ghetto."*

The three roles of the filmmaker intermix and in effect exist only in their relation to each other. Since the narrator is, as such, strictly a witness, his story is restricted to the story of the interviewing: the narrative consists of what the interviewer hears. Lanzmann's rigor as narrator is precisely to speak strictly as an interviewer (and as an inquirer), to abstain, that is, from narrating anything directly in his own voice, except for the beginning—the only moment which refers explicitly the film to the first person of the filmmaker as narrator:

> The story begins in the present at Chelmno . . . Chelmno was the place in Poland where Jews were first exterminated by gas . . . Of the four hundred thousand men, women and children who went there, only two came out alive . . . Srebnik, survivor of the last period, was a boy of thirteen when he was sent to Chelmno . . . I found him in Israel and persuaded that one-time boy singer to return with me to Chelmno [3–4]

The opening, narrated in the filmmaker's own voice, at once situates the story in the present and sums up a past which is presented not yet as the story but rather as a pre-history, or a pre-story: the story proper is contemporaneous with the film's speech, which begins, in fact, subsequent to the narrator's written preface, by the actual song of Srebnik resung (reenacted) in the present. The narrator is the "I" who "found" Srebnik and "persuaded" him to "return with me to Chelmno." The narrator, therefore, is the one who *opens*, or reopens, the story of the past in the present of the telling: But the "I" of the narrator, of the signatory of the film, has no voice: the opening is projected on the screen as the silent text of a mute script, as the narrative voice-over of a *writing* with no voice.

On the one hand, then, the narrator has no voice. On the other hand, the continuity of the narrative is insured by nothing other than by Lanzmann's voice, which runs through the film and whose sound constitutes the continuous, connective thread between the different voices and the different testimonial episodes. But Lanzmann's voice— the active voice in which we hear the filmmaker speak—is strictly, once again, the voice of the inquirer and of the interviewer, not of the narrator. As narrator, Lanzmann does not speak but rather, vocally recites the words of others, *lends his voice* (in two occasions) to read aloud two written documents whose authors cannot speak in their own voice: the letter of the Rabbi of Grabow, warning the Jews of Lodz of the extermination taking place at Chelmno, a letter whose signatory was himself consequently gassed at Chelmno with his whole community ("Do not think"—Lanzmann recites—"that this is written by a madman. Alas, it is the horrible, tragic truth", 83–84), and the Nazi document entitled "Secret Reich Business" and concerning technical improvements of the gas vans ("Changes to special vehicles . . . shown by use and experience to be necessary"; 103–105), an extraordinary document which might be said to formalize Nazism as such (the way in which the most perverse and most concrete extermination is abstracted into a pure question of technique and function). We witness Lanzmann's voice modulating evenly—with no emotion and no comment—the perverse diction of this document punctuated by the unintentional, coincidental irony embodied by the signatory's name: "Signed: Just".

Besides this recitation of the written documents, and besides his own mute reference to his own voice in the written cinematic preface of the silent opening, Lanzmann speaks as interviewer and as an inquirer, but as narrator, he keeps silent. The narrator lets the narrative be carried on by others—by the live voices of the various witnesses he interviews, whose stories must be able to *speak for themselves*, if they are to testify, that is, to perform their unique and irreplaceable first-hand witness. It is only in this way, by this abstinence of the narrator, that the film can in fact be a narrative of testimony: a narrative of that, precisely, which can neither be reported, nor narrated, by another. The narrative is thus essentially a narrative of silence, the story of the filmmaker's *listening*: the narrator is the teller of the film only insofar as he is the bearer of the film's silence.

In his other roles, however, that of the interviewer and of the inquirer, the filmmaker, on the contrary, is by definition a transgressor, and a breaker, of the silence. Of his own transgression of the silence, the interviewer says to the interviewee whose voice cannot be given up and whose silence must be broken: "I know it's very hard. I know and I apologize" (117).

As an interviewer, Lanzmann asks not for great explanations of the Holocaust, but for concrete descriptions of minute particular details and of apparently trivial specifics.[13] "Was the weather very cold?" (11). "From the station to the unloading ramp in the camp is how many miles? . . . How long did the trip last?" (33). "Exactly where did the camp begin?" (34). "It was the silence that tipped them off? . . . Can

---

[13]In this respect, the filmmaker shares the approach of the historian Hilberg: "In all my work," says Hilberg, "I have never begun by asking the big questions, because I was always afraid that I would come up with small answers; and I have preferred to address these things which are minutiae or details in order that I might then be able to put together in a gestalt a picture which, if not an explanation, is at least a description, a more full description, of what transpired" (70).

he describe that silence?" (67). "What were the [gas] vans like? . . . What color?" (80). It is not the big generalizations but the concrete particulars which translate into a vision and thus help both to dispel the blinding impact of the event and to transgress the silence to which the splitting of eyewitnessing reduced the witness. It is only through the trivia, by small steps—and not by huge strides or big leaps—that the barrier of silence can be in effect displaced, and somewhat lifted. The pointed and specific questioning resists, above all, any possible canonization of the experience of the Holocaust. Insofar as the interviewer challenges at once the sacredness (the unspeakability) of death and the sacredness of the deadness (of the silence) of the witness, Lanzmann's questions are essentially desacralizing.

> *How did it happen when the women came into the gas chamber? . . . What did you feel the first time you saw all these naked women?*
>
> . . . .
>
> *But I asked and you didn't answer: What was your impression the first time you saw these naked women arriving with children? How did you feel?*
>
> I tell you something. To have a feeling about that . . . it was very hard to feel anything, because working there day and night between dead people, between bodies, your feeling disappeared, you were dead. You had no feeling at all. [114–116]

Shoah is the story of the liberation of the testimony through its desacralization; the story of the decanonization of the Holocaust for the sake of its previously impossible historicization. What the interviewer above all avoids is an alliance with the silence of the witness, the kind of emphatic and benevolent alliance through which interviewer and interviewee often implicitly concur, and work together, for the mutual comfort of an avoidance of the truth.

It is the silence of the witness's death which Lanzmann must historically here challenge, in order to revive the Holocaust and to rewrite the *event-without-a-witness* into witnessing, and into history. It is the silence of the witness's death, and of the witness's deadness, which precisely must be broken, and transgressed.

> *We have to do it. You know it.*
> I won't be able to do it.
> *You have to do it. I know it's very hard. I know and I apologize.*
> Don't make me go on please.
> *Please. We must go on.* [117]

What does *going on* mean? The predicament of having to continue to bear witness at all costs parallels, for Abraham Bomba, the predicament faced in the past of having to continue to *live on*, to survive in spite of the gas chambers, in the face of the surrounding death. But to have to *go on* now, to have to keep on bearing witness, is more than simply to be faced with the imperative to replicate the past and thus to replicate his own *survival.* Lanzmann paradoxically now urges Bomba to break out of the very deadness that enabled the survival. The narrator calls the witness to come back from the mere mode of surviving into that of living—and of living pain. If the interviewer's role is thus to break the silence, the narrator's role is to insure that the story (be it that of silence) will go on.

But it is the inquirer whose philosophical interrogation and interpellation constantly reopen what might otherwise be seen as the story's closure.

> *Mrs. Pietyra, you live in Auschwitz?*
> Yes, I was born there . . .
> *Were there Jews in Auschwitz before the war?*
> They made up eighty percent of the population. They even had a synagogue here . . .
> *Was there a Jewish cemetery in Auschwitz?*
> It still exists. It's closed now.
> *Closed? What does that mean?*
> They don't bury there now. [17–18]

The inquirer thus inquires into the very meaning of *closure* and of narrative, political and philosophical *enclosure*. Of Dr. Grassler, the ex-assistant to the Nazi "commissar" of the Jewish ghetto, Lanzmann asks:

> *My question is philosophical. What does a ghetto mean, in your opinion?* [182]

Differences

Grassler of course evades the question. "History is full of ghettos," he replies, once more using erudition, "knowledge" and the very discipline of history to avoid the cutting edge of the interpellation: "Persecution of the Jews wasn't a German invention, and didn't start with World War II" (182). Everybody knows, in other words, what a ghetto is, and the meaning of the ghetto does not warrant a specifically *philosophical* attention: "history is full of ghettos." Because "history" knows only too well what a ghetto is, this knowledge might as well be left to history, and does not need in turn to be probed by us. "History" is thus used both to deny the *philosophical* thrust of the question and to forget the specificity—the *difference*—of the Nazi past. Insofar as the reply denies precisely the inquirer's refusal to *take for granted* the conception—let alone the preconception—of the ghetto, the stereotypical, preconceived answer in effect *forgets* the asking power of the question. Grassler essentially forgets the difference: forgets the *meaning* of the ghetto as the first step in the Nazi overall design precisely of the framing—and of the enclosure—of a difference, a difference that will consequently be assigned to the ultimate enclosure of the death camp and to the "final solution" of eradication. Grassler's answer *does not meet* the question, and attempts, moreover, to *reduce* the question's difference. But the question of the ghetto—that of the attempt at the containment (the reduction) of a difference— perseveres both in the speech and in the silence of the inquirer- narrator. The narrator is precisely there to insure that the question, in its turn, will *go on* (will continue in the viewer). The inquirer, in other words, is not merely the agency which asks the questions, but the force which takes apart all previous answers. Throughout the interviewing process the inquirer-narrator, at the side of Grassler as of others, is at once the witness of the question and the witness of the gap—or of the difference—between the question and the answer.

Often, the inquirer bears witness to the question (and the narrator silently bears witness to the story) by merely recapitulating word by word a fragment of the answer, by literally repeating—like an echo— the last sentence, the last words just uttered by the interlocutor. But the function of the echo—in the very resonance of its amplification— is itself inquisitive, and not simply repetitive. "The gas vans came in here," Srebnik narrates: "there were two huge ovens, and afterwards the bodies were thrown into these ovens, and the flames reached to the sky" (6). "To the sky [*zum Himmel*]," mutters silently the interviewer, opening at once a philosophical abyss in the simple words of the narrative description of a black hole in the very blueness of the image of the sky. When later on, the Poles around the church narrate how they listened to the gassed Jews' screams, Lanzmann's repetitious echoes register the unintended irony of the narration:

> *They heard screams at night?*
> The Jews moaned ... They were hungry. They were shut in and starved.
> *What kinds of cries and moans were heard at night?*
> They called on Jesus and Mary and God, sometimes in German ...
> *The Jews called on Jesus, Mary and God!* [97–98]

Lanzmann's function as an echo is another means by which the voice-lessness of the narrator and the voice of the inquirer produce a

and the flames reached to the sky.

question in the very answer, and enact a *difference* through the very verbal repetition. In the narrator as the bearer of the film's silence, the *question* of the scream persists. And so does the *difference* of what the screams in fact call out to. Here as elsewhere in the film, the narrator is, as such, both the guardian of the question and the guardian of the difference.

The inquirer's investigation is precisely into (both the philosophical and the concrete) particularity of difference. *"What's the difference between a special and a regular train?"* the inquirer asks of the Nazi traffic planner Walter Stier (133). And to the Nazi teacher's wife, who in a Freudian slip confuses Jews and Poles (both "the others" or "the foreigners" in relation to the Germans), Lanzmann addresses the following meticulous query:

> Since World War I the castle had been in ruins . . . That's where the Jews were taken. This ruined castle was used for housing and delousing the Poles, and so on.
> *The Jews!*
> Yes, the Jews.
> *Why do you call them Poles and not Jews?*
> Sometimes I get them mixed up.
> *There's a difference between Poles and Jews?*

Oh yes!
What difference?
The Poles weren't exterminated, and the Jews were. That's the differ-
ence. An external difference.
And the inner difference?
I can't assess that. I don't know enough about psychology and anthro-
pology. The difference between the Poles and the Jews? Anyway, they
couldn't stand each other. [82–83]

As a philosophical inquiry into the ungraspability of difference
and as a narrative of the specific differences between the various
witnesses, *Shoah* implies a fragmentation of the testimonies—a fragmentation both of tongues and of perspectives—that cannot ultimately be surpassed. It is because the film goes from singular to
singular, because there is no possible *representation* of one witness
by another, that Lanzmann needs us to sit through ten hours of the
film to begin to witness—to begin to have a concrete sense—both of
our own ignorance and of the incommensurability of the occurrence.
The occurrence is conveyed precisely by this fragmentation of the
testimonies, which enacts the fragmentation of the witnessing. The
film is a gathering of the fragments of the witnessing. But the collection
of the fragments does not yield, even after ten hours of the movie,
any possible totality or any possible totalization: the gathering of
testimonial incommensurates does not amount either to a generalizable theoretical statement or to a narrative monologic sum. Asked
what was his concept of the Holocaust, Lanzmann answered: "I had
no concept; I had obsessions, which is different . . . The obsession of
the cold . . . The obsession of the first time. The first shock. The first
hour of the Jews in the camp, in Treblinka, the first minutes. I will
always ask the question of the first time . . . The obsession of the last
moments, the waiting, the fear. *Shoah* is a film full of fear, and of
energy too. You cannot do such a film theoretically. Every theoretical
attempt that I tried was a failure, but these failures were necessary
. . . You build such a film in your head, in your heart, in your belly,
in your guts, everywhere"(*Interview*, pp. 22–23). This "everywhere"
which, paradoxically, cannot be totalized and which resists theory as
such, this corporeal fragmentation and enumeration which describes
the "building"—or the process of the generation—of the film while it
resists any attempt at conceptualization, is itself an emblem of the
specificity—of the uniqueness—of the mode of testimony of the film.
The film testifies not merely by collecting and by gathering fragments
of witnessing, but by actively exploding any possible enclosure—any
conceptual frame—that might claim to *contain* the fragments and

to fit them into one coherent whole. *Shoah* bears witness to the fragmentation of the testimonies as the radical invalidation of all definitions, of all parameters of reference, of all known answers, in the very midst of its relentless affirmation—of its materially creative validation—of the absolute necessity of speaking. The film puts in motion its surprising testimony by performing the historical and contradictory double task of the breaking of the silence and of the simultaneous shattering of any given discourse, of the breaking—or the bursting open—of all frames.

II

The Impossibility of Testimony

Shoah is a film about testimony, then, in an infinitely more abysmal, paradoxical and problematic way than it first seems: the *necessity of testimony* it affirms in reality derives, paradoxically enough, from the *impossibility of testimony* that the film at the same time dramatizes. I would suggest that this impossibility of testimony by which the film is traversed, with which it struggles and against which it precisely builds itself is, in effect, the most profound and most crucial subject of the film. In its enactment of the Holocaust as the *event-without-a-witness*, as the traumatic impact of a historically ungraspable *primal scene* which erases both its witness and its witnessing, *Shoah* explores the very boundaries of testimony by exploring, at the same time, the historical impossibility of witnessing and the historical impossibility of *escaping* the predicament of being—and of having to become—a witness. At the edge of the universe of testimony which is the universe of our era, at the frontiers of the necessity of speech, *Shoah* is a film about silence: the paradoxical articulation of a *loss of voice*—and of a loss of mind. The film is the product of a relentless struggle for remembrance, but for the self-negating, contradictory, conflictual remembrance of—precisely—an *amnesia*. The testimony stumbles on, and at the same time tells about, the impossibility of telling.

> No one can describe it. No one can recreate what happened here. Impossible? And no one can understand it. Even I, here, now . . . I can't believe I'm here. No, I just can't believe it. It was always this peaceful here. Always. When they burned two thousand people—Jews—every day, it was just as peaceful. No one shouted. Everyone went about his work. It was silent. Peaceful. Just as it is now. [6]

What cannot be grasped in the event-without-a-witness, and what the witness nonetheless must now (impossibly) bear witness to, is not merely the murder but, specifically, the autobiographical moment of the witness's death, the historical occurrence of the *dying* of the subject of witnessing as such.

> *What died in him in Chelmno?*
> Everything died. But he's only human, and he wants to live. So he must forget. He thanks God . . . that he can forget. And let's not talk about that.
> *Does he think it's good to talk about it?*
> For me it's not good.
> *Then why is he talking about it?*
> Because you're insisting on it. He was sent books on Eichmann's trial. He was a witness, and he didn't even read them. [7]

Podchlebnik, in whom "everything died" as a witness, retrospectively gives testimony in the Eichmann trial, but he still would rather keep the witness dead, keep the witness as a (dead) secret from his own eyes by *not reading* anything about his own role in the trial. The desire not to read, and not to talk, stems from the fear of hearing, or of witnessing, oneself. The *will-to-silence* is the will to *bury* the dead witness inside oneself.

But the film is "insisting," here again, that the "Jewish cemetery" (to return to the dialogue with Mrs. Pietyra) cannot be once and for all "closed" (18), that the witness must himself precisely now reopen his own burial as witness, even if this burial is experienced by him, paradoxically enough, as the very condition of his survival.

The Matter of the Witness, or the Missing Body

What would it mean, however, for the witness to reopen his own grave—to testify precisely from inside the very cemetery which is not yet closed? And what would it mean, alternatively, to bear witness from inside the witness's *empty* grave—empty both because the witness in effect did not die, but only died unto himself, and because the witness who did die was, consequent to his mass burial, dug up from his grave and burned to ashes—because the dead witness did not even leave behind a corpse or a dead body? One of the most striking and surprising aspects of *Shoah* as a film about genocide and war atrocities is the absence of dead bodies on the screen. But it is the *missing* corpses which *Shoah* remarkably gives us to witness, in its "travelings" throughout the graveyard with no bodies, and in its persistent exploration of the empty grave which is both haunted and yet *uninhabited* by the dead witness.

> *And it was the last grave?*
> Yes.
> *The Nazi plan was for them to open the graves, starting with the oldest?*
> Yes. The last graves were the newest, and we started with the oldest, those of the first ghetto . . . The deeper you dug, the flatter the bodies were . . . When you tried to grasp a body, it crumbled, it was impossible to pick up. We had to open the graves, but without tools . . . Anyone who said "corpse" or "victim" was beaten. The Germans made us refer to the bodies as *Figuren* . . .
> *Were they told at the start how many* Figuren *there were in all the graves?*
> The head of the Vilna Gestapo told us: "There are ninety thousand people lying here, and absolutely no trace must be left of them" [12–13]

"No one was supposed to be left to bear witness," testifies in turn Richard Glazar (50). The Nazi plan is in effect to *leave no trace* not only of the crime itself of the historical mass murder, but of all those who materially witnessed that crime, to eliminate without trace any possible eyewitness. Indeed, even the corpses of the now dead witnesses or the *Figuren* are still material evidence by which the Nazis might, ironically, be *figured out.* The corpses still continue to materially *witness* their own murderers. The scheme of the erasure of the witnesses must therefore be completed by the literal erasure—by the very burning—of the bodies. The witness must, quite literally, *burn out*, and burn out of sight.

> Suddenly, from the part of the camp called the death camp, flames shot up . . . In a flash . . . the whole camp seemed ablaze . . . And suddenly one of us stood up . . . and facing that curtain of fire, he began chanting a song I didn't know:
> " . . . We have been thrust into the fire before but we have never denied the Holy Law."
> He sang in Yiddish, while behind him blazed the pyres on which they had begun then, in November 1942, to burn the bodies in Treblinka . . . We knew that night that the dead would no longer be buried, they'd be burned. [14]

Testifying from Inside

Is it possible to literally *speak from inside the Holocaust*—to bear witness from inside the very *burning* of the witness? I would suggest that it is by raising, by experiencing and by articulating such a question that the film takes us on its oneiric and yet materially historic trip, and that it carries out its cinematic exploration—and its philosophical incorporation—of the radical *impossibility of testimony*. To put it differently, the very testimony of the film (insofar precisely as it is a groundbreaking testimony) actively confronts us with the question: in what ways, by what creative means (and at what price) would it become possible *for us* to witness the-event-without-a-witness? A question which translates into the following terms of the film: Is it possible to witness *Shoah* (the Holocaust and/or the film) from inside?[14] Or are we necessarily outside (outside the blazes of the Holocaust, outside the burning of the witness, outside the fire that consumes the film) and witnessing it from outside? What would it mean to witness *Shoah* from inside?

It is the implication of this rigorous, tormented question that guide, I would suggest, the topographical investigation of the film and specifically, the inquiry addressed by Lanzmann to Jan Piwonski, the Polish pointsman who directed the death trains from the outside world into the concrete inside of the extermination camp:

> *Exactly where did the camp begin?*
> . . . Here there was a fence that ran to those trees you see there . . .
> *So I'm standing inside the camp perimeter, right?*
> That's right.
> *Where I am now is fifty feet from the station, and I'm already* outside *the camp. This is the Polish part, and over there was death.*
> Yes. On German orders, Polish railmen split up the trains. So the locomotive took twenty cars, and headed toward Chelm . . . Unlike Treblinka, the station here is part of the camp. And at this point we are *inside* the camp. [39, my emphasis]

I would suggest that this precision, this minute investigation and concretization of the film's cinematic space, derives not simply from a geographical or topographical attempt at definition, but from the quest of the whole film to get to witnessing precisely this *inside* of the

[14]I owe the formulation of this last point to Peter Canning, who suggested the insightful wording of the question in the course of a class I was then teaching on the problems of witnessing and on *Shoah*.

death camp. In contrast to the Nazi teacher's wife, who insists on having seen the gas vans only from outside—

Did you see the gas vans?
No . . . Yes, from the outside . . . I never looked inside; I didn't see Jews in them. I only saw things from outside. [82]—

the crucial task and the concrete endeavor that separates *Shoah* from all its filmic predecessors is, precisely, the attempt to witness from inside.

What does it mean, however, once again, to witness from inside a death camp? And supposing such a witnessing could in itself be (or become, thanks to the film,) possible, what would the consequent necessity of *testifying out of that inside* precisely mean? One after the other, Lanzmann explores the philosophical challenges and the concrete impossibilities/necessities that such a testimony from inside the death camp would entail:

1. It would mean *testifying from inside the death, the deadness and the very suicide of the witness.* There are two suicides in the film, of two (unrelated) Jewish leaders.[15] Both suicides are elected as the desperate solutions to the impossibility of witnessing, whose double bind and dead end they materialize. To kill oneself is, in effect, at once to *kill the witness* and to remain, by means of one's own death, *outside the witnessing.* Both suicides are thus motivated by the *desire not to be inside.*[16] How then to bear witness *from inside the desire not to be inside?*

2. Testifying from inside a death camp would mean, at the same time, equally impossibly, the necessity of *testifying from inside the absolute constraint of a fatal secret,* a secret that is felt to be so binding, so compelling and so terrible that it often is kept secret even from oneself.[17] For many reasons, the transgression

[15]One by Czerniakow, the Jewish leader of the Warsaw ghetto, who attempts at first to negotiate with the Germans, but commits suicide when he understands that his negotiations failed, the day after the first transport of the Jews of Warsaw to Treblinka takes place (188–190); the other is by Freddy Hirsch, one of the Jewish leaders of the Czech family camp and specifically the protector of the (hundred) children, who commits suicide when he is urged to participate in the camp's armed resistance, a participation which necessitates his abandonment of the children to their likely death (157, 159–162).

[16]The same is true of the self-blazing of the Warsaw ghetto, which might be seen as yet another suicide, and as yet another materialization of the desire not to be inside (not to be inside the ghetto).

[17]Cf. Podchlebnik's way of refusing to read books about the Eichmann trial, thus keeping his own witness, his own testimony in the trial as a sort of secret from himself (7).

of such secrecy does not seem possible to those who feel both bound and bonded by it. "For we were 'the bearers of the secret,' " says Philip Müller, an ex-Sonderkommando member: "we were reprieved dead men. We weren't allowed to talk to anyone, or contact any prisoner, or even the SS. Only those in charge of the Aktion" (68). Victims as well as executioners[18] come to believe in their elected fate to join a tongue-tied cult of muteness, to be the destined *bearers of the silence*. Because the secret is at once a bondage and a bond, the breach of silence sometimes is no longer at the disposal of a conscious choice, or of a simple (rational) decision of the will. So that concentration camps' survivors will historically maintain the secret, and the silence, even years after the war.

Since the testimony, like the oath of silence, is in turn a speech act, but a speech act that, both in its utterance and in its stakes, is specifically the opposite act to the pledge of secrecy, how would it be possible to testify not just in spite of, but precisely *from inside the very binding of the secret?*

3. In the sequence of concrete and philosophical impossibilities, bearing witness *from inside a death camp* would equally entail the paradoxical necessity of *testifying from inside a radical deception*, a deception that is, moreover, doubled and enhanced by *self-deception*:

(Philip Müller)
All eyes converged on the flat roof of the crematorium. . . . Aumeyer addressed the crowd: "You're here to work for our soldiers . . . Those who can work will be all right.

It was clear that hope flared in those people . . . The executioners have gotten past the first obstacle . . . Then he questioned a woman: "What's your trade?" "Nurse," she replied. "Splendid! We need nurses in our hospitals . . . We need all of you. But first, undress. You must be disinfected. We want you healthy." I could

---

[18]On the German side, see Franz Schalling's narrative:

You weren't in the SS, you were. . .
Police.
Which police?
Security guards . . . An SS man immediately told us: "This is a top-secret mission!"
Secret?
"A top-secret mission." "Sign this!" We each had to sign. There was a form ready for each of us, a pledge of secrecy. We never even got to read it through.
You had to take an oath?
No, just sign, promising to shut up about whatever we'd see. Not say a word. After we'd signed, we were told: "Final solution of the Jewish question." [74]

see the people were calmer, reassured by what they've heard, and they began to undress. [69]

(Franz Suchomel)
We kept on insisting: "You're going to live!" We almost believed it ourselves. If you lie enough, you believe your own lies. [147]

How to attest to the way things were *from within the very situation of delusion and illusion*—from inside the utter blindness to what in reality things were? How to bear witness to historic truth *from inside the radical deception* (amplified by self-deception) by which one was separated from historic truth at the very moment one was most involved in it?

4. Finally, the necessity of testifying *from inside* (the topographical determination to bear witness from inside the death camp) amounts to the film's most demanding, most uncompromising and most crucial question: *How to testify from inside Otherness?*

When the Jews talked to each other . . . the Ukrainians wanted things quiet, and they asked . . . yes, they asked them to shut up. So the Jews shut up and the guard moved off. Then the Jews started talking again, in their language . . . : *ra-ra-ra,* and so on. [30]

Lanzmann, who is listening to the Polish peasant Czeslaw Borowi in the company of his interpreter, knows, as soon as his attentive ears pick up the "ra-ra-ra," that the foreign language he is listening to is no longer simply Polish. He interrupts the Pole and, addressing him through the interpreter without waiting for her complete translation, asks:

What's he mean, la-la-la? *What's he trying to imitate?*
Their language—

answers the interpreter by way of explanation, or translation, not of Borowi's sounds but of his intention. But this is one moment in which Lanzmann *does not want translation.* In response to the translator's explanation, the inquirer insists:

No, ask him. Was the Jews' noise something special?
They spoke Jew—

Borowi replies, misnaming Yiddish but finally returning to the scene of discourse, and gracefully offering a *meaning* to explain the strangeness of his previous sounds and to dispel their unintelligibility.

Does Mr. Borowi understand "Jew"?
No. [30–31]

To testify *from inside Otherness* is thus to be prepared, perhaps, to bear witness from within a "ra-ra-ra," to be prepared to testify not merely in a foreign language but *from inside the very language of the Other*: to speak from within the Other's tongue insofar precisely as the *tongue of the Other* is by definition the very tongue *we* do not speak, the tongue that, by its very nature and position, one by definition *does not understand*. To testify from inside Otherness is thus to bear witness from inside the living pathos of a tongue which nonetheless is bound to be heard as mere noise.

Insiders and Outsiders

It is therefore in reality impossible to testify from inside otherness, or from inside the keeping of a secret, from inside amnesia or from inside deception and the delusion of coercive self-deception, in much the same way as it is impossible to testify, precisely, from inside death. It is impossible to testify from the inside because *the inside has no voice*, and this is what the film is attempting to convey and to communicate to us. From within, the inside is unintelligible, it is *not present to itself*. Philip Müller, who spent years working in the management of the dead bodies in the Auschwitz crematorium, testifies:

> I couldn't understand any of it. It was like a blow on the head, as if I'd been stunned. I didn't even know where I was . . . I was in shock, as if I'd been hypnotized, ready to do whatever I was told. I was so mindless, so horrified . . . [59]

In its absence to itself, the inside is *inconceivable* even to the ones who are already in. "Still I couldn't believe what had happened there on the other side of the gate, where the people went in," says Bomba: "Everything disappeared, and everything got quiet" (47). As the locus of a silence and as the vanishing point of the voice, the inside is *untransmittable*. "It was pointless," says Müller, "to tell the truth to anyone who crossed the threshold of the crematorium" (125). The film is about the relation between truth and threshold: about the impossibility of telling the truth, and about the consequent historical necessity of recovering the truth, precisely past a certain threshold. And it is this threshold that now needs to be historically and philosophically recrossed. Inside the crematorium, "on the other side of the gate" where "everything disappeared and everything got quiet," there is loss: of voice, of life, of knowledge, of awareness, of truth, of the capacity to feel, of the capacity to speak. The truth of this loss constitutes precisely what it means to be inside the Holocaust. But the loss also defines an impossibility of testifying from inside to the truth of that inside.

Who would be in a position, then, to tell? The truth of the inside is even less accessible to an outsider. If it is indeed impossible to bear witness to the Holocaust from inside, it is even more impossible to testify to it from the outside. From without, the inside is entirely *ungraspable*, even when it is not simply what escapes perception altogether and remains invisible as such (as for the Nazi teacher's wife), nor even simply (as in Borowi's case) what is witnessed as pure noise and perceived as mere acoustic interference. To Jan Karski, the most honest, generous and sympathetic outside witness, the wartime messenger who politically accepted, in his mission as an underground Polish courier, to see the Jewish ghetto with his own eyes so as to report on it to the Western allies, his own testimony makes *no sense*. The *inside of the ghetto* in effect remains to him as utterly *impenetrable* as a bad dream, and his bewildered, grieving memory retains the image of this wretched inside only as what makes of him, forever, an *outsider*.

> It was a nightmare for me . . .
> *Did it look like a completely strange world? Another world, I mean?*
> It was not a world. There was not humanity . . . It wasn't humanity. It was some . . . some hell . . . They are not human . . . We left the ghetto. Frankly, I couldn't take it any more . . . I was sick. Even now I don't want . . . I understand your role. I am here. I don't go back in my memory. I couldn't tell any more.
> But I reported what I saw. It was not a world. It was not a part of humanity. I was not part of it. I did not belong there. I never saw such things, I never . . . nobody wrote about this kind of reality. I never saw any theater, I never saw any movie . . . this was not the world. I was told that these were human beings—they didn't look like human beings. [167, 173–174]

Since for the outsider, even in the very grief of his full empathy and sympathy, the truth of the inside remains the truth of an *exclusion*— "It was not a world, there was not humanity"—it is not really possible to *tell the truth*, to testify, from the outside. Neither is it possible, as we have seen, to testify from the inside. I would suggest that the impossible position and the testimonial effort of the film as a whole is to be, precisely, neither simply inside nor simply outside, but paradoxically, *both inside and outside*: to create a *connection* that did not exist during the war and does not exist today *between the inside and the outside*—to set them both in motion and in dialogue with one another.

III

Between the Inside and the Outside: Jan Karski's Trip

The whole testimony of Jan Karski can in fact be read as illustrating this philosophical dynamic, this cinematic exploration of the meaning and the consequences of the act of *crossing* the dividing line between the inside and the outside. What was historically at stake in the political endeavor of Karski's testimony, and what is philosophically at stake in Karski's reiterated, cinematic testimonial narrative, is *the double movement of a trip*, or of a journey, first from the outside to the inside and then, back from the inside to the outside. Upon the request of two Jewish leaders, Karski travels, first, from the outside spheres of the unsuspecting Polish world (the element in Poland which, under the jurisdiction of a government in exile, attempts to maintain its independence from the Nazis) into the inside of the Nazi-dominated Jewish ghetto. This preliminary journey *in* is planned, however, for the sake of a subsequent and crucial journey *out*, a journey whose political mission is precisely to *bring out* the message of the ghetto, to take the inside message of the Jewish leaders outside the boundaries of Nazi hegemony, and to communicate this information and this plea from the inside to the governments outside, to the leaders of the Western Allies who are trying to defeat the Nazis. Karski narrates his initial interview with the Jewish leaders:

> A meeting was arranged outside the ghetto. There were two gentlemen. They did not live in the ghetto. They introduced themselves—leader of Bund, Zionist leader . . . my mission [was] to impress upon all people whom I am going to see that the Jewish situation is unprecedented in history . . .
>
> We understand we have no country of our own, we have no government, we have no voice in the Allied councils. So we have to use services, little people like you are . . . Will you fulfill your mission . . . approach the Allied leaders? We want an official declaration of the Allied nations that in addition to the military strategy which aims at securing . . . military victory in this war, extermination of the Jews forms a separate chapter, and the Allied nations formally, publicly announce that they will deal with this problem, that it becomes a part of their overall strategy in this war. Not only defeat of Germany but also saving the remaining Jewish population. [167–170]

Historically, we know that Karski's mission failed to elicit the political response requested, that his testimony was itself kept secret by the Allied governments (being officially denied and disbelieved), thus having no bearing on the course of military or political events. Karski failed, in this way, to politically (effectively) *transmit* the inside of the Holocaust. But he did accomplish his own autobiographical, uncanny journey toward the Other, his own disorienting, radical displacement, by crossing first the boundary to the inside and by then recrossing it, in an attempt not merely to go back outside but to *reach out to the Outside from within his very eerie visit to the Inside.*

How, indeed, can an outsider such as Karski, and, for that matter, how can anyone reach out, and open up, precisely to the frightening inside of Otherness?

I would suggest that Karski's testimony might provide some answer to the philosophical insistence and to the enigmatic pressure of this question. The striking narrative of Karski's trip into the ghetto is doubled, and to some extent is motivated, by the underlying latent narrative of the occurrence of a unique human encounter. The story of the ghetto unwittingly encompasses the story of the birth of a particular attachment, an attachment that will grow into a singular, compelling human bond, not between the Jews at large and the Pole who they hope will be their advocate, but between two individuals: Jan Karski and the Jewish leader of the Bund.

> Between those two Jewish leaders—somehow this belongs to human relations—I took, so to say, to the Bund leader, probably because of his behavior—he looked like a Polish nobleman, a gentleman, with straight, beautiful gestures, dignified. I believe that he liked me also, personally. Now at a certain point, he said: "Mr. Vitold, I know the Western world . . . It will strengthen your report if you will be able to say "I saw it myself." We can organize for you to visit the Jewish ghetto. Would you do it? If you do, I will go with you to the Jewish ghetto to Warsaw so I will be sure you will be as safe as possible. [171]

Ironically and paradoxically in a story of the encounter with an Other, Karski gets to *like* the Bund leader precisely because of his non-Jewish, Polish (aristocratic) air. He can love the Jew because he recognizes in him something humanly *familiar* ("somehow this belongs to human relations"), because he sees in him, initially, not the Other but (safely) the Same. In the very movement of his sympathy, Karski can thus take the Jew, ironically, outside of Jewishness and bring him into his own world of the Polish nobleman, as an imaginary double, a companion or a brother.

But the Jewish leader offers, precisely out of this mutual responsiveness and in view of what he feels to be a historical necessity, to take in turn Karski out of his aristocratic Polish world and have him visit not only the foreignness of *his* own world, but, beyond the mere fact of the strangeness, precisely the *alienation* of the Jewish ghetto. In return, the Bund leader offers not only companionship, but a companionship intent on providing a *protection*, on precisely making the trip into the alien world *safe*. Thus it is that Karski unsuspectingly is led to his bewildering discovery of Otherness, as well as to his startling recognition that what he took to be *familiar* in the very figure that has focused his particular attachment is in fact quite staggeringly *different* and quite frighteningly *strange*.

> So within the outside walls, practically there were some four units. The most important was the so-called central ghetto. They were separated by some areas inhabited by Aryans . . . There was a building. This building was constructed in such a way that the wall which separated the ghetto from the outside world was a part of the back of the building, so the front was facing the Aryan area. There was a tunnel. *We went through this tunnel* without any kind of difficulty. *What struck me was that now he was a completely different man*—the Bund leader, the Polish nobleman. I go with him. He is broken down, like a Jew from the ghetto, as if he had lived there all the time. Apparently, this was his nature. This was his world. So we walked the streets . . . We didn't talk very much. He led me. [171–172; my emphasis]

Through the formation of a dialogue in walking, as well as through the sharing of a silence, the two companions in the eerie trip unsettle both for us and for themselves the boundaries between the inside and the outside. Karski's testimony is the story of this unexpected intimate relationship with a double from outside the ghetto who (by merely crossing the ghetto's wall) has turned out to be radically Other, an estranged Other who nonetheless continues to be cherished and, as such, continues both to mark a traumatizing lesson and to *inform* a discipleship of Otherness—a genuine discipleship of the inside.

> It was not a world. There was not humanity. Streets full, full . . . Those horrible children . . . It wasn't humanity. It was some . . . some hell . . . Now the Germans in uniform, they were walking . . . Silence! Everybody frozen until he passed . . . Germans . . . Contempt. This is apparent that they are subhuman. They are not human.
>
> Now at a certain point some movement starts. Jews are running from the streets I was on. We jumped into a house. He just hits the door. "Open the door! Open the door!" They open the door. We move in . . . He says: "All right, all right, don't be afraid, we are Jews." He pushed me to the window, says, "Look at it. Look at it." There were two boys, nice-looking boys, Hitler-jugend in uniform. They walked. Every step

they made, Jews disappearing, running away . . . At a certain point, a boy goes into his pocket without even thinking. Shoots! Some broken glass. The other boy congratulating him. They go back. So I was paralyzed. So then the Jewish woman—probably she recognized me, I don't know, that I am not a Jew—she embraced me. "Go, go, it doesn't do you any good, go, go." So we left the house. Then we left the ghetto. [172–173]

Under the protection—but also in the very skin—of his Jewish alter ego ("we are Jews"), Karski, in observing and recording what it means to be the Other, in effect experiences what it means to be *inside the Holocaust*, as well as what it feels, specifically, to be an *insider* of the ghetto. It is ironic that it is precisely Jewish empathy that has to send him back outside, back to the relief of the outsider, so as to prevent his torture and to spare him this particular insidedness of its own humiliation.

In going out, however, Karski has learned an unforgettable—though unanticipated—lesson. He knows, henceforth, that it is not a simple thing to move from one side to the other side of the wall of the ghetto. He has learned that there is a radical, unbreachable and horrifying difference between the two sides of the wall. It is indeed this knowledge, this sense that the outside and the inside are qualitatively so different that they are not just incompatible but *incomparable* and utterly *irreconcilable*, that he expresses in his dismally repeated (quasi-hallucinated) statement: "This was not a world. There was not humanity."

> So then the Jewish woman—probably she recognized me, I don't know, that I am not a Jew—she embraced me. "Go, go, it doesn't do you any good, go, go." So we left the house. Then we left the ghetto. So then he said: *"You didn't see everything; you didn't see too much. Would you like to go again? I will come with you.* I want you to see everything. I will."
> Next day we went again. The same house, the same way. So then again I was more conditioned, so I felt more things. [173; emphasis mine]

The real question raised by Karski's testimony is the following: why does Karski go *a second time* inside the ghetto? His cognitive report as witness is more or less complete after the first time, and his second visit to the inside is not really necessitated by his formal mission as a diplomatic emissary. Moreover, Karski now knows that it is not possible to simply wander to and fro, to simply move between the inside and the outside of the ghetto, without paying a costly price. I would argue that the most significant element of Karski's testimony is precisely this gratuitous *return* to the ghetto—this Orphic repetition of his spectral visit. Karski is persuaded to accomplish this *return* from inside the very intimacy of the singular friendship—of the singular companionship of his estranging and compelling host. I would thus suggest that this visit to the ghetto is nothing less, indeed, than the retracing of a journey equal to an oath of love. In repeating his descent to hell ("This was not a world . . . It was some . . . some hell"), Karski makes a gift to his companion of his fear, of his attention, of his memory, of his emphatic suffering, of his discipleship in trauma, and of the *oath of faithfulness* precisely to his *witness*—of the pledged promise of his future testimony.

> So then we just walked the streets; we didn't talk to anybody. We walked probably one hour. Sometimes he would tell me: "Look at this Jew"—a Jew standing, without moving. I said: "Is he dead? He says: "No, no, no, he is alive. Mr. Vitold, remember—he's dying, he's dying. Look at him. Tell them over there. You saw it. Don't forget." We walk again. It's macabre. Only from time to time he would whisper: "Remember this, remember this" . . . Very many cases. I would say: "What are they doing here?" His answer: "They are dying, that's all. They are dying." We spent more time, perhaps one hour. We left the ghetto. Frankly, I couldn't take it any more. "Get me out of it." And then I never saw him again. I was sick. Even now, I don't want . . . I understand your role. I am here. I don't go back in my memory . . . Then we left. He embraced me then. "Good luck, good luck." I never saw him again. [174–175]

Like the testimony of the Holocaust survivors, Karski's testimony ends with the abruptness of an irrecuperable loss. "Still I couldn't believe," Karski could have said with Bomba, "what had happened there on the other side of the gate, where the people went in: everything disappeared, and everything got quiet" (47). Like the fading of the voice, the vanishing from sight—the sudden disappearance of the Jewish Bund leader from Karski's life—marks Karski's own personal participation in the Holocaust experience: "I never saw him again." This loss is built into the testimony, which is *informed* by its own bereavement—informed, that is, not just from without, but from within. I would suggest precisely that it is the power of Karski's whole testimony to bespeak throughout the whole description of the ghetto the quintessence of its final sentence, to say the disenchantment and the dispossession of the witnessing by this sudden interruption of the cognitive report, by this disruption, this abduction, this expropriation of the seeing for the very witness who accepted to *go in* so as to "see with his own eyes." "I never saw him again."

This final loss and final sentence is, however, also, at the same time, Karski's indirect way of explaining why, historically, once his mission failed and caught within the paradoxes of his own ongoing history, in the end he had no choice but *to leave the Jew behind*.

> *We are humans.* Do you understand it? Do you understand it? [169]

> It was not a world. *There was not humanity* . . . It was not a world. It was not a part of humanity. I was not part of it. [172]

The prisoner of his own oath of speaking, Karski thus becomes, *unlike* the Jew but also, paradoxically, *like* him, as yet another *bearer of the silence*:

> Now . . . Now I go back thirty-five years. No, I don't go back . . . In thirty-five years after the war I do not go back. I have been a teacher for twenty-six years. I never mention the Jewish problem to my students. [167]

Between the Inside and the Outside: Lanzmann's trip

I would now suggest that Lanzmann's own trip is evocative of that of Karski: that Lanzmann, in his turn, takes us on a *journey* whose aim precisely is *to cross the boundary*, first from the outside world to the inside of the Holocaust, and then back from the inside of the Holocaust to the outside world.

On the one hand, it is the spectator of the film who, like Karski, is the visitor from the outside, and Lanzmann is in the position of the Jewish Bund leader, seemingly a "Polish [or French] nobleman," a man of the world, but who knows the tunnel that connects the outside to the inside and who leads us through this tunnel in his film guiding us into a singular and unforgettable experience of a *seeing*, while at the same time whispering, precisely, in his echo-like, ghost-like asides: *"Look at it, look at it"* . . . (173).

> *"Look at this Jew"*—a Jew standing, without moving. I said: "Is he dead?" He says: "No, no, no, he is alive. Mr. Vitold, remember—he's dying, he's dying. *Look at him.* Tell them over there. *You saw it. Don't forget"* . . . "Remember this, remember this." [174; emphasis mine]

On the other hand, Lanzmann at the same time is himself, like Karski, fundamentally a *courier*, and perhaps in turn, of necessity, also something like an *underground courier*: not only the bearer of the silence but, like Karski in his diplomatic mission, the very *bearer of a message* which he has to bring, precisely, from the very voicelessness and silence of the inside to the outside. While Karski failed, however, to *communicate effectively* the inside outcry of the ghetto to the outside world, Lanzmann hopes, by means of the resources of his art, to have an impact on the outside from the inside, to literally *move* the viewers and to actually *reach* the addressees: to make—historically and ethically—a difference. Will the artistic messenger succeed where the political messenger failed? In an interview in *L'Express*, Lanzmann defines the difficulty of the task:

> My problem was *to transmit*. To do that one cannot allow oneself to be overwhelmed by emotion. You must remain detached. This work has plunged me into an immense solitude . . . But it was essential not to be crushed. Or to crush others. I tried rather to reach people through their intelligence.

How to *transmit* at once the pathos and the disconnection, the abyssal *lostness* of the inside, without being either crushed by the abyss or overwhelmed by the pathos, *without losing the outside*? How to be, thus, at the same time inside and outside? And how to guide the audience into an inside which nonetheless can keep in touch with the outside? It is the complexity of this specific question that defines, I would suggest, Lanzmann's paradoxical attempt to "reach people through their intelligence" precisely in a film that produces an effective and affective shock that resonates, as such, in the whole body of the viewer. If the film succeeds in reaching in the viewer the *intelligence* of the emotion, the very *dumbness* of the inside will have been transmitted, and the very shock of the event might generate its own process of historical *intelligibility*.

"To reach people through their intelligence" is thus to bring the darkness of the inside to the physical light of the outside.[19] to literally and effectively *narrate the Holocaust in light*.[20]

. . .

[19]I would suggest here that the very notion of intelligence in relation to *Shoah* is both disoriented and disorienting, and is thus, like the film itself, not a concept ("I was asked what was my concept of the Holocaust: I had no concept," said Lanzmann: "I had obsessions, which is different"), but something like a metaphor: a metaphor similar to that of light, not, however, in the sense of an *enlightenment* (which, ultimately, is not possible) but in the sense of a *physical illumination*. Physical illumination is indeed what the film is about, even though the very process of illumination involves obscurity. The film is itself obscure: it sheds light where we least expect it to, and its heart of darkness is revealed as utterly unknown and perhaps unknowable. The film's role, however, is to physically *shed light*. It is in this way that the film speaks to the intelligence.

[20]The expression is alluding to George Wilson's description of the very art of film. See George M. Wilson, *Narration in Light: Studies in Cinematic Point of View*. Baltimore and London: Johns Hopkins University Press, 1986.

The importance of the role of light in the whole film is itself obliquely, oddly, inadvertently illuminated in the very secrecy (the very incompatibility with light) of the astounding Nazi document discussing, in its purely bureaucratic manner, the technical improvements to be implemented in the lighting system of the gas vans, with the purpose of preventing, quite specifically and quite uncannily, the gas vans' *"load"* (the overload of the dead bodies) from precisely *falling out into the light*:

> Geheime Reichssache (Secret Reich Business)
> Berlin, June 5, 1942 . . .
>   The lighting [in the gas vans] must be better protected than now. The lamps must be enclosed in a steel grid to prevent their being damaged. *Lights could be eliminated, since they are never used.* However, it has been observed that *when the doors are shut, the load always presses hard against them* [against the doors] *as soon as darkness sets in, which makes closing the doors difficult.* Also, because of the alarming nature of darkness, screaming always occurs when the doors are closed. It would therefore be useful to light the lamp before and during the first moments of the operation. [104]

Heart of Darkness

As soon as darkness sets in, the half-dead and half-living bodies in the gas vans rush to the doors—rush to the outside light—in a desperate attempt at once to avoid death and to avoid the very fact of dying in the dark, to avoid, that is, not seeing, and not knowing, their own death. The asphyxiated bodies are attempting not just to prevent their death, but to prevent their death, precisely, from *escaping them*, from taking place without their knowledge or awareness. Pushing toward the light, the gas vans' captives strive for some sort of *intelligence* of their own death, or at least for some sort of physical intelligibility.

This is what the film, in its turn, tries to provide, at the same time that it attempts to testify from *their* position, to bear witness from the very inside of the gas vans. While testifying from within the darkness, the film also tries to reach, precisely, the intelligence provided by an outside light.

As illustrated by the Nazis' own perception of the "operation" of the gas vans, the Nazi project is essentially a project of *containment*: the gas van is designed primarily as a death *container*—as a moving grave and as the enforced confinement of a burial alive. In much the same way as the death camp, the gas chamber, and the walled confinement of the ghetto, the gas van concretizes, once again, the way in which the Other in the Nazi program is at once *enclosed* and literally (in all senses of the term) *framed*. The essence of the sought containment—both physical and metaphysical—is to transform the material frame, the rationale of the container, into a means for the literal obliteration of the Other and a medium for the rationalization of the murder. The ghetto is thus made into an antechamber to the gas chamber and the moving vans are themselves transformed from pragmatic vehicles of transportation into vehicles that go nowhere— vehicles, precisely, of asphyxiation.

As the film shows and as the Nazi document (*Geheime Reichssache*) itself unwittingly reveals, however, light—and the desire for illumination—is *what prevents the closure of the doors* and what disrupts, uncannily, the Nazi project of containment: "the load naturally rushes toward the light when darkness sets in, which makes closing the doors difficult." The Nazi project, on the other hand, is a project in which "lights could be eliminated, since they are never used." But the film *brings the bodies back to light*. In bringing the inside of the darkness (the interior of the gas van, of the mobile grave) to the light of the outside, the film, once again, expands and ultimately bursts the very limits of the grave—explodes the very contours of the frame and of the frame's inherent claim both to define life and to contain (to bury) death.

Since light—the effort toward intelligence and intelligibility—is what prevents the closure of the doors, the film—as a striving for light—struggles to prevent, in turn, its own closure, and bursts open even its own filmic frame. In a discussion of his film at Yale, Lanzmann was addressed by the following question from the floor.

> *Question:* I would be interested to know if there is a relation between the figure of Simon Srebnik—the boy singer, who says at one point; "I thought: 'If I survive, I just want one thing: five loaves of bread' . . . But I dreamed too that if I survive, I'll be the only one left in the world"— and the ending of the film. You end the film with the story of Simha Rottem, one of the members of the failed Jewish uprising of the Warsaw ghetto, who in turn says, "I was alone throughout my tour of the ghetto. I didn't meet a living soul . . . I said to myself: 'I'm the last Jew. I'll wait for morning, and for the Germans.' " I'm sure that was intentional— "the only Jew in the world left." I'm sure you framed that intentionally . . .
>
> *Claude Lanzmann:* It is . . . it is the same end with a slight difference. But the last image of the film is a rolling train. You know, this was a real question, the question of the end. I did not have the moral right to give a happy ending to this story. When does the Holocaust really end?

Did it end the last day of the war? Did it end with the creation of the State of Israel? No. It still goes on. These events are of such magnitude, of such scope that they have never stopped developing their consequences . . . When I really had to conclude I decided that I did not have the right to do it . . . And I decided that the last image of the film would be a rolling train, an endlessly rolling . . . train.[21]

Unlike Karski who, after his visit to the ghetto, gets back outside without disrupting the very boundaries that his own crossing has unsettled, without putting in question the dividing line that separates the inside and the outside, Lanzmann's shuttle movement between the inside and the outside has a far more radical effect. Once he has gotten inside, Lanzmann cannot simply (to borrow Karski's terms) "*get out*,"[22] but has to *break out* and to *break through* from inside the darkness into the physical light of the outside. Unlike Karski, whose trip *leaves the inside behind* while unwittingly continuing to mourn its *loss*, Lanzmann's voyage *takes precisely the inside outside* and, in so doing, breaks the frame which both encloses and closes the inside in keeping it radically separate from the outside.

IV

Between the Inside and the Outside: Biographical Geography

Like Karski, Lanzmann in his turn comes to the Holocaust, however, from the outside and starts his journey toward *Shoah* as a mere outsider: an outsider in the sense that he is not, historically, a Holocaust survivor; in the sense that his relationship with the inside was not for him a given—geographical or biographical—but a taxing journey of discovery, a life process marked, in turn, by the struggle of a groping in the dark and punctuated by its own impossibilities. The film's *narration in light* is at the same time, enigmatically and referentially, a *narration in life*: a narration which consists in the account— and in the performance—of a *journey*, of a life-itinerary with respect to which the film is at once an interpreter and a material witness. As an outsider to the Holocaust Lanzmann will, indeed, like Karski, have to *travel* toward the inside. He, too, will accomplish his own voyage toward the Other, an uncanny voyage made of actual trips and of a

---

[21]Panel Discussion of *Shoah*, Yale University, May 5, 1986. Transcript, pp. 51–52.

[22]"Get me out of here," says Karski to the Jewish Bund leader when he "cannot take it any more" (174).

series of geographical and biographical displacements, of which the film—and the process of its making—are both a replica and the testimonial culmination.

Lanzmann starts his journey as a patriotic Frenchman, attuned to social and political French preoccupations and to contemporary philosophical concerns. "I was not brought up in Jewishness," he pointed out in his 1986 interview at Yale. "My paternal grandfather, who became a French citizen in 1913, at the age of 39, was called up for the French army at the very outbreak of the [First World] war, and fought for four years at the front line with the soldiers who had graduated in the 1913 high school class. He was wounded three times and obtained the highest French military distinctions . . . After the War . . . [my family] thought it had given enough blood for France, cut most of its ties with the Jewish world, and plunged into the ambiguous adventure of assimilation. I say 'ambiguous' because assimilation, in many respects, can be considered as destruction" (*Interview*). Lanzmann, disconnected both from the cultural tradition and from the history of Jews, is educated in French culture and, as a student, specializes in German philosophy.

From this position of exteriority to Jewishness and to the inside of the Holocaust, Lanzmann, during World War II, fights the Nazis as a member of the French Underground and as a student Resistance leader. His father, one of the Resistance leaders in Auvergne, nonetheless teaches his children how, in their capacity as Jews or as potential victims, they should above all be the masters of the art of disappearance. "He would ring the bell of the main entrance of the house we lived in," Lanzmann narrates, "in much the same way as the militia or the Gestapo would have done it. Jolted out of sleep, we had to break speed records—which he would time with a chronometer—to put on our clothes and take refuge in an underground hiding place which he had dug up in the middle of the garden. The house we lived in was the most silent in the world: the hinges of each door were oiled with compulsive regularity and accuracy. Thus our father taught us to escape perception and to remain invisible . . . I was not Jewish by tradition or by education, "but I think that the war as such has made me very much aware of what it is to be a Jew" (*Interview*). This glimpse of the inside is still essentially grasped only from outside: Jewishness is for the first time recognized as a potential threat, but the threat is not experienced as a real danger inside history, but rather, as the frightening inside of the father's thinking and imagination. "My father was a very pessimistic man," Lanzmann explains. "The worst was always sure for him. He had no doubts about it . . . In one way he was insane. But in another way he was . . . absolutely right". The inside of the Otherness of Jewishness is thus unwittingly, obscurely grasped, in the midst of the patriotic freedom struggle of the Frenchman, as the (neither true nor false) enigmatic locus of a fear in the father's fantasy. Out there in history, however, the real danger crucially remains, for the adolescent Lanzmann (who is fifteen years old in November 1940), in the military risks taken by the French Resistance and in the political menace which the Nazis represent for France, for Europe and for the Western world.

After the war, Lanzmann is inspired by the philosophical work of his future friend and mentor Jean-Paul Sartre, who, in 1946, publishes his *Reflexions sur la question juive*.[23] Lanzmann comments on the impact of this publication: "[The] book . . . was absolutely crucial for me . . . It was something, what the greatest French writer had written . . . [on the question of anti-Semitism]. This permitted us to breathe. It was a kind of *reconnaissance*, of acknowledgment . . . The picture of the anti-Semite that Sartre gave is still exemplary today". Via Sartre, the acknowledgment (*reconnaissance*) of the Jewish question can remain, however, an external—as opposed to an internal—recognition, the acknowledgment from the outside of the reality of anti-Semitism but, by the same token, only of the mythic fictionality of the Jew, of the *unreal* negativity of Judaism in the anti-Semite's fiction.

Belatedly, Lanzmann recognizes, on another level, that Sartre's book itself encompasses a remarkable silence, that it omits mentioning the Holocaust in spite of its date of publication at a crucial turning point of history:

> The book was published in 1946 . . . And yet there is not a word in it about the Holocaust; because the Holocaust is an event that was no one at the time could grasp in its full scope. [*Interview*]

After the war, Lanzmann undertakes a series of successive travels, a series of negotiations of the inside and the outside, whose combination constitutes, I would suggest, the itinerary of an existential search whose destination, *a priori*, is unknown and that will eventually lead him to the inside of the film, and to the film as the locus of a true discovery of the inside.

Lanzmann's postwar search begins in Germany. "I went to Germany very early, in 1947. I spent one year in Tubingen . . . I was studying philosophy, this was my field, and Germany was a country of philosophy in spite of the Nazis. There was Kant. There was Leibniz. There was

[23]Translated into English under the title *Anti-Semite and Jew*, New York-Random House, 1965.

Hegel . . . The year after, I was appointed lecturer at Berlin University during the blockade of Berlin . . . Berlin was destroyed completely. I wanted to see the Germans, in plain clothes" (*Interview*). "What do you think impelled you to go to Germany?" the interviewer asks. Lanzmann replies: "I can understand myself only in the process of creation, with a pen . . . or with a camera. Even now it is unclear to me why I went to Germany . . . At the time, and I was not alone—this was the case for most people, even in Europe—we didn't fully grasp the scope—and the immensity—of the catastrophe. We didn't . . . Even the people who returned from concentration camps could not, or did not want to, talk at the time" (*Interview*).

The position of the European scholar—the pure lover of philosophy, or the lover of pure philosophy—which Lanzmann occupies during his stay in Germany, is unknowingly again, in the wake of Sartre, an oblivious theoretical position marked by an unrecognized omission, a modified position of exteriority to the insiders of the Holocaust and of pragmatic, practical outsidedness to the reality and the immediacy of Jewish European history. From this stay in Germany as a professional philosopher Lanzmann recalls, however, one incident that, from the midst of his cosmopolitan engagement, returned him unwittingly to "the Jewish question":

When I was a lecturer in Berlin I was giving a course . . . about Sartre (*Being and Nothingness*) and about Stendhal (*The Red and the Black*) . . . One day a group of German students came to me . . . and . . . asked me if I would hold with them a seminar on anti-Semitism. I said why not, yes . . . We started to [conduct] this [seminar]. After three weeks, I was called by the French military commander in Berlin, General Ganvel . . . [who] told me: "I forbid you to hold this seminar . . . Berlin is a sensitive town, at the . . . crossroad of five nationalities: the Americans, the British, the Russians, the French and the Germans . . . This [seminar on anti-Semitism] is politics, and you are not supposed to engage in politics." [*Interview*]

In response to the German students' expressed wish to face history and to confront themselves, in an attempt to understand anti-Semitism as a driving force which guided Germany throughout the war—and its meaning for them now—Lanzmann sets out—under the aegis of philosophy—to ask a real question and to make a real impact, to meditatively engage with history so as to move it forward, toward a change, toward a lesson of the war, or at least toward the process of a dialogue and of a historicization of the trauma. But the Franco-German seminar on anti-Semitism is irrevocably prohibited by the

French military command, which forbids precisely Lanzmann to engage (to intervene) in historical, political processes. Later, Lanzmann will identify in this diplomatic prohibition the Allies' share in the forgetting—and in the denial—of the war: the closing of the seminar is itself a symptom of the Western world's inability to face the Holocaust, an allegory of the postwar historical repression of historical processes by the Allies. "I always have maintained, and I still do today," says Lanzmann, "that if the Germans of today are unable to face their past, to integrate it into their history, if the de-Nazification [of Germany] was made so badly, it is not only the fault of the Germans: it is the fault of the Allied powers too" (*Interview*, p. 17).

At the time, however, Lanzmann is surprised by the political repercussions of his professional philosophical concerns: "We were real philosophy students. This is what counted for us most . . . We were discussing Plato and Descartes and Kant. We were working hard in the field. The political side was secondary in a way, even with what happened" (*Interview*, p. 17). Politics thus catches Lanzmann unawares. In the split Berlin, he unexpectedly discovers politics as something he unwillingly comes up against from within his very passionate engagement in philosophy. He discovers that, in some obscure way, politics—apparently an outside business—has to do with the *inside*. But he is still too much outside, still an outsider to his own discovery. From the Franco-German philosophical exteriority to the immediacy of Jewish history, "at the [inadvertent] crossroads of five nationalities," the unrecognized inside of the Jewish question ironically returns, still only theoretically, still only from outside (from France), but in the form of the absolute constraint of a practical reality and in the lived predicament of an unforgettable and irrevocable pragmatic prohibition. Even though he is outside France, France is unwittingly reminding Lanzmann that he is not outside the question, nor is the question—or the asking of philosophy—outside the impact, or the processes, of politics.

The next stage in Lanzmann's existential voyage is East Germany. Out of a strong desire to work out an understanding of the Communist bloc, and to understand the Russians who have helped to bring about the victory over the Nazis, Lanzmann applies for a visa to East Berlin.[24]

[24]"One has to understand first of all," Lanzmann explains, "what the Russians meant for Europeans. It was much more important than the Americans. When the war broke out between Germany and . . . the Soviet Union, it was a fantastic relief, because we thought that the liberation would come thanks . . . to the Russians. I remember very well Stalingrad, which was a turning point in the story of the war . . . We were extremely grateful to the Russians. It was a kind of sky over our head . . . a protection. You must understand the feelings toward the Communists at the time. They were fighters and

He is denied the visa, but nonetheless accomplishes the trip without permission, *underground*, and publishes (in ten articles in *Le Monde*) the first French newspaper reportage on East Germany during the Cold War.

Lanzmann's next trip is to Israel, where he goes with a similar goal in mind: to send a reportage on the problems of the Middle East to the same French newspaper, which has in fact solicited it. The successive biographical positions of the wartime *French patriotic activist* and of the *European (cosmopolitan) philosopher*, are thus replaced by the position of the *international reporter*, in this consistent movement toward the outside and toward the Other, a movement which repeatedly combines geographical displacements with the formulation of some philosophical and analytical reflections. These analytical reflections—these persistent philosophical and epistemological displacements—are both triggered and enabled, each time, by the recurrent movement of the *physical transgression of a boundary*.

In Israel, however, this crossing to the outside abruptly and unsettlingly reveals an inside: the inside of Jewishness which is, for the first time, recognized as a reality in its own right, and a reality which, furthermore, has resonance inside himself. The voyage outside toward the Other inadvertently comes up against the inside of the Other in himself.

> I went to Israel for the first time in 1952 and it was a real shock for me to discover that there was a real Jewish world, to discover, let us say, the Jewish positivity . . . I had many debates with Israelis, because I saw it according to Sartre, [and thought] that the Jew was a pure creation of the anti-Semite . . . I discovered that this was not true. I felt immediately these Israelis as my brothers, [and thought] that I was born French by pure chance. [*Interview*]

they were fighting against the Germans" (*Interview*).

If one remembers, in addition to the significance of the Russians during the war, the fact that Lanzmann's grandfather had originally come to Paris from White Russia, after having spent a period of his life, as a transition, in Berlin (*Interview*, p. 1), one realizes that Lanzmann's itinerary—from Paris to Berlin to East Berlin (as an attempt to understand the Russians)—reenacts unwittingly the Grandfather's itinerary *in reverse*. Of all the possible significations of the direction of his journey, Lanzmann is aware only of the fact that it is a trip toward anxiety, a retracing in reverse of the obscure itinerary of a *flight*. Both the later journey of the film *Shoah* and Lanzmann's biographical itinerary embody, thus, a *reaching out toward anxiety* in a drive to search and to explore its source, its origin and its dynamic: "But if you ask me," Lanzmann comments, "why I wanted to go to Germany, I have another answer too. I wanted to go east, because I am afraid of the east . . . When I drive my car, when I want to go outside of Paris . . . my first movement is to go west. I feel at ease when I go west, and. . .it scares me to travel to the East. And Germany for me was the East . . . The obsession of the East [is in the film] . . . When I was in Poland . . . in one way I like Poland and I like Russia too. But there is a movement Eastward which is frightening" (*Interview*).

From Israel, the traveler also discovers that he can no longer simply write as a reporter, simply expedite to France a reportage. Unexpectedly, the inside is encountered as a *resistance to*—and an unsettlement of—*theory*. "I spent four months there," Lanzmann testifies, "but I was unable to write this report . . . I could not write about Israel as if I would have written about India or any other kind of country. I could not" (*Interview*). In other words, Lanzmann discovers that he can no longer simply *write as an outsider*, simply *testify from the outside*. But he does not yet entirely possess the meaning of the difficulty.

Why Israel

At first he thinks that it is simply the medium which is at fault, that journalism is not the appropriate realm for his philosophical attempt at understanding. He consequently sets out to write, instead of the reportage, a book. But the book, of which he writes about a hundred pages, will turn out to be equally impossible, lacking focus and simultaneously pursuing too many directions. The material of the difficulty would itself become, belatedly, both the substance and the subject of Lanzmann's first film. At the time of the endeavor of the book, however, Lanzmann finds himself blocked and entangled:

> I could not go on because [the book] raised too many questions that I was not able to answer . . . It was an aborted book . . . It was only twenty years later that this unrealized reportage and this aborted book became the film *Pourquoi Israel* ("Why Israel"), which I created very fast, almost without preparation. I knew exactly what I wanted to say . . . The questions which are unresolved in the book are solved in the film, but not on the same level . . . I had to grow up and there are questions that . . . become meaningless in the course of life . . . You give the answers, but on another level. [*Interview*]

Film would thus seem to be the very medium which accommodates the simultaneous multiplicity of levels and directions, a medium that can visually *inscribe*—and cinematically bear witness to—*the very impossibility of writing*. The film is not merely an overcoming of the actual impossibility, but specifically, a testimony to it. Very like the necessity of "going on" for the Holocaust survivors, the film also speaks about what is impossible and yet what *must be done*: "We have to do it. You know it."

This impossibility which Israel embodies for Lanzmann, first in the actual impossibility of writing and later in the very possibility of film as a testimony to—and an inscription to—that same impossibility, is, I would suggest, the impossibility, on the one hand, of *saying the inside from the outside*, and, on the other hand, the imperative necessity of speaking from inside *to* the outside; the contradictory and yet compellingly intransigent necessity of being outside and inside at the same time.

As in Karski's case, however, Lanzmann's journey into the inside and into the reality of Otherness is equally made possible by the creation of a "we" ("Don't be afraid, we are Jews"),[25] by a loving dialogue engaged with an insider who is also, on another level, like himself in some way an outsider, a companion who thus mediates the difficult negotiation of the inside and the outside and facilitates the trip inside by transforming it, here as in Karski's case, into the very journey of an oath of love. "It's really complicated, Lanzmann says, "because I'm not sure I would have done this film had I not met in Jerusalem my [future] wife":

> She was not my wife at the time, she was a strange woman and she was half German-Jewish, a writer. She introduced me to the world of the German Jews in Israel, and it was for me a revelation to see these people who had left Germany between 1933 and 1939 with libraries full of Schiller, Goethe, Kant, and the entire German culture. It was a connection with my first years in Germany and it was a real estrangement for me and I liked this very much. I did the film [*Pourquoi Israël*] because I was in love with her and because it was the only way for me to be able to go to Israel and see her. I dedicated the film to her. [*Interview*]

The uniqueness of his first film opens for Lanzmann the possibility of addressing the unconscious question of his search—and the unknown direction of his journey—in yet another film, when his Israeli friends—resonating to his own unformulated cinematic message—charge him with the task of undertaking *Shoah*: of continuing the taxing and creative journey toward the inside and the progression backwards, by setting out to undertake, equally in an unprecedented way, on the still less accessible subject of the Holocaust—on this *unspeakable* insidedness of Jewish history—a film that would nonetheless be really *telling*: a film that would *speak*, this time, no longer simply from inside the Jewish (national, political and military) self-determination marked by Israel—from Israel as the embodiment of

---

[25]"We jumped Into a house," Karski narrates. "He just hits the door: 'Open the door! Open the door! They open the door. We move in . . . He says: 'All right, all right, don't be afraid, *we* are Jews' " (173; emphasis mine).

the postwar, post-Holocaust Jewish regeneration and national *resistance to annihilation*—but rather, from inside the very trap of the *absolute exposure to annihilation*, from within very process of undergoing—with no defense, no ally and no recourse whatsoever—one's own radical historical and physical erasure. Lanzmann's problem thus becomes the following: how to *speak* about—and *from inside*—erasure, without being reduced to silence, without being oneself erased; how *to be heard* about—and from inside—erasure; how to make a film from inside annihilation that would speak with equal force, however, *both to insiders and to outsiders*; how to make a film that would speak, indeed, in a performatively liberating way, not merely by dynamically *undoing* the *exclusion of the inside*, but by actively *enabling*, at the same time, the *inclusion of the outside*.

Toward a Black Sun

Shoah—this ultimate stepping inside, this unprecedented *face-to-face with the inside* and, most specifically, with the inside's *resistance to be faced*—is in this way conceived, ironically enough, as yet another task proposed to Lanzmann from outside, as yet another undertaking triggered or initiated not by Lanzmann's own direct possession and acknowledgment of the sense of his own movement, but by his friends' perception of the true *direction* of his journey, by the Israelis' notion of where it was that Lanzmann—with his unique audacity and his transgressive creativity—was truly heading.

> The Israelis . . . asked me if I would consider undertaking a film about the Holocaust . . . I said yes rather quickly, without thinking very much . . . After I started, it became impossible to stop. [*Interview*, p. 21]

Thus begins Lanzmann's eleven-year involvement with the process of the making of the film, a process which itself inaugurates as yet another journey, a new research[26] and a renewed, continued stubborn search: a constant struggle to assemble—and to reassemble—the material and financial means for the production[27], the stubborn

---

[26]Covering fourteen countries, and materializing into 350 hours of film, edited into the nine and a half hours of the actual movie.

[27]"*Shoah* cost between three million dollars and four million dollars—all from France and Israel. Lanzmann took out a loan of four million francs to finish the film. 'No American investors could be found,' he says." *The Boston Globe*, Nov. 3, 1985, p. 3.

tracking of survivors commonly believed to be dead[28]; the audacious hunting of ex-Nazis and their surreptitious filming by a secret camera.[29] At one point, Lanzmann's secret filming is discovered by a reluctant Nazi witness (a former member of the *Einsatzkommando*): Lanzmann is beaten up and has to be hospitalized for a month. His camera and film are taken away. But Lanzmann recovers and comes back to continue the creation of the film, now haunted by the fear that his own death might interrupt his work before the work is finished.

But the making of the film, replicating in this way the biographical itinerary of the *travel toward anxiety*, has reached, by now, a point of no return.[30] The production of the film becomes itself, thus, both a race against time and a race against death.[31]; a contest in which something must at all costs be historically, decisively *won*; a race, however, which admits no compromise, no shortcuts[32]. "*Shoah* is a film full of fear—and of energy too," Lanzmann says in looking back, in recalling both the obstacles and the momentum, both the urgency and the endurance of his own long-distance race toward the realization of the film: "It was a work of patience, but it was a mixture of patience and emergency together" (*Interview*). The unusual combination, the different trainings and lucidities of all the previous biographi-

---

[28]"Almost as soon as I began making the film in 1974, it vanished from me," Lanzmann narrates. "I knew I needed a very special kind of survivor—the people of the special work detail—Jews who were forced to transport the corpses from the gas chambers to the crematorium. They were the direct witnesses of the death of their own people . . . They were all kids, but there are now not many of them left . . . I went to research institutes in Israel, New York and London, and got names [of survivors] from researchers in the Holocaust field. The real question was to convince them to talk. This was not easy" (*Ibid.*).

[29]"Every Nazi in the film was a miracle," Lanzmann says. "I negotiated with Suchomel for a year. Finally, I agreed to pay him. I have film showing him getting paid. I succeeded by telling him, 'Listen, I am not a prosecutor. I am not a judge. I am not a Nazi-hunter.' " Suchomel agreed to be taped, but not filmed. Lanzmann filmed him . . . using a camera concealed in a bag of what Suchomel thought was sound equipment ("I was afraid he would see sunlight reflecting off the lens"). The signal was beamed to an unmarked truck parked just outside, containing TV equipment. "I had under my shoulder a very flat transmitter and a microphone in my tie. Even in the hottest weather, I had to wear a suit jacket. I had to sweat, out of heat, but also out of fear" (*Ibid.*).

[30]"There is a point of no return in this world," Lanzmann says: "it's like when you climb the . . . unexplored North face, and you have to invent the way. There is a moment you cannot retreat. Either you have to reach the summit or fall" (*Interview*).

[31]"If one sees the film, one senses a feeling of real emergency, not only because I felt the people would disappear or die, but because the more I was advancing in the film, the more I feared my own death without finishing. I had some difficult nights about this" (quoted in "A Monument against Forgetting," *The Boston Globe*, Nov. 3, 1985, p. 3).

[32]"If somebody would have told me," Lanzmann says, "If you don't finish at such a date, you would have had your head cut,' . . . I would have had my head cut" (*Interview*).

cal positions that were given up ultimately for the film's sake (the wartime activist, the continental scholar, the professional philosopher, the international reporter, the underground visitor, the political and philosophical investigator) are in fact implicitly maintained and productively included in the film's journey and achievement. Between the quick decision, the light acceptance and the unawareness of the start and the race, the anguish of the finish, between the obstacles—the impossibilities of going on and the impossibility of stopping—a work of an unprecedented scope and of an incommensurate dimension is most lucidly and yet unwittingly created.

Unlike the previous biographical and existential voyages, here Lanzmann's movement for the first time knows from the beginning the real destination of the journey: to go *toward the Holocaust*; to *go inside* the history of an erasure. And yet the journey, here again, reveals to what extent its own supposed knowledge of its destination is in reality illusory. Lanzmann discovers the many ways in which he *does not know* what, at the starting point, he unfoundedly believed he knew:

> When I started to work on *Shoah* . . . I was like many Jews, I thought I knew: I thought I had this in my blood, which is a stupidity . . . When I read Hilberg, for instance, I discovered that in spite of the fact that I had read already many books, I was perfectly ignorant. [*Interview*, p. 16]

Lanzmann discovers, thus, the way in which the Jews themselves are also *mere outsiders* to their own history—to their own Holocaust. The ignorance unwittingly discovered does not proceed, in fact, from a deficiency in erudition—from not yet having read the best books on the subject—but from the way in which the Holocaust reveals itself as incommensurate with knowledge, the way in which the Holocaust unconsciously and actively conjures up its own forgetting and resists—above all—its own knowing from inside. "The Holocaust," says Lanzmann, "is very difficult to face":

> It is like a black sun, and you always have to struggle against yourself in order to go on. It's what happened during the process [of the making] of the film. I had to struggle against my own irrepressible tendency to forget what I had done. It happened . . . while I was building some scenes, in spite of the fact that I knew . . . that I had shot them, [in spite of the fact] that I had typed all the words, and so on . . . Suddenly I was reading and I said, 'But I never saw this.' It was not true. It was repression." [*Panel Discussion*, p. 39]

I always had to fight in myself a tendency to repulse what I was doing.
It was very difficult to face. It was like a black sun. I had to go deep
inside myself.[33]

The journey toward the film, the struggle toward a narration of the
Holocaust *in light*, is thus not simply a historical, unprecedented
journey toward erasure, but a journey, at the same time, both *into*
and *outside of* the black sun inside oneself. To understand *Shoah* is
not to *know* the Holocaust, but to gain new insights into what *not
knowing* means, to grasp the ways in which *erasure* is itself part of
the functioning of our *history*. The journey of *Shoah* thus paves the
way toward new possibilities of understanding history, and toward
new pragmatic *acts* of historicizing history's erasures.

V

A Point of Arrival

The crucial testimony about the sense and the direction of Lanzmann's journey is, however, not external but internal to the film itself.
It addresses the spectator, right away, in Lanzmann's own voice, from
within the very writing on the screen which constitutes the film's
silent opening.

> Of the four hundred thousand men, women and children who went
> there, only two came out alive: Mordechaï Podchlebnik and Simon
> Srebnik. Srebnik, survivor of the last period, was a boy of thirteen when
> he went to Chelmno . . .
> I found him in Israel and persuaded that one-time boy singer to
> return with me to Chelmno. [3–4; emphasis mine]

Something is found, here, in Israel, which embodies in effect a point
of arrival in Lanzmann's journey, as well as the beginning—or the
starting point—of the journey of the film. "*I found him in Israel.*" I
would suggest that the artistic power of the film proceeds, precisely,
from this *finding*: the *event* of *Shoah* is an event of finding. Unlike
Karski, whose journey into the inside and into Otherness has left him
only with the memory of the acute experience of a *losing* ("I never
saw him again."), Lanzmann's journey—even if it has, undoubtedly,
encountered losses on its way—has amounted to a crucial *finding*.

[33]Quoted in *The Boston Globe*, Nov. 3, 1985, p. 3.

What is it exactly that Lanzmann, at the outset of the film, *finds*? He finds, I would suggest, the *paths* to finding; he finds some further questions which unfold uncannily before him the obscure direction of his own pursuit. He finds, especially, the depth and the complexity, the nonsimplicity and the committed interminability involved in the very process of arriving, reaching, finding. The inaugural event of finding is itself already constituted by a number of implied—and incommensurable—discoveries, which the film sets out to explore on different levels.

1. The *finding*, first and foremost, is the finding of Simon Srebnik, the astonishing winning survivor, "that one-time boy singer" who was literally executed (shot in the head) and yet miraculously, more than once, fooled death and survived:

   With his ankles in chains, like all his companions, the boy shuffled through the village of Chelmno each day. That he was kept alive longer than the others he owed to his extreme agility, which made him the winner of jumping contests and speed races that the SS organized for their chained prisoners. And also to his melodious voice: several times a week . . . young Srebnik rowed up the Narew, under guard, in a flat-bottomed boat . . . He sang Polish folk tunes, and in return the guard taught him Prussian military songs . . .

   During the night of January 18, 1945, two days before Soviet troops arrived, the Nazis killed all the remaining Jews in the "work details" with a bullet in the head. Simon Srebnik was among those executed. But the bullet missed his vital brain centers. When he came to, he crawled into a pigsty. A Polish farmer found him there. The boy was treated and healed by a Soviet Army doctor. A few months later Simon left for Tel-Aviv along with other survivors of the death camps.

   I found him in Israel and persuaded that one-time boy singer to return with me to Chelmno. [3–4]

2. The *finding* is thus also, at the same time, the finding of a *site* of entering, the discovery of the unique significance of a *place*: the discovery of Israel as the place where, on the one hand, the remnants of the extinguished European Jewery could gather (find each other), and where, on the other hand, Lanzmann, coming from outside, can for the first time look inside and discover the reality of the Jews (as opposed to the anti-Semites' fictions)—a reality materially created and conditioned as the outcome of a history. The discovery of Israel is thus the finding of a place which enables Lanzmann, for the first time, to *inhabit* his own implication of the story of the Other (Srebnik's story).

3. The finding is the *finding of testimony*—of its singular significance and functioning as the story of an *irreplaceable historical
   performance*, a narrative performance which no statement (no
   report and no description) can replace and whose unique enactment by the living witness is itself part of a *process of realization*
   of historic truth. Insofar as this realization is, by definition, what
   cannot simply be reported, or narrated, by another, Lanzmann
   finds in Israel, precisely, that which cannot be reported: both
   the general significance and the material, singular concretiza-
   tions of the testimony (Srebnik's testimony, as well as others').

4. Israel becomes the place from which Lanzmann can himself, for
   the first time, testify from the inside (as both an inside and an
   outside witness), the place, in other words, in which Lanzmann
   for the first time finds a voice with which he can say "I" and with
   which he can articulate his own testimony: "*I found* him in Israel
   and *persuaded* that one-time boy singer to return with me . . ."
   The finding is the finding of the power and the function of
   Lanzmann's "persuasion," the finding of his own unique voice
   and of the necessity and irreplaceability of his own testimony.

5. Finally, the finding is *the finding of the film* itself: *Shoah* rethinks,
   as well, the meaning and the implications of the advent (of the
   event) of its own finding. To find the film is to find a new
   possibility of sight, a possibility not just of vision—but of revision. While for Karski, the trip inside means first the gaining,
   but then the losing, of the possibility of seeing and specifically,
   of "seeing again" ("I never saw him again"), Lanzmann finds
   precisely in the film the material possibility and the particular
   potential of *seeing again* someone like Srebnik whom, after his
   shooting, no one was likely or supposed to ever see again. Even
   more astonishingly, the finding of the film provides in general,
   in history, the possibility of *seeing again* what in fact was never
   seen the first time, what remained *originally unseen* due to the
   inherent blinding nature of the occurrence.

The Return

The film does not stop, however, at the site of its own finding(s),
does not settle at its initial point of arrival, but rather, uses the arrival
as a point of departure for another *kind* of journey, a *return trip* which,
going back to the originally unperceived historical scene, takes place
as a journey to another frame of reference, entering into what Freud

calls "eine andere Lokalität"—into another scale of space and time: "I found him in Israel and persuaded that one-time boy singer to *return with me to Chelmno.*"

Why is it necessary to return to Chelmno? What is the return about? Who, or what, returns?

> We are, I am, you are
> by cowardice or courage
> the one who find our way
> back to this scene[34]
> carrying a knife, a camera
> a book of myths
> in which our names do not appear.[35]

The return in *Shoah* (and in Lanzmann's trip) from Israel to Europe (Poland, Chelmno), from the place of the regeneration and the locus of the gathering of Holocaust survivors back to the prehistory of their oppression and suppression, back to the primal scene of their annihilation, is at once a spatial and a temporal return, a movement back in space and time which, in attempting to revisit and to repossess the past is also, simultaneously, a movement forward toward the future. "I did not want to go to Poland," Lanzmann narrates. "I had a deep refusal in me to go to Poland. I thought that one can talk about this from everywhere, from any place—from Paris, from Jerusalem, from New Haven . . . And I said, 'what will I see in Poland, I will see the nothingness, I will see the absence.' And I did not want to go. And I went there, really, at the very end, and I had to beat myself. But something extraordinary happened . . . When I arrived in Poland I was really loaded with knowledge, with inquiries I had made before—I was loaded like a bomb. But the fuse was missing. And Poland was for me the fuse of this bomb."[36] The *return to Chelmno*, therefore, is

---

[34]"The film," Lanzmann says, "is at moments a crime film . . . [on the mode of] a criminal investigation . . . But it is a Western too. When I returned to the small village of Grabow, or even in Chelmno . . . Okay. I arrive here with a camera, with a crew, but forty years after . . . This creates an incredible . . . event, you know? Well . . . I am the first man to come back to the scene of the crime, where the crime has been committed" (*Panel Discussion*, p. 53).

[35]Adrienne Rich, *Diving into the Wreck*, New York and London: W. W. Norton, 1973, p. 22.

[36]And I started to explode," Lanzmann continues, describing the effect of Poland on his creative journey. "And to explode means that for years afterward, and during the whole shooting of the film, I was possessed and I hallucinated. I have filmed these stones of the Treblinka camp for days and days in every season, because the seasons are very important in this film . . . And I remember my camera man telling me, 'But you are insane! We have already hundreds of shots of these stones, what do you want to do with it? These are only stones!' But the stones were for me the killed Jews, the human beings. I had nothing else to film except the stones, and I filmed them with such

both a historical return (a return in time) of Srebnik and a no less difficult biographical and geographical return (a return in space) of Lanzmann. Lanzmann's force of persuasion exercized on Srebnik (". . . and I *persuaded* that one-time boy singer to return") had to be equally exercised, no less energetically and forcefully, on himself, for the return to be put into effect, in this new initiation of a dialogic journey motivated, once again, by the creation of a "we" ("I persuaded [him] to return *with me* to Chelmno").

The Return of the Dead

The return to Chelmno by the boy singer for whom the Chelmno period ended with a bullet in the head concretizes at the same time, allegorically, a historical return of the dead. In a way, the returning forty-seven-year-old Srebnik ("He was then forty-seven years old", 4), reappearing on the screen at the site of the annihilation, the improbable survivor who returns from Israel to the European scene of the crime against him, is himself rather a ghost of his own youthful performance, a returning, reappearing ghost of the one-time winner of chained races and of the boy singer who moved the Poles and charmed the SS, and who, like Scheherazade, succeeded in postponing his own death indefinitely by telling (singing) songs. Thus, if Srebnik on the screen at forty-seven, in the scene of Chelmno of today, embodies a return of the dead, his improbable survival and his even more improbable return (his ghostly reappearance) concretizes allegorically, in history, a return of the (missing, dead) witness on the scene of the event-without-a-witness.

Srebnik had, during the Holocaust, witnessed in effect himself, in Chelmno, a return of the dead—a return to life of the half-asphyxiated bodies tumbling out of the gas vans. But he witnessed this revival, this return of the dead, only so as to become a witness to their second murder, to an even more infernal killing (or rekilling) of the living dead, by a burning of their bodies while those are still alive and conscious of their burning, conscious of their own encounter with the flames by which they are engulfed, devoured:

> When [the gas vans] arrived, the SS said: "Open the doors!" . . . The bodies tumbled right out . . . We worked until the whole shipment was burned.

---

a feeling of emergency that they became for me the human beings and that they have become now for the viewers the human beings." (*Evening* pp. 4–5).

> I remember that once they were still alive. The ovens were full, and the people lay on the ground. They were all moving, they were coming back to life, and when they were thrown into the ovens, they were all conscious. Alive. They could feel the fire burn them. [101–102]

Srebnik's witness dramatizes both a burning consciousness of death, and a crossing (and recrossing) of the boundary line which separates the living from the dead, and death from life. But when Srebnik saw all that, he was not really a (living) witness since, like Bomba[37], like Podchlebnik,[38] he too was already *deadened.*

> When I saw all this, it didn't affect me . . . I was only thirteen, and all I'd ever seen until then were dead bodies. Maybe I didn't understand, maybe if I'd been older, but the fact is, I didn't. I'd never seen anything else. In the ghetto in Lodz I saw that as soon as anyone took a step, he fell dead. I thought that's the way things had to be, that it was normal. I'd walk the streets of Lodz, maybe one hundred yards, and there'd be two hundred bodies. They went into the street and they fell, they fell . . .
>
> So when I came . . . to Chelmno, I was already . . . I didn't care about anything. [102–103]

Therefore, it is only now, today that Srebnik can become a witness to the *impact* of the falling (and the burning) bodies,[39] only today that he can situate his witnessing in a frame of reference that is not submerged by death and informed solely by *Figuren*, by dead bodies. It is therefore only now, in returning with Lanzmann to Chelmno, that Srebnik in effect is returning from the dead (from his own deadness) and can become, for the first time, a witness to himself, as well as an articulate and for the first time fully *conscious* witness of what he had been witnessing during the war.

The Return of the Witness

Urged by Lanzmann, Srebnik's return from the dead personifies, in this way, a historically performative and retroactive *return of witnessing* to the witnessless historical primal scene.

[37]Bomba: "I tell you something. To have a feeling about that . . . it was very hard to feel anything, because working there day and night between dead people, between bodies, your feelings disappeared, you were dead. You had no feeling at all" (p. 116).

[38]Podchlebnik: *"What died in him in Chelmno?* Everything died" (p. 6).

[39]On the impact of the falling body, in conjunction with an innovative theory of reference, see Cathy Caruth's remarkable essay "The Claims of Reference," in The Yale Journal of Criticism, vol. 4, no. 1, Fall 1990. See also her *Empirical Truths and Critical Fictions: Locke, Wordsworth, Kant and Freud*, Baltimore, Johns Hopkins University Press: 1990.

Srebnik recognizes Chelmno.

It's hard to recognize, but it was here. They burned people here . . . Yes,
this is the place. No one ever left here again . . . It was terrible. No one
can describe it . . . And no one can understand it. Even I, here, now . . .
I can't believe I'm here. No, I just can't believe it. It was always this
peaceful here. Always. When they burned two thousand people—
Jews—every day, it was just as peaceful. No one shouted. Everyone
went about his work. It was silent. Peaceful. Just as it is now. [6]

Chelmno recognizes Srebnik. The Polish villagers remember well
the child entertainer who "had to . . . [sing when] his heart wept" (p.
6), and they identify and recognize the pathos and the resonance, the
lyrics and the melody of his repeated singing:

He was thirteen and a half years old. He had a lovely singing voice, and
we heard him.
> "A little white house
> lingers in my memory
> Of that little white house
> I dream each night." [4]

"When I heard him again," one of the Polish villagers remarks, "my
heart beat faster, because what happened here . . . was a murder. I
really relived what happened" (4).

Lanzmann places Srebnik in the center of a group of villagers before
the church in Chelmno, which, at the time, served as a prison-house
for the deported Jews and as the ultimate waystation on their journey—via gas vans—to the forest, where the (dead or living) bodies
were being burned away in so-called ovens. The villagers at first
seem truly happy to see Srebnik, whom they welcome cheerfully and
warmly.

Are they glad to see Srebnik again?
Very. It's a great pleasure. They're glad to see him again because
they know all he's lived through. Seeing him as he is now, they are very
pleased. [95]

Why does the memory linger? the inquirer would like to know. What
motivates this livelihood of the remembrance?

Why does the whole village remember him?
They remember him well because he walked with chains on his
ankles, and he sang on the river. He was young, he was skinny, he
looked ready for the coffin . . . Even the [Polish] lady, when she saw
that child, she told the German: "Let that child go!" He asked her:

"Where to?" "To his father and mother." Looking at the sky [the German] said: "He'll soon go to them." [95–96]

When Lanzmann gets, however, to the specific subject of the role of the Church in the past massacre of the Jews, the Polish testimony becomes somewhat confused. The evocation of the memories becomes itself unknowingly tainted with fantasies.

> *They remember when the Jews were locked in this church?*
> Yes, they do . . .
> *The vans came to the church door! They all knew these were gas vans, to gas people?*
> Yes, they couldn't help knowing.
> *They heard screams at night?*
> The Jews moaned, they were hungry . . .
> *What kind of cries and moans were heard at night?*
> They called on Jesus and Mary and God, sometimes in German . . .
> *The Jews called on Jesus, Mary and God!*
> The presbytery was full of suitcases.
> *The Jews' suitcases?*
> Yes, and there was gold.
> *How does she know there was gold? The procession! We'll stop now.*
> [97–98]

Like the Nazi teacher's wife (who only "sees things from outside"; 82), the Poles embody outside witness—present an outside view of the Jewish destiny, but an outside view which nonetheless believes it can account for the inside: in trying to account for the inner meaning of the Jewish outcry from inside the church, and in accounting for the

The procession.

inner, unseen content of the robbed possessions of the Jews inside
the confiscated suitcases, the Poles bear in effect *false witness*. Out of
empathy in the first case, with respect to the imagined moaning of
the Jewish prisoners of the church, out of hostile jealousy and of
competitive aggression in the second case, with respect to the imaginary hidden treasures and envied possessions, the Poles distort the
facts and *dream their memory*, in exemplifying both their utter failure
to imagine Otherness and their simplified negotiation of the inside
and the outside, by merely projecting their inside on the outside. It is
to their own fantasy, to their own (self-)mystification that the Poles
bear witness, in attempting to account for historical reality. Their
false witness is itself, however, an objective illustration and concretization of the radically delusional quality of the event.

The scene is interrupted by the silence—and the sound of the
bells—of the procession, a church ritual executed by young girls
dressed in white, which celebrates the birth of the Virgin Mary.

This ritual celebration of the images of youth and the predominance
of white in the religious ceremony connote the innocence of childhood, the pure integrity and the intactness of virginity, which the
ritual is evoking as the attributes of the Holy Virgin. And yet, the
presence of Srebnik at the scene reminds us of another kind of child-

hood, and the contiguity of this rather unvirginal and violated child-hood (of the child who had to sing when his heart wept) with the immaculate virginity here enacted, of itself creates an almost sacrile-gious, and desacralizing, resonance, in an astounding, a vertiginous and a breath-taking cinematic condensation and juxtaposition of dif-ferent dimensions, of different registers of space and time, of different levels of existence and experience. The sudden, unexpected superim-position of the Holocaust in which the church served as a death enclosure (as the antechamber to the gas vans) and of the present Christian celebration of the birth of the Virgin Mary, brings out a terrible and silent irony, of a church that in effect embodies a mass tomb, at the same time that it celebrates a birth, of a site whose history is stained with blood, at the same time that it is the stage of an oblivious celebration of an ethical virginity and of an intactly white immaculateness. Very like the whiteness of the snow covering the forests of Sobibor, Auschwitz and Treblinka, the whiteness of the ritual itself turns out to be an image which, quite literally, covers up history, as the embodiment (and as the disembodiment) of a *white silence.*

Viewing the procession, one recalls Benjamin's discussion of con-temporary art and, particularly, of photography and film as vehicles, specifically, of desacrilization, as accelerating agents in the modern cultural process of the "shattering"—and of the "liquidiation"—of the *cult-values* of tradition:

> We know that the earliest art works originated in the service of a ritual—first the magical, then the religious kind . . . [Now] for the first time in world history, mechanical reproduction [photography and film] emancipates the work of art from its parasitical dependence on ritual . . . The total function of art is reversed. Instead of being based on ritual, [art] begins to be based on another practice—politics.[40]

It has been a long but sure way from the moment at which Lanz-mann, at the head of the Franco-German Seminar on Anti-Semitism in postwar Berlin, was surprised (caught unawares) by the political repercussions of his philosophical considerations, to this surprise translation, by his camera, of the religious into the artistic and of the artistic into the political, to this sudden exhibition, and this uncanny evidence of unexpected depths of political significance in the very ritual of the procession.

[40]Walter Benjamin, "The Work of Art in the Age of Mechanical Reproduction," in *Illuminations,* trans. Harry Zohn, ed. Hannah Arendt, New York: Schocken Books, 1968, pp. 223–224.

The Return of History

After the procession, Lanzmann—who does not forget—returns to the interrupted subject of the inside of the Jewish suitcases.

> *The lady said before that the Jews' suitcases were dumped in the house opposite [the church]. What was in this baggage?*
> Pots with false bottoms.
> *What was in the false bottoms?*
> Valuables, objects of value. They also had gold in their clothes . . .
> *Why do they think all this happened to the Jews?*
> Because they were the richest! Many Poles were also exterminated. Even Priests. [99]

Lanzmann's tour de force as interviewer is to elicit from the witness, as in this case, a testimony which is inadvertently no longer in the control or the possession of its speaker. As a solicitor and an assembler of the testimonies, in his function as a questioner but mainly, in his function as a listener (as the bearer of a narrative of listening), Lanzmann's performance is to elicit testimony which exceeds the testifier's own awareness, to bring forth a complexity of truth which, paradoxically, is *not available as such* to the very speaker who pronounces it. As a listener, Lanzmann endows the interlocutor with speech. It is in this way that he helps both the survivors and the perpetrators to overcome their (very different kind of) silence. Facing Lanzmann, the Polish villagers, in turn, exhibit feelings that would normally be hidden. But the silent interviewer and the silent camera urge us not simply to see the testimony, but to see *through* it: see— throughout the testimony—the deception and the self-deception which it unwittingly displays, and to which it unintentionally testifies.

> *Why do they think all this happened to the Jews?*
> Because they were the richest! Many Poles were also exterminated. Even Priests.

In response to Lanzmann's question, Mr. Kantorowski, the player of the organ and the singer of the church, finds his way out of the crowd which surrounds Srebnik and, pushing himself in front of the camera, overshadows Srebnik and eclipses him:

> Mr. Kantorowski will tell us what a friend told him. It happened in Myndjewyce, near Warsaw.
> *Go on.*
> The Jews there were gathered in a square. The rabbi asked an SS man: "Can I talk to them?" The SS man said yes. So the rabbi said that

around two thousand years ago the Jews condemned the innocent Christ to death. And when they did that, they cried out: "Let his blood fall on our heads and on our sons' heads." Then the rabbi told them: "Perhaps the time has come for that, so let us do nothing, let us go, let us do as we're asked."

He thinks the Jews expiated the death of Christ?

He doesn't think so, or even that Christ sought revenge. The rabbi said it. It was God's will, that's all.[41] [99–100]

Through the voice of the church singer which seems to take on the authority to speak for the whole group, and through the mythic mediation both of archetypal stereotypes of anti-Semitism and of the Christian story of the Crucifixion, the Poles endow the Holocaust with a strange comprehensibility and with a facile and exhaustive compatibility with knowledge: "It was God's will, that's all . . . That's all. *Now you know!*" (100). It is by dehistoricizing the events of recent history, and by subsuming them under the prophetic knowledge of the Scriptures, that the Poles are literally washing their hands of the historical extermination of the Jews:

So Pilate washed his hands and said: "Christ is innocent," and he sent Barabas. But the Jews cried out: "Let his blood fall on our heads!"

That's all. Now you know. [100]

Thus the Poles misrepresent, once more, the Jews from the inside and the objective nature of the Jewish destiny and slip, once more, across

[41]On the generalizable historical significance of this passage, see Peter Canning's remarkable analysis in "Jesus Christ, Holocaust: Fabulation of the Jews in Christian and Nazi History": "The compulsive ritual of accusing the Jews of murder (or betrayal, or well-poisoning, or desecration of the Host) and attacking them is inscribed with bodies in history; it is not prescribed but only implicitly suggested in the New Testament, which preaches love and forgiveness. In the Gospel it is 'the Jews' who call down the wrath of God on themselves: 'Let his blood be on us and on our children!' (Mt. 27:25) Reciting this text, the Polish villagers whom Claude Lanzmann interviewed . . . excuse themselves, the Germans and God—all are absolved of responsibility for the Holocaust. Once again, 'the Jews brought it on themselves.' The Crucifixion was their crime. The Holocaust was the punishment which they called down on their own heads, and on their children.

"The Biblical myth functions as an attractor, not only of other narratives but of ongoing events which it assimilates. What I must risk calling the Holo-myth of Christianity—divine incarnation, crucifixion, resurrection—is not the one source or cause of the Holocaust, it 'attracted' other causal factors to it (the war, inflation, political-ideological crisis, socio-economic convulsions), absorbed them and overde-termined their resolution . . . Those other critical factors, and their resolution in a fascist syncretism, were not alone capable of turning anti-Semitism into systematic mass murder. Nazism reactivated the cliché it had inherited from the Christian Holo-myth and its re-enactment in the event of ritual murder, but transformed it into a regular, mechanized destruction process." (*Copyright* 1, *Fin de siècle 2000*, Fall 1987, pp. 171–172).

Mr. Kantorowski speaking.

the boundary line between reality and fantasy: they unwittingly begin again to dream reality and to hallucinate their memory. In testifying to a murder which they go as far as to call suicide, the Poles bear once again false witness both to the history of Nazism and to the history of the Jews.

But once again, this misrepresentation (this false witness) is itself attributed precisely to the Jews and represented as *their* inside story. Like the Nazis, who make the Jews *pay* for their own death traffic and participate—through "work details"—in the management of their own slaughter, the Poles pretend to have the Jews provide their own interpretation of their history and their own explanation of their murder. Kantorowski thus claims that his own mythic account is in fact the Jews' own version of the Holocaust.

> *He thinks the Jews expiated the death of Christ?*
> He doesn't think so, or even that Christ sought revenge. The rabbi said it. It was God's will, that's all [100]

In forging, so to speak, the rabbi's signature so as to punctuate his own false witness and to authorize his own false testimony, Kantorowski disavows responsibility for his own discourse. In opposition to the act of signing and of saying "I" by which the authentic witnesses assume at once their discourse, their speech act and their responsibility toward history ("I found him in Israel and persuaded him to return . . . ," says Lanzmann; "I understand your role, I am here," says Karski; "I can't believe I'm here," says Srebnik), Kantorowski's testimony, like the secret Nazi document discussing the improvements of the gas vans ("Secret Reich Business"), is equally destined to remain unsigned.

Mr. Kantorowski, after all, does indeed in some ways remain silent. Not only because, as he claims, it is the words of the dead rabbi that *speak for him*. But because what *speaks through him* (in such a way as to account for his role during the Holocaust) is, on the one hand, the (historic) silence of the church and, on the other hand, the silence of all given frames of explanation, the nonspeech of all preconceived interpretative schemes, which dispose of the event—and of the bodies—by reference to some other frame. The collapse of the materiality of history and of the seduction of a fable, the reduction of a threatening and incomprehensible event to a reassuring mythic, totalizing unity of explanation, is in effect what all interpretive schemes tend to do. Mr. Kantorowski's satisfied and vacuous interpretation stands, however, for the failure of all ready-made cultural discourses both to account for—and to bear witness to—the Holocaust.

The film's strategy is not to challenge the false witness, but to *make the silence speak* from within and from around the false witness: the silence within each of the testimonies; the silence *between* various silences and various testimonies; the irremediable silence of the dead; the irremediable silence of the natural landscapes; the silence of the church procession; the silence of the ready-made cultural discourses pretending to account for the Holocaust; and above all, in the center of the film, Srebnik's silence in front of the church, in the middle of the talkative, delirious, self-complacent Polish crowd. The church scene is an astounding emblem of the multiplicity and the complexity of layers which unfold between this central silence and the various speeches which proceed from it and encroach upon it. Like a hall of mirrors, the church scene is a hall of silences infinitely resonant with one another. "There are many harmonies," says Lanzmann, "many concordances in the film. I knew very quickly that the film would be built in a circular way, with a stillness at the center, like the eye of a hurricane."[42]

---

[42]Quoted in "A Monument against Forgetting", *The Boston Globe*, Nov. 3, 1985, p. 3. Cf. Lanzmann's remarks in his interview with Roger Rosenblatt, for Channel 13 (Public Television WNET) in 1987: "When one deals with the destruction of the Jews, one has to talk and to be silent at the same moment . . . I think there is more silence in *Shoah* than words."

The silence reenacts the event of silence. "It was always this peace-ful here," Srebnik had said, "Always. When they burned two thousand people—Jews—every day, it was just as peaceful. No one shouted. Everyone went about his work. It was silent. Peaceful. Just as it is now" (p. 6).

Indeed, the church scene is not just a hall (a mirroring) of silences, but the very stage of the performance—of the execution and the repetition—of an act *act of silencing.* Although Srebnik here personi-fies the return of the witness—the return of witnessing into the very scene of the event-without-a-witness, what the church scene puts into effect and plays out, not in memory but in actual fact (and act), is how the real witness, in returning back to history and life, is once again *reduced to silence,* struck *dead* by the crowd. The scene is even more complex, since what the crowd points out as the Jews' crime and as the reason for the Holocaust is the Crucifixion, or the Jews' murder of Christ. But the Polish villagers are not aware that they themselves are in turn acting out precisely such a *ritual murder story*[43]; they are unaware of the precise ways in which they themselves are actually *enacting* both the Crucifixion and the Holocaust in *annihilat-ing Srebnik,* in *killing once again the witness* whom they totally dispose of, and *forget.*

What Kantorowski's testimony chooses to deny—*his* signature, *his* voice, the Poles' responsibility—it thus performs, reenacts before our eyes. What is not available in words, what is denied, what cannot and what will not be remembered or articulated, nonetheless gets realized. What takes places in the film, what materially and unexpectedly *occurs* and what returns like a ghost is *reference itself,* the very object—and the very content—of historical erasure.

I would suggest that what the film shows us here, in action, is the very process of the *re-forgetting of the Holocaust,* in the repeated murder of the witness and in the renewed reduction of the witnessing to silence. The film makes the testimony *happen*—happen inadver-tently as a second Holocaust. The silent Srebnik in the middle of this picture—with his beautifully dignified and tragic mute smile, and with his mutely speaking face (a face signed by his silence) is in effect a ghost: a ghost which, as such, is essentially *not contemporaneous;* which is contemporaneous, in reality, neither with the voices of the crowd which surrounds him, nor even with himself—with his own muted voice. What the church scene dramatizes is the only possible

[43]For an acute description of the functioning of the "ritual murder story" in history, see again Peter Canning, "Jesus Christ, Holocaust: Fabulation of the Jews in Christian and Nazi History," pp. 170–173.

encounter with the Holocaust, in the only possible form of a *missed encounter.*[44]

I would suggest precisely that the film is about the essence of this *missed contemporaneity* between Srebnik and the semi-circle which surrounds him, between Srebnik's voice and his own silence, and fundamentally, between the Holocaust experience and the witness of the Holocaust experience.

Shoah addresses the spectator with a challenge. When we are made to witness this re-enactment of the murder of the witness, this second Holocaust that appears spontaneously before the camera and on the screen, can we in our turn become *contemporaneous* with the meaning and with the significance of that enactment? Can we become contemporaneous with the shock, with the displacement, with the disorientation process that is triggered by such testimonial reenactment? Can we, in other words, assume in earnest, not the finite task of making sense out of the Holocaust, but the infinite task of encountering *Shoah*?

VI

The Return of the Song

If the church scene is thus punctuated, signed by Srebnik's silence, where is Srebnik's testimony, here lost, to be found? The film includes, indeed, an element through which the very silencing of Srebnik's voice can be somehow reversed, through which the very loss of Srebnik's testimony can be somehow recovered, or at least resist its own forgetting and itself be re-encountered, in the repetition of the melody and in the return of Srebnik's "melodious voice" in his reiterated singing. In spite of his own silencing and of his silence, the return of the witness undertaken by the film nonetheless persists, takes over, and survives in the return of the song. In the absence—and the failure—of the contemporaneity between the Holocaust and its own witness, the song nevertheless creates a different kind of contemporaneity between the *voice* and the historical (revisited) *site* of the voice, between the song and the place at which the song is (and was) heard,

[44]Cf. Lacan's conception of "the Real" as "a missed encounter" and as "what returns to the same place." *Le Séminaire, livre XI, Les Quatre concepts fondamentaux de la psychanalyse*, Paris: Seuil, 1973 (translated from the French by Alan Sheridan as *The Four Fundamental Concepts of Psychoanalysis*, New York: W. W. Norton, 1978) chapters III–V. See also Chapter 2, III: Undoing the Entrapment: Psychoanalytic work with trauma."

between the *voice* and the *place* to which, at the beginning of the film, the song in fact *gives voice*:

. . . it was here . . . Yes, this is the place. [5]

The song creates, indeed, an unexpected contemporaneity between its reiterated resonance and the very silence of the place.

It was always peaceful here. Always . . . It was silent. Peaceful. Just as it is now. [6]

At the same time, this contemporaneity between present and past, between the singing voice and the silent place remains entirely incomprehensible to, and thus noncontemporaneous with, the witness.

No one can understand it. Even I, here, now . . . I can't believe I'm here. No, I just can't believe it. [6]

It is in hovering between the ways in which it is at once contemporaneous with the place and noncontemporaneous with the witness (with the singer) that the song returns to the inconceivable historical site of its own singing, and that the harmonies and the disharmonies of this return of the song provide an entrance, or a threshold, to the film. It is the song which is the first to testify, the first to speak after the voiceless opening of the narrator. The song encroaches on—and breaks—at once the silence of the landscape and the muteness of the writing on the screen. Through Srebnik's voice, the film introduces us into the soothing notes and the nostalgic lyrics of a Polish folk tune which itself, however, dreams about, and yearns for, another place.

> A little white house
> lingers in my memory
> Of that little white house
> each night I dream. [4]

The White House

Srebnik's voice inhabits his own song. But does anyone inhabit the "white house" of which he sings? Who can enter the white house? Does the "I" of Srebnik (the "I" who "can't believe he's here") inhabit what his voice is so dreamily and yearningly evoking? What in fact is there inside the "little white house"? What is there beyond the threshold, behind the whiteness of the house?

The longing for the white house recalls the white virginity of the procession. The white house seems as safe, as wholesome, as immaculate in its invitation and its promise, as the white procession of the youthful virgins. And yet, we know that it is not only virginity, but an aberrant violation of lives and of the innocence of childhood, that is implied ironically and silently by the juxtapositions of the church scene, and by the whiteness of the ritual ceremony.

Virginity is what is not written upon. The white is, on the one hand, the color of the virgin page before the writing—the white house sung before the writing of the film—but also, on the other hand, the very color of erasure.[45] For the viewer who has seen the film, and who has come full circle—like the film, like the song—to start again at the beginning, the "white house" brings to mind not just the snow that, whitely covering the peaceful meadows, covers up the emptied graves from which the dead bodies were disinterred so as to be reduced to ashes, burned away, but similarly in a different sense, the later image of white houses in the Polish village of Wladowa, a village once inhabited by Jews but whose Jewish houses have been since vacated (like the graves under the snow) by their original inhabitants (obliterated in extermination camps) and are now occupied, owned and inhabited by Poles. The little white house yearned for thus turns out to be itself, ironically enough, a ghost house; a ghost house that belongs at once to dreaming ("Of that little white house / Each night I dream") and to memory ("A little white house / lingers in my memory").

Calling us into a dream, the white house, paradoxically, will also force us to wake up. Plunged into the dreamy beauty of the landscape and into the dreamy yearning of the melody of the white house, the spectator as a witness—like the witnesses of history—has to literally *wake up* to a reality that is undreamt of, wake up, that is, into the unthinkable realization that what he is witnessing is not simply a dream. We will be called upon to see the film—and to view perception—critically, to discriminate reality from dream, in spite of the confusing mingling of memory and dream, in spite of the deceptive quality of what is given to direct perception. On the borderline between dreaming and memory, the song—as a concrete, material residue of history—is that "small element of reality that is evidence that we are not dreaming."[46] The residue of an implicit violence (the unquantifiable ransom with which Srebnik has to keep buying his life)

[45]White is thus, for instance, the color the blank page of forgetfulness on which the ex-Nazi commissioner of the Warsaw ghetto, Dr. Grassler, claims to "take notes" to "refresh" the total blankness of his memory about his Nazi past.

[46]As Lacan puts it in an altogether different context; see "Tuché and Automaton," in *The Four Fundamental Concepts of Psychoanalysis*, p. 60.

which at the same time is luringly soothing, the song incorporates the real both in its literal, and yet also, in its deceptive quality. As a purveyor of the real, the song invites us, at the threshold of the film, to cross over from the landscape and the white house into an encounter (a collision) with the actuality of history. It melodiously invites us to a crossing of the distance between art and reference. And no one can suspect that this melodious invitation was in history, and is now in the film, an invitation to the shock of an awakening; of an awakening to a reality whose scrutiny requires a degree of vigilance, of wakefulness of and of alertness such that it exceeds perhaps human capacity. No one can suspect that what awaits us from behind the white house is not simply a nightmare, but the urgency of waking up into a history and a reality with respect to which we are not and perhaps cannot be, fully and sufficiently awake.

The place from which the song invokes us at the threshold of the film and to which it points, at the same time as the locus of the real and as the origin of singing, designates, I would suggest, the place of art within the film: the song becomes itself a metaphor for the whole film which is inaugurated by its melody, and which registers the impact and the resonance of its returns. Opened by the song, the film does not simply show itself: it calls us. It calls us through the singing it enacts. It is asking us to listen to, and hear, not just the meaning of the words but the complex significance of their return, and the clashing echoes of their melody and of their context. The film calls us into hearing both this clash and its own silence. It calls us into what it cannot show, but what it nonetheless can point to. The song inaugurates this calling and this act of pointing.

Yes, this is the place . . .

Shoah begins with the apparent innocence of singing, only to thrust us more profoundly and astonishingly into the discrepancy between the lyrics and their context, only to point us more sharply toward the ambiguity that lies behind that innocence:

> A little white house
> lingers in my memory . . . [4]

repeats sweetly the song. But another voice proceeds to speak over the resonance of the song:

> When I heard him again, my heart beat faster, because what happened
> here . . . was a murder. [5]

271

Srebnik singing.

Thus testifies, in Polish, the first voice-over—whose origin is not immediately identifiable, locatable—in the words of one of the by-standers, one of the Polish witnesses of history.

Then Srebnik's face in a close-up—the face that carries both the lightness, the enticing sweetness of the song and the weight, the outrage and the cruelty, of history—twists the silence of its pain into a smile and gazes vacantly, incredibly, incredulously through survival, death and time, through piles of vanished burned bodies into the green trees, the brown earth, and the perspective of the blue horizon:

Yes, this is the place . . . No one ever left here again. [5]

Darum, Warum

The contradictions riddling the very beauty of the first song are aggravated, underscored and sharpened with the second song which, narratively, is a singing replica—or a melodious counterpart—to the first song but which, rhetorically and musically, sets up a dissonance and a sharp contrast with the harmonies and with the innocence of the initial invitation.

He sang Polish folk tunes, and in return *the guard taught him Prussian military songs.* [3]

> You, girls, don't you cry,
> don't be so sad, for the dear summer is nearing . . .
> and with it I'll return.
>
> A mug of red wine, a piece of roast
> is what the girls give their soldiers.
>
> Therefore.—Why? Therefore.—Why?
> [Darum.—Warum?, Darum.—Warum?]
>
> When the soldiers march through the town,
> the girls open their doors and windows.
>
> Therefore. Why? Therefore. Why?
> Only because of this [sound]
> *Tschindarrassa / Bum!* [Cymbals, drum] (6) [47]

The two songs sung by Srebnik are contrasted and opposed in many ways. Although they are both folk tunes and are both—by implication or explicitly—about returns, the dialogue between the tune in Polish and its counterpart in German is more than a mere dialogue of foreign tongues. Whereas the song about the white house concretizes a dream of arrival—an implicit dream of reaching—the Prussian military song is marked by a departure and a passage and is a ritual, not of arriving or of coming to inhabit, but of leaving. The act of leaving, at the same time, is disguised, denied and masked by a discursive rhetoric of coming back and by a promise of returning. Apparently, the Prussian song is as sweet in its yearning and as harmless as the Polish song. And yet, the elements of lure on the one hand, and on the other hand of a subordinating force become (almost) apparent. By virtue of its function as a military march, and through the forceful beats of its percussions ("Tschindarrassa, Bum!"; "*Darum, Warum*"), the Prussian song[48] incorporates the latent rhythms of artillery and bombs. Hinting at both the malignancy of the deception and the violence to come, the song implicitly includes the military connotations—and the metaphoric, tactile contiguity—of war, of bloodshed ("a mug of red wine"), of brutality ("a piece of roast") and of physical invasion ("the girls open their doors and windows"). The whole song, with the beats of its repeated rhymes between its ques-

---

[47]Translation modified and expanded, transcribing all the German lyrics that are clearly audible in the film.

[48]In my analysis of the Prussian song, I owe both gratitude and inspiration to Dr. Ernst Prelinger, who has provided me with a sophisticated explanation of the original German lyrics of the song, an explanation which informs my discussion of it here.

tions and its answers ("Darum, Warum"), and with its metaphoric female gifts of drinking, eating, and of opening ("the girls open their doors and windows"), is a figure for a sexual interplay; but the interplay is one of conquest and of transitory military and sexual occupation. It is as though the enigma of the white house—the enigma of a space that is inviolate and intimate, sung in the first song—were, so to speak, invaded, cancelled out, forced open by the second. No wonder that, behind the lure of its enticing surface, the charm of the German song (which primarily plays out a sexual tease) turns out to be itself a sadistic tool by which the singing child becomes a hostage to the Germans, an instrument of torment and abuse through which young Srebnik is reduced by his adult spectators to a chained, dancing marionette transformed—playfully and cruelly—into a singing toy.

The Word of Our Commander

It is in this way that the shift between the Polish song and its German reply ("and in return, the guard taught him Prussian military songs") is accomplished at the threshold of the film, as a subtle—and yet ominous—transaction, an invisible—yet audible—exchange between the music of the victim and the music of (and from the point of view of) the perverse oppressor.

Another song which, later in the film, will mark Nazi perversity and violence much more explicitly and in which the victim, equally, will have to sing the point of view of the oppressor, is the song whose singers are today entirely extinguished and to which only the ex-Nazi Suchomel is able to bear witness, by singing it to Lanzmann. In much the same way as the singers of the song sang it in a voice that was not theirs—the voice of the oppressor—Suchomel, inversely, now reproduces the forced singing of the victims in the alien and jaunty voice of the ex-Nazi. It is thus that Suchomel repeats to Lanzmann the Treblinka hymn that the camp prisoners were forced to sing, for the guards' pleasure:

> Looking squarely ahead, brave and joyous, at the world,
> the squads march to work.
> All that matters to us now is Treblinka.
> It is our destiny.
> That's why we've become one with Treblinka.
> in no time at all.
> We know only the word of our commander,
> we know only obedience and duty,

we want to serve, to go on serving,
until a little luck ends it all. Hurray!

"Once more, but louder," Lanzmann requests, in response to Sucho-mel's completed singing. Suchomel obliges Lanzmann. "We're laugh-ing about it," he says with a mixture of complicity and condescension, "but it's so sad."

> *No one is laughing.*
> Don't be sore at me. You want history—I'm giving you history. Franz wrote the words. The melody comes from Buchenwald. Camp Buchenwald, where Franz was a guard. New Jews who arrived in the morning, new "workers Jews," were taught the song. And by evening they had to be able to sing along with it.
> *Sing it again.*
> All right.
> *It's very important. But loud!*
>> Looking squarely ahead, brave and joyous, at the world,
>> the squads march to work.
>> All that matters to us now is Treblinka.
>> It is our destiny.
>> That's why we've become one with Treblinka.
>> in no time at all.
>> We know only the word of our commander,
>> we know only obedience and duty,
>> we want to serve, to go on serving,
>> until a little luck ends it all. Hurray! [105–106]

Having thus repeated once again this song, Suchomel, proud and bemused at his own memory, concludes:

> Satisfied? That's unique. No Jew knows that today! [106]

The self-complacency, the eagerness of Suchomel in obliging Lanz-mann suggests that he, too, in effect enjoys and takes implicitly sadis-tic pleasure in the act of his own singing, in his own staged, imitative musical performance and in the inconceivable discrepancy of his own representation of the victims. "You want history—I'm giving you history." Can history be *given*? How does Suchomel *give* history, and what does the act of "giving"—the gift of reality—here mean? Ironically enough, the song is literally history insofar as it conveys this historical discrepancy and this sadistic pleasure, at the same time that it speaks through the historical *extinction* of the message and the *objectification* of the voice. As a literal residue of the real, the song is history to the extent that it inscribes within itself, precisely, this historical discrepancy, this incommensurability between the voice of its sadistic author and the voice of its tormented singers. What is historically "unique" about the song is the fact that it is a Nazi-authored Jewish song that "no Jew knows today." "You want history—I'm giving you history." In the very outrage of its singing doubly, at two different moments (in the camp and in the film, by the victims and by Suchomel) in a voice that is not, and cannot become, its own, the song is, so to speak, the opposite of a signed testimony, an *anti-testimony* that consists, once more, in the absence and in the very forging of its Jewish signature. Like Mr. Kantorowski's mythical account of the Holocaust, the Nazi narrative of the Jews' victimization (both in the camp song and in Suchomel's revoicing of it) is a speech act that can neither own its meaning nor possess itself as testimony. "You want history—I'm giving you history." As the extinction of the subject of the signature and as the objectification of the victim's voice, "history" presents itself as anti-testimony. But the film restitutes to history—and to the song—its testimonial function. Paradoxically enough, it is from the very evidence of its enactment as an anti-testimony that the song derives the testimonial power of its repetition, and the historic eloquence of its unlikely and ghostly return: "*Sing it again . . . It's very important. But loud!*"

The Quest of the Refrain, or the Imperative to Sing

I would suggest that the imperative, "Sing it again," is the performative imperative that artistically creates the film and that governs both its structure and its ethical and epistemological endeavor: to make truth happen as a testimony through the haunting repetition of an ill-understood melody; to make the referent come back, paradoxically, as something heretofore unseen by history; to reveal the real as the impact of a literality that history cannot assimilate or integrate as knowledge, but that it keeps encountering in the return of the song.

"Our memory," writes Valéry, "repeats to us what we haven't understood. Repetition is addressed to incomprehension."[49] We "*sing again*" what we cannot know, what we have not integrated and what, consequently, we can neither fully master nor completely understand. In *Shoah*, the song stands for the activation of the memory of the whole film, a memory that no one can possess, and whose process of collecting and of recollecting is constantly torn apart between the pull, the

[49]Valéry, "Commentaire de *Charmes*," in *Oeuvres*, Paris: Gallimard (Bibliothèque de la Pléiade), 1957, Vol. I, p. 1510; my translation.

pressure and the will of the words and the different, independent pull of the melody, which has its own momentum and its own compulsion to repeat but which does not know what in fact it is repeating.

The whole film, which ends only to begin again with the return of the song, testifies to history like a haunting and interminable refrain.[50] The function of the refrain—which is itself archaically referred to as "the burden of the song"—like the burden of the vocal echo which, as though mechanically, returns in the interviewer's voice the last words of the discourse of his interlocutors, is to create a difference through the repetition, to return a question out of something that appears to be an answer: *Darum—Warum?* ("Therefore.—Why?"). The echo does not simply reproduce what seems to be its motivation, but rather puts it into question. Where there had seemed to be a rationale, a closure and a limit, the refrain-like repetition opens up a vacuum, a crevice and, through it, the undefined space of an open question.

> The flames reached to the sky.
> *To the sky ...* [6]

The Singer's Voice

What gives this refrain-like structure of the film—the repetition of the song and of its burden, the return of the resonance of the refrain— the power not merely to move us but to strike and to surprise us, the power each time to astonish us and to impact upon us as though for the first time? When Srebnik sings the two songs of the opening, and when the echo of the second song puts into question the apparent harmony and innocence of the first tune, what constitutes the power of the singing and the strength—the eloquence—of Srebnik's testimony through it, is neither the lyrics nor even the music (someone else's music), but the uniqueness of the singing voice. The uniqueness of the voice restores the signature to the repeated melody and to the cited lyrics, and transforms them from anti-testimony into a compelling and unequaled testimony. What makes the power of the testimony in the film and what constitutes in general the impact of the film is not the words but the equivocal, puzzling relation between words and voice, the interaction, that is, between words, voice, rhythm, melody,

---

[50]*"Shoah"*, says Lanzmann, "had to be built like a musical piece, where a theme appears at a lower level, disappears, comes back at a higher level or in full force, disappears, and so on. It was the only way to keep several parameters together." (*Panel Discussion*, p. 44)

images, writing, and silence. Each testimony speaks to us beyond its words, beyond its melody, like the unique performance of a singing, and each song, in its repetitions, participates in the searching refrain and recapitulates the musical quest of the whole film. Like Lanzmann, Srebnik facing an unspeakable event at thirteen and a half, and again at the beginning of the film—as a singer who remained alive because of his "melodious voice"—is in turn a sort of artist: an artist who has lost his words but who has not lost the uniqueness of the singing voice and its capacity for signature. What is otherwise untestifiable is thus transmitted by the signature of the voice. The film as a visual medium hinges, paradoxically, not so much on the self-evidence of sight as on the visibility it renders to the voice, and on the invisibility it renders tangible, of silence. The film speaks in a multiplicity of voices that, like Srebnik's, all transmit beyond what they can say in words. In much the same way as the singing crematorium witnessed and evoked by Philip Müller, the film resonates like a whole chorus of testimonies and of voices that, within the framework of the film, sing together:

> The violence climaxed when they tried to force the people to undress. A few obeyed, only a handful. Most of them refused to follow the order. Suddenly, like a chorus, they all began to sing. The whole "undressing room" rang with the Czech national anthem, and the *Hatikvah*. That moved me terribly . . .
> That was happening to my countrymen, and I realized that my life had become meaningless. Why go on living? For what? So I went into the gas chamber with them, resolved to die. With them. Suddenly, some who recognized me came up to me . . . A small group of women approached. They looked at me and said, right there in the gas chamber . . . : "So you want to die. But that's senseless. Your death won't give us back our lives. That's no way. You must get out of here alive, you must bear witness to . . . the injustice done to us." [164–165]

The singing of the anthem in the crematorium signifies a common recognition, by the singers, of the perversity of the deception to which they had been all along exposed, a recognition, therefore, and a facing, of the truth of their imminent death. The singing, in this way, conveys a repossession of their lost truth by the dying singers, an ultimate rejection of their Nazi-instigated self-deception and a deliberately chosen, conscious witnessing of their own death. It is noteworthy that this is the only moment in the film in which a community of witnessing is created physically and mentally, against all odds. Erasing its own witnesses and inhibiting its own eyewitnessing, the historical occurrence of the Holocaust, as we have seen, precluded by its very structure any such community of witnessing.[51] But this is what the film tries precisely to create in resonating with the singing chorus of the dying crematorium, whose many signatures and many voices are today extinguished and reduced to silence. The film, as a chorus of performances and testimonies, does create, within the framework of its structure, a communality of singing, an odd community of testimonial incommensurates which, held together, have an overwhelming testimonial impact.

The Disappearance of the Chorus

Müller wishes to die so as to belong, to be part of this community, to join the singing. But the dying singers have it as their last wish to exclude him from their common death, so that he can be not an extinguished witness like them, but a living witness to their dying and their singing. The singing challenges and dares the Nazis. The act of singing and of bearing witness embodies resistance. But for Müller, the resistance cannot mean giving up life; it has to mean giving up death. Resistance spells the abdication of suicidal death and the endurance of survival as itself a form of resistance and of testimony. Resistance signifies the price of the historical endurance—in oneself—of an actual return of the witness. As a returning delegate of the dead witnesses, Müller's act of testifying and his testimonial afterlife can no longer be, however, part of a living community. Facing his singing compatriots in the crematorium, Müller understands that the gift of witness they request from him, and his responsive, mute commitment to bear witness, leave him no choice but to stand alone, to step outside of the community[52] as well as of shared cultural frames of reference, outside of the support of any shared perception. The holding and the inner strength of the common singing empowers Müller and allows him to escape and to survive. But his survival

---

[51]See above, Chapter 7, I, "The Occurrence as Unwitnessed."

[52]Compare Rudolph Vrba's decision to escape, after the suicide of Freddy Hirsch that aborts the Resistance plan for the uprising of the Czech family camp: "It was quite clear to me then that the Resistance in the camp is not geared for an uprising but for survival of the members of the Resistance. I then decided to act . . . [by] leaving the community, for which I [was] co-responsible at the time. The decision to escape, in spite of the policy of the Resistance movement at the time, was formed immediately . . . As far as I am concerned, I think that if I successfully manage to break out from the camp and bring the information to the right place at the right time, that this might be a help . . . Not to delay anything but to escape as soon as possible to inform the world" (195–196).

cannot simply be encompassed by a common song, and his afterlife of bearing witness can no longer lose itself in a choral hymn. If his living voice is to speak for the dead, it has to carry through and to transmit, precisely, the cessation of the common singing, the signature of the endurance, the peculiarity and the uniqueness of a voice doomed to remain alone, a voice that has returned—and that speaks—from beyond the threshold of the crematorium.

Müller, Srebnik, and the others, spokesmen for the dead, living voices of returning witnesses that have seen their own death—and the death of their own people—face to face, address us in the film both from inside life and from beyond the grave and carry on, with the aloneness of the testifying voice, the mission of the singing from within the burning.

> Suddenly, from the part of the camp called the death camp, flames shot up. Very high. In a flash, the whole countryside, the whole camp, seemed ablaze . . . And suddenly one of us stood up. We knew . . . he'd been an opera singer in Warsaw . . . His name was Salve, and facing that curtain of fire, he began chanting a song I didn't know:
> > "My God, my God,
> > why has Thou forsaken us?
> >
> > We have been thrust into the fire before
> > but we have never denied the Holy Law".
>
> He sang in Yiddish, while behind him blazed the pyres on which they had begun then, in November 1942, to burn the bodies in Treblinka . . . We knew that night that the dead would no longer be buried, they'd be burned. [14]

A Winning Song

The entire film is a singing from within the burning of a knowledge: "We knew that night . . . " The knowledge of the burning is the knowledge—and the burning—of the singing. At the beginning of the film, Srebnik's song incorporates the burned bodies with whose death and with whose burning it still resonates. In singing, on the one hand, as he has been taught, about the girls "opening the doors" to soldiers who pass by, in the very way that he himself, uncannily, is commanded by the SS to "open the doors" of the arriving gas vans so as to receive— and to unload—the bodies to be burned; in singing also, on the other hand, his original melodious yearning of and for the sweetness of white house, Srebnik's singing and his singular, compelling voice, is the bearer of a knowledge—and a vision—not just of the ashes but of

the living burning, of the burning of the living—a vision of the half-asphyxiated bodies coming back to life only to feel the fire and to witness, conscious, their encounter with, and their consumption by, the flames:

> When [the gas vans] arrived, the SS said: "Open the doors!" We opened them. The bodies tumbled right out . . . We worked until the whole shipment was burned . . .
>
> I remember that once they were still alive. The ovens were full, and the people lay on the ground. They were all moving, they were coming back to life, and when they were thrown into the ovens, they were all conscious. Alive. They could feel the fire burn them . . .
>
> When I saw all this, it didn't affect me. I was only thirteen, and all I'd ever seen until then were dead bodies. [101–102]

The deadening of the live witness, the burn of the silence of the thirteen-year-old child who is "not affected," passes on into his singing. The unique expression of the voice and of the singing both expresses and covers the silence, in much the same way as the unique expression of the face—of Srebnik's figure at the opening of the film—both covers and expresses the deliberate and striking absence of dead bodies from *Shoah*'s screen. It is indeed the living body and the living face of the returning witness that, in *Shoah*, becomes a speaking figure

for the stillness and the muteness of the bodies, a *figure* for, precisely, the *Figuren*. What the film does with the *Figuren* is to restore their muteness to the singing of the artist-child, to revitalize them by exploring death through life, and by endowing the invisibility of their abstraction with the uniqueness of a face, a voice, a melody, a song. The song is one that has won life for Srebnik, a life-winning song which, framed within the film and participating in the searching repetition of its refrain, wins for us a heightened consciousness and an increased awareness, by giving us the measure of an understanding that is not transmittable without it. As a fragment of reality and as a crossroad between art and history, the song—like the whole film—enfolds what is in history untestifiable and embodies, at the same time, what in art captures reality and *enables* witnessing. In much the same way as the testimony, the song exemplifies the power of the film to address, and hauntingly demands a hearing. Like Müller coming back to testify and speak—to claim an audience—from beyond the threshold of the crematorium, Srebnik, though traversed by a bullet that has missed his vital brain centers by pure chance, reappears from behind the threshold of the white house to sing again his winning song: a song that, once again, wins life and, like the film, leaves us—through the very way it wins us—both empowered, and condemned to, *hearing*.

When I heard him again, my heart beat faster, because what happened here . . . was a murder. [5]

He was thirteen and a half years old. He had a lovely singing voice, and *we heard him*. [4]

> "A little white house
> lingers in my memory.
> Of that little white house
> each night I dream."

Index